The Afrikaner as Viewed by the English

1795—1854

MICHAEL STREAK
M.A., D.Litt. et Phil.

*

C. STRUIK (PTY) LTD.
CAPE TOWN
1974

C. Struik (Pty) Ltd.
Africana Specialist and Publisher

By the same author

LORD MILNER'S IMMIGRATION POLICY FOR THE TRANSVAAL, 1897–1905

ISBN 0 86977 039 X

*Originally submitted for the degree D.Litt. et Phil.
at the Rand Afrikaans University, Johannesburg.*

Printed by Printpak (Cape) Ltd., Dacres Avenue, Epping, Cape.

In memory of Tom King

Acknowledgements

I wish to express my thanks to the following people: Professor F. A. van Jaarsveld, now of the University of Pretoria, who, as my promoter, guided me through this thesis; my wife, Valerie, and my mother, Mrs. G. C. Loubser, for their continual support, both moral and financial; and the Rand Afrikaans University and the Human Sciences Research Council for financial assistance which helped me to undertake research in the United Kingdom. Finally, a word of sincere thanks to my publisher.

Contents

Introduction

These days much is heard of the Afrikaners, and commentary on them as a group, whether from within South Africa or abroad, is generally hostile. It is commonplace to hear that the state of affairs within the country, especially with regard to those matters concerning race, is of their doing and that the situation is beyond redemption as long as the Afrikaners, as a group, hold the reins of political power.

This hostility towards the Afrikaners or, in the case of criticism from abroad, towards the White population as a whole, is nothing new. Indeed, the attitudes prevailing today differ little from those held by the British when they first came into contact with the Dutch settlers of the Cape Colony as far back as 1795 and not only is the same criticism levelled at the white inhabitants of South Africa today but, irrespective of the changes that have taken place in South Africa over the past 150 years, today's critics follow the same trends as their forebears in making their views public: an almost hysterical appeal to the emotions based on so-called examples of the 'heinous' South African way of life – examples which more often than not are the exception rather than the rule; a soul-stirring cry for the relief of the 'oppressed' Blackman; sombre predictions that the situation within the country can never rectify itself through a process of 'natural change'; that a Black uprising is imminent; and always, but always, an appeal to the powers that be (formerly in Britain but now in other countries, too) to apply pressure of one kind or another on the authorities in South Africa.

With this close parallel between the past and the present regarding adverse opinion of South Africa it is not difficult to follow the development of public opinion of the Afrikaner during the first half of the nineteenth century for, first and foremost, both pre-suppose that the Blacks are the oppressed and the Afrikaners are the oppressors.

This work sets out to trace the growth of public opinion of the Afrikaners between 1795 and 1854. It attempts to trace the English relationship with the Afrikaners and provide the basis upon which Englishmen arrived at their conclusions respecting them, as well as trying to show the reasons for Englishmen becoming divided amongst themselves on both their opinion of the Afrikaners and upon colonial events as they unfolded. It also attempts to show that the criticism levelled against the Afrikaners was determined more by the fluctuating political philosophy of the British than by the actual actions of the Afrikaners themselves. Lastly, it is hoped that by looking back at the experiences of the past century the reader will pause to consider more objectively the influences governing public opinion of both South Africa and the Afrikaners today.

* * *

I would like to draw attention to the fact that in a work of this nature the two basic problems to contend with are objectivity and perspective and the degree to which these have been achieved *in the eyes of the reader* must largely be determined by whether or not he is critical of the Afrikaners. And if personal attitudes towards the Afrikaners can influence the *reader,* how much more so does this not hold good for the *writer*. For this reason, I feel justified in taking the step of entering briefly into my personal background as obviously this will have shaped me and have had a great deal to do with my attitudes towards the Afrikaners. It is hoped that the reader will then perceive that I have no axe to grind respecting the Afrikaners nor, indeed, do I set myself up as an apologist for them.

To begin with, my mother is of Afrikaner stock, while my father's line can be traced back to the 1820 British Settlers. My maternal grandmother who, during her life, married de Villiers, Thom and Louw, grew up in a British concentration camp during the Anglo-Boer War. My "Oupa" Louw naturally fought for the Republics. My grandmother did not live to see the creation of Republic in 1961 but my grandfather did and it represented to him the culmination of a life-long political interest – an interest, incidentally, which had been characterised by an implacable hatred towards "die blêrrie Engelse". My paternal grandfather, on the other hand, a Chief Justice of Natal, was true to the British tradition of things and would, I am sure, have voted strongly against the creation of the Republic in 1961 had he been alive. I received my schooling in Cape Town at English-medium schools and by some twist of fate I received my university education at Afrikaner or Afrikaner-orientated institutions. As I understand things, this makes me neither an Afrikaner nor an Englishman but rather, as I like to believe, part of the broad mass of people who comprise the white population of South Africa.

A final comment is necessary to clarify certain terms used in this work. In the first place, who were the Afrikaners or 'Boers' and how did their names evolve? Obviously, their origin is to be found in the first free burghers of the Cape settlement who, as Dutch East India Company officials in 1657, were granted land for the purpose of supplying the Cape market. The outcome of this was that by 1660 it was already possible to distinguish between the farmer and the town dweller and as time went on the occupation of the country people came to describe them as a group – hence 'Boers' (or farmers). As for the origin of the term 'Afrikaner', as early as the seventeenth century reference to the 'Africaan', 'Africaander' and 'Africaaner' are to be found in the manuscript collections of the Cape Archives; while by 1806 Janssens was able to draw a line between Hollanders of Europe and the local 'Africanen' or 'Zuid-Africanen' as people who already then were conscious of their African connection.

Throughout this work reference is made to the "Cape Dutch" (i.e. colonists of the Cape of Dutch extraction) and "Afrikaners". These refer to the colonial-born, white inhabitants of the Cape Colony who had as their language 'Dutch' or Afrikaans and who knew no other home but the Cape. For purposes of this study, however, and because of the political significance that the interior farmers (or Boers) assumed in the formation of the present-day Afrikaner people, the term "Afrikaner" is applicable particularly to those who upheld the Afrikaner traditions as manifested by the Great Trek. Whilst the inhabitants of Cape Town and its environs could be called Cape Dutchmen *and* Afrikaners both prior to and after the events of 1836, those who emigrated to Natal and beyond with the Great Trek, because of their political significance, must be thought of as *only*

Afrikaners. Because of their political significance, then, it will be noticed that a greater emphasis is placed upon the interior and frontier Afrikaners than the Cape Dutch who did not proceed on the Trek.

The application of the term "English" is more simple since it refers to all the inhabitants of the United Kingdom whether Welsh, Irish, Scottish or English as well as referring to the British officials, immigrants and missionaries who settled in South Africa.

New York, December 1973. M.S.

CHAPTER ONE

First Acquaintances
1795–1802

> "If the condition of man," observed an early English traveller, "was to be estimated entirely by the means it possessed of supplying an abundance, or preventing a scarcity, of the necessary articles of life . . . the European colonists of the Cape of Good Hope might be pronounced amongst the happiest of men. But as all the pleasures of this world are attended with evils, like roses placed on stems that are surrounded by thorns, so these people in the midst of plenty unknown in other countries, can scarcely be considered as objects of envy. Debarred from every mental pleasure arising from the perusal of books or the frequent conversation of friends, each succeeding day is a repetition of the past, whose irksome sameness is varied only by the accidental call of a traveller, the less welcome visits of the Bosjesmans, or the terror of being put to death by their own slaves, or the Hottentots in their employ. The only counterpoise to this wearisome and miserable state of existence, is a superfluity of the necessities of life, as far as regards the support of animal functions, which all, of every description among the colonists, have the means of acquiring with little exertion either of body or mind."[1]

By the time the Cape of Good Hope came to be occupied by Great Britain in 1795 the British had, by virtue of their internal political development, arrived at a far more advanced stage of democracy than had their European neighbours, and together with the lead they had obtained in the Industrial Revolution and owing to their widespread interests in the East, they had established themselves as the number one trading nation in the world. However, the rise to

1. John Barrow, *An Account of Travels into the Interior of Southern Africa in the Years 1797 and 1798,* ii, pp. 385–386.

prominence of the doctrines of Adam Smith's school of Free Trade, intensified in some respects by the American and French Revolutions, meant that by the time the Cape of Good Hope came to be occupied by Great Britain in 1795, the national attitude of the British had come to be characterised by a growth in the power of moral sentiment, as opposed to the purely mercantile outlook of the past when material gain had been the sole test of policy.[2] The establishment of temporary rule at the Cape came at a time when the writings of the French philosophers Rousseau and Montesquieu, and the British poet James Thompson as well as John Wesley's Methodism (all with their appeal to the heart), had added weight to the foundations of British philanthropy[3] and when the protests of English humanitarians against the slave trade had won powerful support throughout the country and when forces which were later to reshape the rest of the world were generated. The vital link provided by the middle class in keeping the industrial war machine going against Napoleon impressed upon that sector of society the indispensable nature of their role within the nation – a realisation which was to bring a reaction against the accumulated evils of the Industrial and Agrarian Revolutions and was to challenge the entire social structure of the land. Parallel with this was the introduction of religious and humanitarian motives into both home and colonial policy, which promised that compassion for the depressed and ill-used, both at home and throughout the empire, would not be overlooked.[4] In particular, the philanthropic desire to rescue the black African from a state of barbarism loomed large and had direct bearing on and greatly influenced what English opinion of the Afrikaner would be.

The most characteristic activity of the trend in Christian humanitarianism was the founding of missionary[5] and other societies,[6] for it

---

2. J. A. Williamson, *A Short History of British Expansion,* pp. 14–20.
3. C. F. J. Muller, *Die Britse Owerheid en die Groot Trek,* pp. 9–10; G. D. Scholtz, *Die Ontwikkeling van die Politieke Denke van die Afrikaner, Deel II, 1806–1854,* p. 25.
4. Williamson, *A Short History of British Expansion,* pp. 22–23; *C.H.B.E.*, ii, *(The Growth of the New Empire, 1783–1870),* p. vi.
5. The first missionaries to the Cape Colony were the Moravian Brethren who, following a short period of missionary work between the years 1737–1744, permanently established themselves in 1792. They were soon followed by the London Missionary Society (1798), the Baptist Church and Wesleyan missionaries, and various Scottish societies.
6. Such as the Clapham Sect and the Society of Friends (Quakers).

was asserted that British imperialists were responsible for the widespread oppression of the weaker races whose material and spiritual salvation should be pursued together. In the case of the Cape of Good Hope it was argued that expansion had from the first been immoral since it could only have taken place at the expense of lands rightfully belonging to the natives. Furthermore, it was maintained that expansion had resulted in the deplorable disruption of the tribal way of life of Rousseau's "noble savage", a fact which was evidenced in the subordinate position he held within the European controlled Colony. Particular condemnation was levelled at the frontiersmen of the Colony, the Boers, for the treacherous means by which, it was alleged, they had reduced the aborigine to what was considered an ignoble and oppressed state.

Whatever the relationship between the conquering British and the local Dutch inhabitants of the Cape Colony would be, it can safely be argued that it would to a great degree depend upon their respective national attitudes or cultures, which would further be manifested through their systems of government, the condition of the people, their habits and customs and, most important, their attitudes towards the Blackman. In particular, the national attitudes of the Cape Dutch and English would determine whether their relationship would be characterised by a movement towards integration and co-operation or by a separation and rejection of one by the other.

From the outset three factors emerged to influence or determine English opinion of the Afrikaner people, the interplay of which, in fact, forms the basis of this study. First were the political aspirations held by a certain section of the Cape Dutch; second was the relationship between the Cape Dutch and the Blackman; and third was the relationship between the Cape Dutch and the English themselves. These factors at once not only highlighted the differences in the national interests of both parties, at the same time reflecting their respective national attitudes, but also provided the cornerstone of what the English came to refer to most commonly as the "South African problem", the root cause of which, more often than not, was attributed to the so-called "character" of the Afrikaner.

In 1795 English cognizance of South African affairs was entirely confined to those who were directly involved in the administration of the Colony. It should be remembered that it had been purely the strategic importance of the settlement as a refreshment station which had drawn the British there in the first instance — a prize which Britain could not afford to let fall into French hands — and they, like the Dutch East India Company before them, had had no intention of developing a large colony. This is borne out by the fact that the population increase of the white inhabitants came mainly from within the settlement itself and accounts for the fact that, until the arrival of the Settlers from Britain in 1820, the British public considered the Cape as nothing more than a port of call — a conclusion underlined by the lack of concern shown by the British press and parliament in the internal affairs of the Colony until that time.[7]

Internally, the socio-political structure of Britain in 1795 did not lend itself to the British being a nation well-informed. The town and country labourers who made up the majority of the English populace had little or no political organisation while, as already stated, it was not until the close of the Napoleonic Wars in 1815 that the middle class began to appreciate the social and political advantages their economic importance had brought them. Journalism in 1795, although of a higher standard than in most countries, enjoyed little or no status and generally speaking the circulation of the press was low. Public opinion as such, then, was confined to the established dominant upper class who looked upon the colonies as a mere burden, for, as Shelbourne, a former minister of colonial affairs, reflected: "It appeared a madness to think of colonies after what had passed in North America."[8] They might, perhaps, have been useful for absorbing excess population, but no more than that. Economically, too, the colonies had not proved themselves valuable as a market. It is therefore understandable that little notice would have been taken of the Dutch colonists of the Cape of Good Hope for, like the French in Quebec, they had no English connection. Furthermore, whatever interest might have been shown in the Cape would have been largely frustrated by the absence of a local press to refer to, and with poor communications and the lack of press correspondents, the British journalists could provide only a limited coverage of the affairs of the Cape Colony based upon whatever source was

7. As late as 1839 *The Spectator* (5 Jan.) was able to state that the Cape Colony had occupied little place in the "public mind" in Britain. See also *The Cape Town Mail,* 23 April 1842.
8. Quoted by *C.H.B.E.,* ii, p. 1.

available to them. Under these circumstances the field of opinion-making was left wide open to the travellers.

The evangelical revival which swept Western Europe during the second half of the eighteenth century and which showed itself in the policy of melioration towards the Blackman came to a climax in the abolition of slavery in 1834. It was this evangelical movement that had brought the missionaries to the Cape Colony during the closing years of the Dutch East India Company's administration and, supported by the semi-educated, evangelically minded and entirely vocal British middle class, was later responsible for wresting the conservative Cape Colony from its state of isolation. The abolition of the slave trade in Britain in 1807 convinced philanthropists that they should work for the ending of slavery itself and, with the backing of the up-and-coming middle class, they took upon themselves the cross of the Blackman. The accounts of travellers such as Barrow (1797–1798), Lichtenstein (1806), Campbell (1815), Philip (1828)[9] and others, supplemented by the reports from the missionary societies, made available for the first time detailed information and provided them with their evidence of the abuse the Blackman allegedly suffered at the hand of the colonists.

The first and by far the most significant English traveller to the Cape Colony for the period ending in the Great Trek – and probably of all times – was John Barrow.[10] Christopher Lloyd, his bio-

---

9. Of course Campbell and Philip were not travellers but missionaries who spent many years in the Colony. However, it is quite feasible to group them with the general body of travellers because of the similarity of their views respecting race relations between White and Black within the Colony.
10. John Barrow, afterwards Sir John, 1764–1848. Of humble birth, John Barrow was a self-made man. After a voyage on a Greenland whaler, Barrow spent three years as a mathematics master at Greenwich where, in his spare time, he taught the son of Sir George Staunton, the life-long friend of Lord Macartney, a connection which took him to China in 1792 and to the Cape as Macartney's private secretary in 1797. Here he became auditor-general and married a local girl, Anna Maria, the cousin of Johannes (later Sir John) Truter. He purchased Newlands House and it was his intention to settle there "as a country gentleman in South Africa" but on the restoration of the Cape to the Dutch he returned to England. In 1804, he became Second Secretary to the Admiralty, a position which he held for forty years. In 1835 a baronetcy was conferred on him. Besides his work on the Cape Colony, he published *Travels in China* and biographical works on Macartney, Anson and Howe. Barrow

grapher, wrote: "if ever there was a self-educated man who made a success of life by the industrious cultivation of his talents it was John Barrow,"[11] while Lady Anne Barnard, a personal acquaintance, remarked "one of the pleasantest, best-informed and most eager-minded young men in the world about everything curious or worth attention"[12] – opinions endorsed by Vernon S. Forbes;[13] nonetheless, Barrow has received unanimous condemnation by Afrikaner historians on grounds of an intractable hatred on his part towards the Afrikaners as a result of being influenced by philanthropists such as Maynier, the deposed landdrost of Graaff-Reinet.

It was Barrow who brought before the English nation the first comprehensive survey of the state of the Cape Colony as it was in 1797/98 and it was he who provided the Cape Colony with its most detailed and accurate map as well as its first proper census. However, irrespective of the undeniable value of this work, Barrow made his mark in the history of South Africa with his descriptions of the Cape inhabitants and the relationship between its various population groups. In particular he was the first Englishman to attribute the problems of the Colony (its lack of development, the friction between the colonists and the natives, and the conditions under which the latter lived) to the actions of the Afrikaners and, with his work bearing something of an official stamp owing to his position of responsibility within the colonial government, Barrow provided those English travellers who succeeded him with a solid basis for continuing the critical attack on the Afrikaners when the relationship between White and Black within the colonies was looked upon with more interest in Britain. It is of great importance to realise that

---

was the founder of the Royal Geographic Society and the greatest promoter of arctic exploration.
The first volume of his narrative on the Cape was based on an extensive tour of inspection of the eastern districts which he undertook as political adviser to landdrost Bresler of Graaff-Reinet who had been despatched to pacify the malcontent burghers of the district; the second volume is based on independent travels to the north-western regions of the Colony. Barrow's *Travels* should be viewed as an attempt to provide Macartney with facts and figures needed to back Dundas' argument that the Cape was of great importance to Britain. He argued that the Colony showed great strategic and economic potential.

11. C. Lloyd, *Mr. Barrow of the Admiralty,* p. 16.
12. As quoted by Lloyd, *ibid.,* p. 52.
13. V. S. Forbes, *Pioneer Travellers of South Africa, 1750–1800,* p. 132.

due to his close association with Macartney, Lady Anne Barnard[14] and others at the Castle in Cape Town throughout the duration of the first occupation, Barrow's opinions can be accepted as expressing the feelings of the English as a whole towards the Afrikaner during this period.

Barrow's significance cannot be over-emphasised for, as Scholtz correctly maintains, "die beskrywings wat Barrow van die Afrikaner gegee het, is in soverre van betekenis dat dit die beeld is wat daar dwarsdeur die negentiende eeu in Brittanje van hom bestaan het".[15] In later years, when his work came to be regarded as a textbook by the philanthropic school of thought in both South Africa and Britain,[16] opinions of the Afrikaner split noticeably into two camps: those who accepted Barrow as an accurate recorder of the affairs of the Cape and those who did not. So powerfully, in fact, did he impress his English and Dutch readers that on the issue of Cape Dutch/English unity within the Colony during the 1820's — and even during the 1830's — his very name was still sufficient to stir up prejudices in the Cape press.[17]

Until the arrival of the 1820 Settlers the English population of the Cape Colony was minimal and comprised only the principal public servants, some Cape Town merchants, the naval staff at Simonstown, a few farmers, a few missionaries and approximately two hundred mechanics and labourers. The English — all Tories, with the "virtues and failings of their kind"[18] — would have been in a decided minority in Cape Town where the Dutch population totalled some 6 000 Whites. It is therefore with this awareness that the initial contact between the English and Afrikaners should be

14. It is interesting to note that although Barrow married a woman born and bred at the Cape, he did not allow this to "shackle his pen" as Lady Anne Barnard feared might happen as the result of such a union. *Vide* D. Fairbridge, *Lady Anne Barnard at the Cape of Good Hope, 1797–1802,* p. 228.
15. Scholtz, *Politieke Denke,* i, p. 348.
16. This was amply illustrated in 1834 when Buxton, on supporting the motion which ultimately led to the Select Committee on Aborigines (1836), had the following to say: "In reference to South Africa . . . I will refer to an authority which few gentlemen in this House will be disposed to question — I mean Mr. Barrow of the Admiralty." (*Vide Hansard,* Part XXIV, 1 July 1834, cols. 1061–1063.)
17. The collision between *The South African Commercial Advertiser* and *The Graham's Town Journal* during 1832–1844 attests to this fact. *Vide infra,* Chapts. V and VIII.
18. E. A. Walker, *A History of South Africa,* p. 144.

considered and in so doing it is of paramount importance to bear in mind that a characteristic of the British nation (so described by a present-day Commonwealth historian) was that while they showed a genius for business and government and had developed a strong protective instinct, the British showed themselves lacking in the "imaginative insight needed if they were to understand and be understood by civilised races different from themselves".[19] For this and a variety of reasons which will be discussed later, the initial contact was not destined to get off to a good start.

Through the eyes of the first Englishmen who wrote on the Cape for the British public at the beginning of the 1800's the day of a typical Cape Town Dutchman[20] commenced "when the husband, having slept the greatest part of the day, finds his bed irksome".[21] He would then drink a solitary cup of coffee, or sometimes he would have a *sopie* or, perhaps both. Then, "with a long pipe stuck into his mouth", he would lounge about in his *slaap mutz* and *nagt cabaay,* either in the house or on the stoep.[22] In the meantime the good woman of the house, having risen alone, would proceed with the household occupations, "which consist of scolding and driving about their slaves" to their daily tasks.[23] The head of the house would then commence with the business of the day which usually entailed attending a *vendutie.* While the inhabitants must obviously have also pursued their various forms of employment, there were no less than three or four of these sales each day in and about Cape Town. Barrow described them as "a kind of a lottery. A man buys a set of goods in the morning, which he again exposes to sale in the evening, sometimes gaining and sometimes losing . . ."[24] In the event of there

19. *C.H.B.E.,* viii, *(South African, Rhodesian and the High Commission Territories),* p. 200; *vide infra,* pp. 41–42.
20. The description which follows does not *pretend* to be an accurate portrayal of Cape living. What is hoped is that it will convey something of the *attitude* which the early Tory English in Cape Town maintained towards the Dutch inhabitants.
21. Barrow, *Travels,* ii, p. 104.
22. *Ibid.*
23. C.O. 48/38, anonymous, undated treatise, "Observations on the Cape of Good Hope," f. 310 (vol. dated 1818). It is possible that the author of this work was R. B. Fisher.
24. Barrow, *Travels,* ii, p. 387. Barrow maintained that in the course of four consecutive months during 1801 the amount of property sold by public auction equalled the total amount of paper money in circulation in the Colony. O. F. Mentzel, in *A Geographical and Topographical Description*

being no sale the man of the house would continue to loll about in a state of undress until midday or, "if the weather be tempting, or any news stirring, he walks out to meet his comrades"[25] and together they would "smoke their pipes and drink wine and *bitters* to edge their appetites and qualify themselves to set a good family example".[26] The hours between 12 and 2 p.m. was the time set aside for the midday dinner. The meal,[27] of which "it is impossible to imagine the quantities of fat that floats on every dish", was followed by a sleep lasting two or three hours.[28] Then, at 6 o'clock the second half of the day began. This was the time of social intercourse. The men would separate from the women and attend their societies or coffee rooms, or else they would congregate at private houses where they would smoke their pipes and *"sit* to *see motions",*[29] while *"things necessary* for *supper"*[30] were ordered. Meanwhile the ladies would have gathered in groups of a dozen or two where young and old alike would "talk over the scandal of the day".[31] Those not so engaged would, after having made themselves look "decent", parade up and down the stoeps of houses either alone or in groups, so that they could "exhibit themselves". During this "show" the "young sparks" of the town would lounge about the streets on foot or, "mounted on papa's horse [would] prance from *stoop to stoop* . . . uttering soft speeches at the feet of their enchantresses".[32] Throughout "the poor children scramble as well as they can among the slaves, to whom they are consigned".[33] At 9 o'clock the evening gun would fire "and,

of the Cape of Good Hope (Van Riebeeck Society, No. 6), ii, p. 78, remarked: ". . . no article of merchandise is free from these speculative ventures."

25. Barrow, *Travels,* ii, p. 104.
26. C.O. 48/38, undated, anonymous treatise, "Observations on the Cape of Good Hope", f. 310.
27. *Ibid.*
28. It is interesting to note that Mentzel, on referring to the strictures the French traveller, La Caille, brought against the type of food eaten by the Cape inhabitants, said: "We must remember that Monsieur is a Frenchman whose palate has been tickled with fricassées, ragoûts and roasts . . . we can read between the lines the Frenchman's disgust for such low taste." (Mentzel, *Description of the Cape of Good Hope,* ii, p. 103.)
29. C.O. 48/38, undated, anonymous treatise, "Observations on the Cape of Good Hope", f. 310.
30. *Ibid.,* f. 311.
31. *Ibid.*
32. *Ibid.*
33. Barrow, *Travels,* ii, p. 105.

as if electrified by it, hundreds of lights are seen at once in motion and in every direction seem to glide about the streets; the parties now break up, and all return, preceeded by a black carrying a lantern, to their respective homes, and for a quarter of an hour the town has quite a magic appearance when . . . every family shuts up within themselves, on *point of eating* . . .".[34] Thus day after day, said Barrow:

> "The lazy glutton safe at home will keep,
> Indulge his sloth, and fatten with his sleep."[35]

A consequence of such living was that few persons had any taste for reading, while no interest at all was shown in the cultivation of the fine arts. Nowhere was a bookshop to be found. A recently opened social club had aspired to a collection of books but owing to the main pursuits of most of the members of "drinking, smoking and gaming" the project was abandoned.[36] The Dutch Church, too, had boasted a fine library but had suffered a similar fate; and although the town possessed an excellent theatre, public response had been such that performances had had to be discontinued. Music was hardly better received for it was found that owing to the Dutch (and a section of the English) inhabitants preferring "a common fiddle accompanied with a pipe and tubor" to serious music, the only way the several "celebrated amateurs" were able to perform before an audience was by assuring their listeners that "their gloomy attention would be recompensed by a gay afterpiece".[37]

Barrow maintained that the underlying problem of the Colony was that the youth grew to maturity in an environment barren of

---

34. C.O. 48/38, undated, anonymous treatise, "Observations on the Cape of Good Hope", f. 311.
35. Barrow, *Travels,* ii, p. 104.
36. Mentzel, who visited the Cape in 1785, in his *Description of the Cape of Good Hope,* had occasion to refute an allegation that "drinking, smoking and gaming" were the general habits of the people. He pointed out that there were two kinds of public houses. The first was where "the usual frequenters . . . [were] soldiers, sailors and slaves" (p. 86), whereas the establishments frequented by "non-commissioned officers and men of similar standing" were entirely different. There "quiet card games" were well played and drinking was not enjoyed to excess (pp. 86–87).
37. Br. Mus., ADD. MSS. 30097, vol. 3, 1805–1806, "Journal of Sir Robert Wilson", f. 52.

opportunity and incentive.[38] To begin with, living in a society which offered no more in the way of education than the teaching of the three R's was, to say the least, a disadvantage. The only alternative open to those parents who insisted upon their children receiving a more advanced education was to send them abroad – a luxury few could afford. However, with or without a formal education, a young man could aspire to no higher calling than that of a clerk within the government service and this was small inducement to self-improvement as the poor salaries offered could not, under any circumstances, be looked upon as a reward for ability. Other than a career in the public service, a young man's dreams could carry him no further than following in the footsteps of his father. Even those who had been fortunate enough to receive an education in Europe, tended to "relapse into the common habits of the colonists" upon their return.[39] One might not choose to agree with the chastisement of the English traveller, Percival, that "money is the idol of the Dutch",[40] yet on consideration, apart from the life of a civil servant, there was not a great deal more to occupy the town dweller than assuming the role of a boarding house *cum* inn keeper, a kind of "Jew broker" *cum* agent to the country Boers, or attending the auction sales and speculating as a "petty dealer".

Of course, Cape Town was not the whole Colony and it played a relatively unimportant part in the fashioning of the Afrikaner as a people. Further afield, the descendants of the French Huguenots – the burghers of Stellenbosch and Drakenstein – occupied the more established farming areas of the Colony, but as far as the opinion-making process of the English was concerned, owing to their situation between Cape Town (where all English/Afrikaner contact took place) and the politically significant frontier districts, these colonists were not of much importance to the travellers in 1800 and therefore did not receive much attention, although these colonists of French descent were recognised as the superior class of Cape farmers. In the same way, the wheat farmers of Swellendam received comparatively little attention from the travellers but unlike the former, though

---

38. Barrow, *Travels,* i, pp. 47–48.
39. *Ibid.,* ii, pp. 393–394.
40. Robert Percival, *An Account of the Cape of Good Hope,* p. 185. Percival was a naval officer stationed at the Cape during the first British occupation, 1795–1802.

found living in good circumstances, they were much condemned for not taking greater advantage of what was thought to be the excellent opportunities afforded them by their surroundings and generally they were looked upon as the "most miserable" of the agricultural class. As far as the personality of these Swellendam farmers was concerned they were held to have much in common with the Boers of the more distant frontier district of Graaff-Reinet.

It is regrettable that, owing to the many generalisations indulged in by those who wrote on the Colony, the burghers of Graaff-Reinet, considered the "least advanced in civilization",[41] were portrayed in such a manner as to create the impression that they were typical of the Cape Colonists as a whole. Barrow was undoubtedly the chief culprit and excelled himself in his descriptions of Cape frontier society and the Graaff-Reinet Boer.[42] He wrote:

> "Placed in a country where not only the necessities, but almost every luxury of life might by industry be procured, he has the enjoyment of none of them. Though he has cattle in abundance he makes very little use of milk or of butter. In the midst of soil and climate most favourable to the cultivation of the vine, he drinks no wine. He makes use of few or no vegetables nor roots. Three times a-day his table is loaded with masses of mutton, swimming in the grease of the sheep's tail. His house is either open to the roof, or covered only with rough poles and turf, affording a favourable shelter for scorpions and spiders; and the earthy floors are covered with dust and dirt, and swarm with insects . . . His apartments, if he happens to have more than one, which is not always the case among the grazing farmers, are nearly destitute of furniture. A great chest that contains all his moveables, and two smaller ones that are fitted to his wagon, are the most striking articles. The bottoms of his chairs consist of thongs cut from a bullock's hide. The windows are without glass; or if there should happen to be any remains of this article, it is so patched and daubed as nearly to exclude the light it was intended to admit. The boor notwithstanding has his enjoyments: he is absolute master of a domain of several miles in extent; and he lords it over a few miserable slaves or

41. Barrow, *Travels*, ii, p. 401.
42. It should be appreciated that whatever the condition or character of the Afrikaner frontiersmen might have been at the close of the 18th century or even throughout the whole of the 19th century, they were by no means unique and in fact were true to the universal type of frontiersman found, for instance, in North America and Australia.

Hottentots without control. His pipe scarcely ever quits his mouth, from the moment he rises till he retires to rest, except to give him time to swallow his *sopie*, or a glass of strong ardent spirit, to eat his meals, and to take a nap after dinner. Unwilling to work, and unable to think; with a mind disengaged from every sort of care and reflection, indulging to excess in the gratification of every sensual appetite, the African peasant grows to an unwieldy size, and is carried off the stage by the first inflammatory disease that attacks him.

How different is the lot of the labouring poor of England, who for six days in the week are doomed to toil for twelve hours in every day, in order to gain a morsel of bread for their family, and the luxury of a little animal food for the seventh day!"[43]

And,

"The women of the African peasantry pass a life with the most listless inactivity. The mistress of the family, with her coffee-pot constantly boiling before her on a small table, seems fixed to the chair like a piece of furniture. The good lady, born in the wilds of Africa, and educated among slaves and Hottentots, has little idea of what, in a state of society, constitutes female delicacy. She makes no scruples of having her legs and feet washed in warm water by a slave before strangers; an operation that is regularly performed every evening. If the motive of such a custom were cleanliness, the practice of it would deserve praise; but to see the tub with the same water passed round through all the branches of the family, according to seniority, is apt to create ideas of a different nature. Most of them go constantly without stockings and shoes, even when the thermometer is down to the freezing point. They generally, however, make use of small stoves to place their feet on. The young girls sit with their hands before them as listless as their mothers. Most of them, in the distant districts, can neither read nor write, so that they have no mental resources whatsoever. Luckily, perhaps, for them, the paucity of ideas prevents time from hanging on their hands. The history of the day is that of their whole lives. They hear nor speak of nothing but that such-a-one is going to the city, or to church, or to be married, or that the Bosjesmans have stolen the cattle of such-a-one, or the locusts are eating their corn. The young people have no meetings at fixed periods, as in most country-places, for mirth and recreation. No fairs, no dancing, no music, nor amusement of any sort. The cold phlegmatic temper and inactive way of life may perhaps be owing to the prolific tendency of all the African

43. Barrow, *Travels*, i, pp. 76–78.

peasantry. Six or seven children in a family are considered as very few; from a dozen to twenty are not uncommon; and most of them marry very young, so that the population of the colony is rapidly increasing . . ."[44]

Isolated as they were at the southern extremity of Africa, the Cape Colonists lived in a conservative world hardly touched by the wave of enlightenment which had transformed the thinking of eighteenth century Europe. The contrast, then, between the people of an isolated and essentially rural Cape and those of an industrialised Europe with its liberal trends stemming from its more developed, metropolitan society was great.

It was the apathetic disposition displayed by the people of the Cape to their country's natural wealth and the commercial possibilities which so richly abounded that first drew criticism from the British during their temporary occupation of the Colony in 1795–1802 and it continued to be one of the main criticisms levelled at the local white Dutch inhabitants throughout the first half of the century. To such people as Barrow and Percival who had witnessed the hardships attendant upon a Europe emerging from the Industrial Revolution (and it will be remembered how Barrow compared the lot of the working class in Britain to that of the Cape Dutchman) the difference in the way of life in a slave-holding colony must have been enormous. In fact, the introduction of slavery was held by Barrow to have been one of the greatest mistakes in the history of the Colony. Besides the evil of slavery itself it had proved particularly detrimental to the character of the slave owners for, in keeping with slave-holding colonies elsewhere, the view had taken root that most types of manual labour were unsuitable for Whitemen. As a result, Barrow complained, the spirit of Batavian industry — a spirit which had once raised a wealthy republic and established a powerful trading empire — was not to be found in a single Dutch colony. In fact, in Barrow's opinion, the colonial Dutch were "the most indolent and prodigal of all nations" for, as soon as they had the means they purchased slaves and stopped working themselves.[45] The result was that the Cape Dutch had become a nation subsisting chiefly upon the labour of slaves, preferring not to work so as "to

---

44. Barrow, *Travels,* i, pp. 80–81.
45. *Ibid.,* ii, p. 29.

avoid any trouble".[46] Nor was Barrow alone in his criticism of the idleness of the Cape Dutch. Percival in 1804 had much to say on the matter[47] and even the sympathetic Lichtenstein referred to the Cape Dutch as "men who have no excitement to activity".[48]

Percival had pointed out that the lax condition of the Colony was very largely due to "the want of patriotic and energetic public characters" and reprimanded the Dutch authorities for not having developed the Cape in case it appeared too attractive to other European powers.[49] John Barrow had also recognised similar tendencies when he outlined what he considered Dutch East India Company policy to have been towards the colonists. He maintained that, in keeping with the contemporary European sentiment towards colonies, the authorities, finding it unnecessary to limit the expansion of the Cape Colony, had placed no bounds on the natural propensity of its White subjects to spread themselves wide over the country for, in so doing,

> "it foresaw that a spirit of industry, if encouraged in a mild and temporate climate, and on fertile soil, might oneday produce a society impatient of the shackles imposed on it by the parent state. It knew that to supply to its subjects the wants of life without the toil of labour or the anxiety of care; to keep them in ignorance, and to prevent a ready intercourse with each other, were the most likely means to counteract such a spirit."[50]

---

46. Barrow, *Travels,* ii, p. 386.
47. Percival, *An Account of the Cape of Good Hope,* pp. 180, 189, 204, 219–220.
48. Henry Lichtenstein, *Travels in Southern Africa in the Years 1803–1806,* p. 364. Lichtenstein was a German traveller to the Cape during the period of the Batavian Republic administration, 1802–1806. He was criticised for certain sympathetic comments he passed on the Cape Dutch inhabitants by the British journal, *Quarterly Review,* Dec. 1812, pp. 391–392.
49. Percival, *An Account of the Cape of Good Hope,* p. 212.
50. Barrow, *Travels,* i, p. 7. The Secession of the Thirteen American Colonies in 1763 confirmed the view that colonies ripened to independence as soon as they grew wealthy and developed interests of their own. In *The Memorandum of Commissary J. A. de Mist* (Van Riebeeck Society, No. 3), p. 195, attention is drawn to the fact that the D.E.I.C. had also adopted this approach towards the Cape Colonists. However, De Mist maintained that in the case of the Cape Colony both geographic and political factors had acted to negate any such action, and the popuplar fear of the colonists becoming too powerful was without foundation. It stemmed, he claimed, from a sense of insecurity arising from the authorities realising that the system of government at the Cape was inadequate.

The implications of such an analysis are great since it may be argued (as it was during the late 1830's) that Barrow recognised something in the make-up of Cape society wherein, under certain conditions, the personality of the frontier Afrikaner would react in such a manner as to remove "the shackles imposed upon it by the parent state". Accepting that the Great Trek represented, as Walker maintains, the rejection of "changing times"[51] in preference for the life to which they were accustomed, is it not possible that Barrow in 1797 was speaking of the Great Trek of 1836? Was he not describing, or diagnosing the ills (perhaps somewhat too zealously) of a particular *type of society* or way of life which had stemmed from a particular environment – one which thrived on freedom of action without interference, freedom of thought possibly and, most important, freedom to move as it chose or, in short, what Walker has termed the *"lekker lewe"?* In view of the collision of interests which the Great Trek manifested in 1836 and the controversy which surrounded it at the time – *particularly* regarding the *causes* of the Great Trek – Barrow's comments upon the state of Cape society in 1797/98 cannot be taken lightly since his main contention was that the Boers represented a wild, undisciplined society, the characteristics of which showed themselves in the people's attitudes towards government, the Blackman, progress, etc. To those who adhered to the liberal or philanthropic school of thought during 1836–1844 the Great Trek was the result of and manifestation of this particular kind of society, an inevitable reactionary movement against the "shackles" imposed by the British Government. Barrow's comments on the state of Cape society should therefore be viewed in this context and that the Great Trek did, in fact, occur is sufficient reason to consider this opinion of his seriously.

As it has been pointed out, the history of the Colony during the

---

51. Walker in *The Great Trek,* pp. 59–105, outlines the character and requirements of the Cape frontiersmen or pastoralists, attributing the causes of the Great Trek to the nature and needs of the mobile society of the interior districts of the Colony. In the *C.H.B.E.,* viii, p. 325, he states that the basis of the colonial frontiersman's way of life was characterised by three main traditions: first, a farm must consist of 6 000 acres of land; second, the redeeming feature of government was that it must be distant; and third, seventeenth century Calvinism – the basis of the religious life of the colonists – demanded that the existing barrier between White and Black be upheld. "The Great Trek" Walker maintains, "took place when and how it did because all these three fundamental traditions were challenged simultaneously".

seventeenth and eighteenth centuries should be looked upon as the "dark night in which the South African nation had its birth"[52] for, by the time the British took possession, the Cape Colony had already developed a society distinctly its own, albeit a conservative one. However, the advent of the British marked the end of isolation for the distant Cape, bringing as they did those ideas which had long been circulating Europe during the second half of the eighteenth century.

From the outset differences in background gave rise to sharp critical attack on the part of the English. For instance, while the appearance of Cape Town was unanimously praised by the early travellers, the listless inactivity in which its white inhabitants were content to live was continually under attack as the "result of ignorance and a proof of the total lack of educational and mental improvement".[53] Thus, Percival spoke of the Cape Dutch as "ignorant", "prejudiced", "indolent", exercising a "perverse bigotry to their own customs".[54] In Barrow's opinion, nowhere on earth was there to be found so large a proportion of "unwieldy and bulky people", nor was there a place where "animal appetites were indulged with less restraint", and where "the powers of body and mind were less capable of exertion".[55]

During 1802 the British press referred to a "most satisfactory" account having been received from the Cape of Good Hope from a gentleman who had been sent on a tour of inspection.[56] Who else could this have been but John Barrow who had then just published the first volume of his *Travels* undertaken during 1797 and 1798. On the strength of Barrow's account the press expressed an attitude which was to pursue the Afrikaners off and on throughout the nineteenth century:

> "Humanity shudders in contemplating the deplorable situation to which the bulk of the native inhabitants, and rightful owners, of this country, have been reduced by the arts and machinations of such lawless miscreants as these [the Cape Dutch]."[57]

52. E. G. Malherbe, *Education in South Africa (1652–1922)*, p. 19.
53. C.O. 48/38, undated anonymous treatise, "Observations on the Cape of Good Hope", f. 312.
54. Percival, *An Account of the Cape of Good Hope*, pp. 204, 217, 219.
55. Barrow, *Travels*, ii, p. 103.
56. *The Observer*, 30 May 1802. This newspaper attached more importance to Barrow's *Travels* than did its counterpart, *The Times*. Further mention is made of Barrow in *The Observer*, 28 Feb. 1802, 18 July 1802.
57. *The Observer*, 18 July 1802.

Barrow informed his British reading public that there could be little doubt that the expansion of the Colony had been at the expense of the aborigine, especially the Hottentots – "the rightful owners" of the land. The Hottentots, considered a "weak and peaceable people", offering little resistance to the advance of the colonists had, as it were, been gradually "cheated" out of their birthright. For, explained Barrow, the Cape Dutch colonists had been quick to learn that "a bottle of brandy was a passport through every horde" and, "with this and tobacco, iron, and a few paltry trinkets, they [the Dutch] purchased a part of the country and of their flock of cattle, and then took the rest by force".[58]

The state of affairs which the British press had commented upon stemmed from the reported intractable and lawless character of the white frontiersmen who, because of their distance from the seat of authority in Cape Town, had been able to extend their territorial possessions at will and without control, completely disregarding any rights the aborigines might have had to the land.[59] Under such circumstances might had been right and, as Pallandt had remarked:

> ". . . this freedom, this spirit of independence and false liberty . . . has made of the South African farmer a tyrant in his domain, and has rendered him so insensible to honest law that he even threatens the Government with sheer disobedience."[60]

While in the vicinity of Algoa Bay, Barrow remarked that, according to the travellers of some twenty years earlier, the virgin country beyond the Gamtoos River (then the colonial limit) had been dotted with Hottentot kraals. In 1797, however, Barrow reported that in all the extensive district of Graaff-Reinet not one independent tribe remained and there was, perhaps, no more than a score of individuals who were not in the employ of the colonists. The 'deplorable situation' which Barrow had sketched referred specifically to "the most wanton and barbarous manner, [in which the Boers held] an absolute power over these poor wretches", and to the decrease of the Hottentot (and Bushman) population which Barrow attributed mainly to

58. Barrow, *Travels*, i, p. 5.
59. *Ibid.* See also A. van Pallandt, *General Remarks on the Cape of Good Hope*, pp. 11–12. Pallandt was private secretary to the governor during the administration of the Colony by the Batavian Republic.
60. Pallandt, *General Remarks on the Cape of Good Hope*, p. 12.

"the cruel treatment they received from an inhuman and unfeeling peasantry", and in fact he predicted that the Hottentots would become an extinct race.[61]

According to Pallandt, "the unfortunate habit" which the frontier Boers had contracted of fighting enemies who were "more timid and ill-natured than dangerous" had reduced frontier relations to a critical state.[62] Barrow informed his English reading public that "the farmer thinks he cannot proclaim a more meritorious action than the murder of one of these people [the Bushmen]" and that their deaths were considered with as much "indifference" as if they were "partridges".[63] He maintained that there was scarcely a cruelty said to have been committed against the slaves of the West Indies that could not find its parallel in the more remote regions of the Cape Colony. Here Boers often resorted to "beating and cutting" the Hottentots in their employ with a kind of whip called a *shambos,* the number of lashes being given according to the system of flogging by pipes,[64] while even firing lead shot into the legs and thighs of their victims was not unheard of.[65] Little wonder that the Bushmen and Hottentots despised the Dutch colonists and were "excited to revenge".[66] Neither could race relations on the frontier hope to improve until the commandos were outlawed – expeditions which were characterised by the most wanton cruelties, including the "inhuman practice of carrying into captivity their women and children . . ."[67]

Of major importance to the subsequent history of South Africa was the attitude held towards the Blackman by the colonists.[68] The

---

61. It is of no small significance to note that John Barrow, and the traveller/missionary body in general failed, either through lack of knowledge or for reasons of their own, to take note of the fact that the decrease in the Hottentot numbers was due to the ravages of two major smallpox epidemics in 1713 and 1755 which almost wiped them out.
62. Pallandt, *General Remarks on the Cape of Good Hope,* pp. 11–12.
63. Barrow, *Travels,* i, p. 85.
64. This system was adopted in the absence of clocks. The offender would not be given a set number of lashes but would be whipped for a set period of time, this time being determined by how long it took to smoke a pipe of tobacco. The number of pipes smoked was dependent upon the magnitude of the crime.
65. Barrow, *Travels,* i, p. 145.
66. *Ibid.,* p. 236.
67. *Ibid.,* p. 290.
68. It must be realised that whatever the basis of the Boers' philosophy was towards the Non-White of the Cape Colony, it was by no means a unique outlook. J. C. Furnas in *The Americans* (pp. 55–56, 92–94, 128) shows

Cape Dutch made no pretence about discriminating between what they referred to as *Christien mensch* and the *Zwarte Natie* considering, as Wilson pointed out, that Nature had drawn a determined line between White and Black and that she had intended "in her partiality that the latter should always be dependents".[69] However, it was not quite as simple as that for, as Scholtz points out, only part of the background to race relations in the Cape Colony of 1795 can be considered home-spun.[70] MacCrone provides greater detail in this connection when he remarks upon the influence religion had on human attitudes from the time when the age of expansion was in full swing. "Religion" he says, "was not an affair merely of the individual or even of the community, but the State as well, so that the religious wars which convulsed Europe during the 16th and 17th centuries had finally to be settled on the principle of *cuius regio eius religio.* Religious intolerance and religious persecution, however, continued not only in the form of anti-Catholic and anti-Protestant prejudice but also in the form of controversies and opposing sects. This state of affairs within Europe was reflected in the attitudes and actions of the Europeans wherever contact was established with non-Europeans."[71] The Afrikaners' strong Calvinist background therefore promised that they, too, would adopt the then current attitude held in Europe towards all men of colour. In addition, the Afrikaners' attitude towards the Non-Whites must be attributed to their constant contact with the Hottentots and Bushmen[72] – "a contact between civilised and non-civilised people – between men who had already climbed high on the ladder of civilisation and those who had not yet put their foot on to the first rung of the ladder".[73] What this meant in practice was that experience having taught them the superiority of the Whiteman, the attitude of the colonists assumed a rigidity wherein persons of colour were looked upon as grossly inferior.

---

the U.S. colonists to poor advantage in this respect: "How to handle the Indians, for example, usually came to mean how to get rid of the Indians." On another occasion he referred to the colonists' attitude towards the Indians as "inhuman" (pp. 128, 55).

69. Br. Mus., ADD. MSS. 30097, vol. 3, 1805–1806, "Journal of Sir Robert Wilson", f. 60.
70. Scholtz, *Origin and Essence of the Race Pattern in South Africa*, p. 3.
71. I. D. MacCrone, *Race Attitudes in South Africa,* p. 6.
72. *Vide infra*, pp. 29–30.
73. Scholtz, *The Origin and Essence of the Race Pattern in South Africa,* p. 4.

Barrow relates an anecdote which well demonstrates how the Cape Dutch did, in fact, consider people of colour to be of a lower status than themselves. While on a tour of inspection on the frontier, General Dundas came across a young black boy who for no apparent reason had been severely beaten. He tells how, on being arrested and placed in the Graaff-Reinet goal for this deed, the responsible Boer had, for a period of three days and night, cried: "Myn God! is dit een maniere om *Christien mensch* te handelen!" and how his shouts had not been cause by physical pain but rather by the degradation of being placed on the level with the *Zwarte Natie*.[74]

Pallandt epitomised the then prevailing attitude of the Cape Dutch towards the Blackman when, referring to the situation in the interior of the Colony, he wrote:

> "Who would believe in Europe that it is difficult, not to say impossible, to make an African farmer, who has been brought up amidst the barbarous treatment which his parents used to inflict upon the natives [the Hottentots] and sometimes upon the unhappy Bushmen, realise that these creatures, on whom he bestows the name of heathen, are his equals by the laws of nature; and that this truth, so simple, appears so ridiculous to them that one of them having been brought to justice a year or so ago in connection with a case of homicide, with which crime a Hottentot charged him (one of his parents having been killed), thought his defence complete and the accusation completely answered by a mere contradiction, to which he added a text from the Holy Bible where it is said of the heathen, *the truth is not in them.* A number of similar facts accounts for the deliberate and wilful evasions of law by these misguided men. All their letters contain pious introductions and conclusions, whereas the main portion only too often contain tales of atrocities. This unfortunate contrast greatly surprised the good Governor on his travels in the interior, and after the story which has just been given it can be said that this fanaticism of the farmers is more troublesome to the Government than the barbarism of the natives. The Governor in the course of his travels drew the attention of several farmers to the fact that their conduct deserved the greatest condemnation, and was amazed beyond measure when one of them, anxious to defend his conduct, showed the Governor, by a process of reasoning of his own, that the natives are directly descended from

74. Barrow, *Travels,* ii, p. 98.
Walker, in *A History of Southern Africa,* p. 207, regards this as the "cause *par excellence*" of the Great Trek. See also Walker's *The Great Trek,* pp. 59–105.

> Ham, and that the threats that had been pronounced against that race entitled the farmers to treat them as a people hated by God himself . . ."[75]

When the British abandoned the Cape Colony in 1802, lasting impressions had been formed. Against an official background of little or no genuine concern for the Afrikaners, the relationship between the English and Afrikaners could not possibly have got off to a worse start. With the exception of Percival, Barrow was the only Englishman at the Cape during the period of the first occupation to publish an account of the Colony and its peoples, and owing to his close personal association with the officials at the Castle and the opportunities afforded him by his official position as secretary to the Governor, he was looked upon as something of an authority on the interior Afrikaners. Moreover, besides the impression he created of the Afrikaners, he did, as has already been stated, commence a tradition of criticism of the Afrikaners which was to persist throughout the nineteenth century; also, from his *Travels* it becomes obvious that when the term 'Afrikaner' was applied in English circles, this invariably meant the frontier Afrikaner of the District of Graaff-Reinet and beyond and also, to a lesser extent, to the Afrikaners of the District of Swellendam.

On only three points did John Barrow find something good to say of the Afrikaners of the Cape Colony. First, he allowed them what one British journal termed the "savage virtue of hospitality";[76] second, they produced fine grapes and third, they bred excellent goats. He informed the British nation that the colonists of the Cape of Good Hope were an indolent, phlegmatic and backward race of people and created the impression that the undeveloped state of society was to be attributed to the lack of order and the general absence of discipline among the colonists, a state which was reflected in the attitude held by the colonists towards the Blackman, which relationship had come to be characterised by extreme cruelty and abuse on the part of the "loathsome" Afrikaners.

---

75. Pallandt, *General Remarks on the Cape of Good Hope,* p. 12. See also *The Memorandum of Commissionary J. A. de Mist,* pp. 256–257; John Campbell, *Travels in South Africa,* p. 344.
76. *Quarterly Review,* Dec. 1812, p. 391.

CHAPTER TWO

Perspective
1795–1812

In order to gain an understanding of the Afrikaners it is necessary to be aware of certain essential aspects of their history for, as it has been suggested, "no one can know or appreciate the Boer who does not know his past; for he is what his past has made him".[1]

By 1795, when Great Britain occupied the Cape Colony, isolation at the extremity of the dark continent, the African sun and the lethargy of an inward-looking mercantile government had caused the 15 000 Europeans[2] of predominantly Dutch origin then comprising the Afrikaner people to so thoroughly adapt to the South African environment that they had emerged as an entirely distinctive group having their own identity which was neither wholly Dutch nor African. Whatever, then, might be said of the Cape Colony, or more particularly of the Afrikaner at the beginning of the nineteenth

---

1. E. G. Malherbe, *Education in South Africa (1652–1922)*, p. 20.
2. Malherbe (*ibid.*, p. 41) provides most useful statistics for the white colonial population for the period 1652–1855:

1652	100 (about)	1672	221
1687	612	1700	1 245
1715	1 886	1722	2 212
1740	3 920	1754	5 510
1772	8 300 (about)	1775	8 669
1778	9 507	1783	11 064
1786	11 829	1793	13 830
1795	14 952	1798	21 746
1803	25 260	1813	33 968
1819	42 217	1821	47 280
1830	55 355	1849	88 490
1855	102 156		

century, certain factors need to be considered against which the Boer personality and any comments it invited need to be weighed. The shaping of the Afrikaner character and the progress of the Afrikaners towards nationhood must be seen in the light of two overall factors: their European origin and their African environment.

When the Cape of Good Hope was established as a halfway station between Europe and the East there was not the remotest intention of forming a colony — a fact which was to prove detrimental to its development and was also to have bearing upon the size and composition of its White population. While Holland might have been the leading nation of Europe — an outward-looking Christian society germinating that rational spirit which was to sweep Europe later during the eighteenth century — and while it might have been at the zenith of its cultural attainments and in the heyday of its commercial power, the infant Cape settlement was endowed with none of the practical advantages such an association might have brought. Seen against the background of Company policy, realistically the settlement could not possibly have hoped to be more than a halfway house, since in practice it was found that men with ability remained in the Netherlands and rarely entered the service of the Dutch East India Company where "the pay was bad and the death rate high",[3] (giving some foundation to the remarks passed by Percival regarding "the want of patriotic and energetic public characters"[4]). In fact, remarked the German traveller Mentzel in 1785, "men who enlist as soldiers or sailors under the conditions offered by the Company are as a rule down at heel and practically destitute".[5] What Hartz concludes from this information is that while the first free burgher population might have been drawn from the highly talented Dutch nation, it was nonetheless drawn exclusively from discharged Company employees, such as Mentzel described. However, Hartz con-

---

The Non-White numbers were as follows: there were more than 25 000 slaves, 80% of whom were found in and about Cape Town and Stellenbosch, while the District of Graaff-Reinet accounted for no more than 2 000. According to the 1798 census compiled by Barrow, there were some 15 000 Hottentots living within the Colony, 14 000 of whom were residing within the Districts of Swellendam and Graaff-Reinet. As far as the Bushmen were concerned, no records are available although it can be assumed that their numbers were small.

3. Louis Hartz (ed.), *The Founding of New Societies*, p. 182.
4. *Vide supra*, p. 15.
5. Mentzel, *Description of the Cape of Good Hope*, ii, p. 21.

tinues, whatever qualities might have been absent from the free burghers as a group, "what were present were the toughness of the peasant and the unsuccessful townsman [and] their capacity to endure adverse circumstances . . . Those qualities were invaluable in their struggle to adapt themselves to a harsh environment, where wild animals were a constant menace, Bushmen and Hottentots were liable to steal their property, the rainfall was unreliable, the soil was generally poor, crops and livestock were subject to strange deseases, and the government was not much concerned with their welfare."[6]

Of course, towards the end of the seventeenth century the Cape Colony had attracted the French Huguenots to its shores, people who had been motivated by religious idealism, but Company policy being what it was and aimed at forming a single Dutch community, within two generations the 160-odd Frenchmen had completely submerged their national identity and adopted the characteristics of their new environment.[7] As Le Vaillant remarked in the 1780's, "banished from France, they have even forgotten the language".[8] Something of their heritage must have remained, though, to distinguish them from their neighbours since it will be remembered that the travellers to the Cape round about 1800 singled out the descendants of the Huguenots as the superior class of colonial farmers. However, asserts Hartz,[9] by far the largest section of the progenitors of the Afrikaners was drawn from elements which had failed to prosper in the free, competitive society of the Netherlands,[10] and while the French and other immigrants undoubtedly contributed to the quality of Cape society they were, nonetheless, totally assimilated.

---

6. Hartz, *The Founding of New Societies,* p. 182.
7. Without exception, in 1800 all travellers bore testimony to the fact that the Huguenots had lost their French identity. See, for instance, Mentzel, *Descriptions of the Cape of Good Hope,* ii, p. 100.
8. Le Vaillant, *Travels into the Interior Parts of Africa,* i, p. 33.
9. Hartz, *The Founding of New Societies,* p. 182.
10. It is necessary to point out that Hartz is a renowned critic of the Afrikaners. His views respecting the composition of the Dutch free burgher population are not held by Afrikaner historians where the emphasis is rather placed on the inherent qualities of a European heritage and the ensuing effect of a mercantile government upon it. See van Jaarsveld, *The Awakening of Afrikaner Nationalism,* pp. 9–12; Scholtz, *Politieke Denke,* i, pp. 53, 115–130. Scholtz, a patriot historian, shows the Afrikaner interpretation of the question clearly: "Die behoorlike vermeerdering van die vryburgers sou vanaf die begin voor een besondere moeilikheid stuit. Dit was om mense te vind wat voldoen het aan die eise wat 'n

Undoubtedly the biggest setback to the development of the Colony, however, lay not so much in the actual composition of the European population of the Cape Colony, for whatever disadvantages they might have had resulting from their status in Europe, this would and could be redeemed (as subsequent events showed) by *opportunity,* but rather in the smallness of their numbers. In practice this meant two things: first, they were unable to assert themselves as their American cousins had done against oppression by a mercantile government; and second, because they lacked a wide cross-section of European society, the Cape Colonists would need to start from scratch, as it were, in the construction and development of a colonial society. Under these circumstances it would take generations to reach the point at which the American colonists had started.

The physical disadvantages facing the Dutch colonists were great and, as if revelling in its primitive state, the country offered few natural advantages which might have assisted development – something which makes comparison with the American Colonies difficult. In the first place, the coast was most unfavourable for shipping and there was not a single river mouth which would admit sea-going vessels of even modest dimensions. Then the navigability of the rivers themselves proved a further drawback to the development of the interior as the only river in Southern Africa with any value for shipping was the Zambesi – small comfort to the Cape Dutch – and while a number of other rivers could accommodate small vessels for short distances, no commercial benefit could be derived from these at all. Transportation by means of coastal shipping and inland waterways proving impossible, it fell to the tedious oxwagon to facilitate the development of the country. A far cry from the internal canal system of Europe and certainly nothing like the great rivers and lakes of the North American continent.

With the absence of those natural means of communications which might have made possible a ready intercourse with the interior, the widely dispersed farmers became even more isolated the further they settled from Cape Town, and owing to the physical character of the country in the interior and the mode of farming pursued, farms of

---

nuwe land stel. Suid-Afrika het hom nie maklik laat tem nie . . . Die manne wat hulle by hierdie omstandighede kon aanpas, moes sowel geestelik as liggaamlik oor besondere eienskappe beskik. Sulke manne was nie volop nie" (p. 53).

6 000 acres or more were typical.[11] The greatest obstacle of all to the development of the Cape, however, was the absence of a steady stream of immigrants to boost the meagre European population.[12] While in 1795 there had been approximately 15 000 Whites (or 21 000 in 1798), some 6 000 of whom resided within Cape Town, had there been a white population of, say, even 50 000 within Cape Town and a proportionate number within the districts, the Cape Colony, of necessity, would have been a very different place by the time the British arrived. What the Patriot Movement at the Cape might have developed into is difficult to say, yet it can be conjectured that had the movement managed to get off the ground there could have developed in embryo an economic situation at the Cape strongly resembling that of the U.S. Colonies, with the Afrikaners asserting themselves and establishing the Cape Colony as a trading nation. On the other hand, the success of such an attempt is doubtful since it would have proved almost impossible during the eighteenth century to convert the Cape into a thriving colony owing to the economic disadvantages it had to contend with and the fact that at that time Europe had no need to import foodstuffs. Unlike the settlers of the British North America colonies who were free to grow what produce they liked and were at liberty to sell it to the highest bidder and within the best available market, the Cape Colonists found themselves continually at loggerheads with the economic interests of the Dutch East India Company whose policy it had been to establish itself as the sole buyer of colonial produce and maintain its inviolable prerogative to monopolise oversea trade.[13] The colonists, therefore, unable to assert their interests, turned their backs on the sea and looked inland where, beyond the limits of the settlement, Africa lay beckoning. The Company did not impede the expansion of its colonists and in return for small annual licences it gave out large tracts of

---

11. *C.H.B.E.*, viii, p. 5. Under these circumstances the isolation of the leading pioneers was to be expected. However, as Scholtz points out (*Politieke Denke*, i, p. 116) the danger existed that these persons might lose their European identity and sink to the level of their wild and African environment.
12. M. Whiting Spilhaus in *South Africa in the Making, 1652–1802*, p. 191, brings to notice a most interesting statistic. She writes that while the European population of the Cape Colony in 1795 was under 16 000 and widely scattered over 135 000 square miles, the USA, only a generation older, had a settler population of 3 million.
13. *C.H.B.E.*, viii, p. 119; S. D. Neumark, *The South African Frontier*, p. 16.

land in the interior. From here grew the trekboer or pastoralist who so greatly influenced the future character of South Africa.

When the highly significant, though small, trading operations were initiated by the Cape merchants towards the end of the eighteenth century it represented a momentous step forward in the development of the Cape Colony but, as in the past the mercantile interests of the Company had been placed above those of the colonists, so also the jealously guarded British trading interests required that the venture be stifled.[14] If only the Cape Colony could have experienced a flood of European immigration similar to that of the United States, then the history of South Africa would have taken a very different course, but realistically the Cape, situated at the southern tip of 'Darkest Africa', was altogether a different proposition to America which had established itself in the public mind as the 'New World'. The Cape Colony was destined therefore to make its way slowly in the world. In fact, development would take place only as rapidly as her natural physical obstacles allowed, and her limited European population was able. As a country, then, the Cape Colony was poor, distances were great and the European population small – not to mention the effects of drought or the ravages of locusts – and in 1795 when Great Britain occupied the Cape Colony markets were poor, there were few roads, no bridges and no mail service, the lack of which had special bearing on the moulding of the personality of the rural farming population.

In addition to these retarding factors, the Cape Colonists were the victims of a highly conservative policy pursued by the Dutch East India Company which, anxious to avoid any possibility of a political uprising by the colonists and, of course, also for reasons of economy, had withheld from the inhabitants training for the assumption of political responsibility. The effect this policy had was that in and about the Cape Peninsula where the interests of the Company chiefly lay and where its influence was the greatest, the people, being denied

---

14. It is interesting to consider what was required of the Cape Colony to assert itself as an independent trading nation. Like the example set by the U.S. Colonies, which broke into and disrupted the previously British monopolised North Atlantic trade triangle (between London, the West Indies and the U.S. Colonies) and which had been the economic foundation of the first British Empire, so the Cape of Good Hope with its 20 000 colonists would have needed to threaten and disrupt the basis of the modern British Empire, viz. the trade triangle lying between India, the River Plate and London. Of course, no such possibility existed.

a proper say in the machinery of government, developed little or no sense of political responsibility[15] – hence their attitude: "the Government knows best, Sir", which later drew comment from the English.[16] On the other hand, where the Company had no interests the situation was the reverse. In the interior the Boers were left entirely to their own devices, and where the effective influence of the government was absent respect for its authority dwindled to nothing. The sparseness of the population and their limited contact with church and school further added to isolate Boer communities from each other and from external influences, all of which contributed to provide the sociological foundations of the Afrikaner people and went far to create a conservative state of mind and a strong feeling of self-reliance among them.

It would have been strange indeed had the Afrikaners not been influenced by their surroundings. In Cape Town – the only real town in the Colony – petty traders and innkeepers sprang up whose prosperity rose and fell with the size of the garrison and the number of ships in harbour. The agriculturalists who were close enough to the town sold what they could to the market and in order to guard against unsatisfactory market conditions, produced as much of their own needs as possible. As for the trekboer, the cattle farmer of the interior, his needs were few and he lived virtually independently. He might once a year or so visit Cape Town to purchase supplies but even this might not have been necessary since agents visited him where he was.

Environment may also be taken as going a long way to explaining the relationships established by the Afrikaners between themselves and the Blackman. Outnumbered and isolated as they were, and feeling the need to maintain their European identity, the basis of their attitude stemmed from their belief that the Blackman – the descendants of Ham – cursed with the 'Mark of Cain', had been subjected to the inferior position of 'hewer of wood and drawer of water' by God Himself and that compared to them, the Afrikaners were a chosen people.[17] The further away from Cape Town the stronger this

---

15. Hartz, *The Founding of New Societies,* p. 185; Scholtz, *Politieke Denke,* i, p. 220.
16. Such as the *Commercial Advertiser,* 15 March 1826.
17. Scholtz (*Politieke Denke,* i, pp. 217–218) refers to the concept that the Blackman was, in fact, considered the descendant of Ham and states that this has ". . . waarlik soos 'n swaar meulsteen aan die nek van die Afri-

belief became where the threat of the natives was more real and where isolation had precluded participation in the religious revival or Enlightenment of eighteenth century Europe. Primitive Calvinism with its doctrine of predestination, its emphasis upon the Old Testament, its rejection of emotionalism and its appeal to nationalism had consolidated the Afrikaner attitude towards the native within the first decades of the settlement being established – an attitude which was further strengthened by the relationship which existed between white master and black slave and which, common to all slave-holding colonies, had given rise to the concept that manual or domestic labour was unfit for the Whiteman, which outlook had resulted in the absence of an Afrikaner artisan class. In the eyes of the early colonists, by the unalterable decrees of God, the Blackman had been provided for their use, and it was therefore necessary that, when dealing with the Hottentots, Bushmen and Bantu, these people of colour should at all times be impressed with the superior authority of the Whiteman. In other words, the Blackman would be kept *'op sy plek'*. In addition to all this was the fact that the Afrikaners were tremendously outnumbered and with the government not assuming its responsibility to govern, it became necessary for them to take the affairs of the frontier into their own hands.

By 1795 the European roots of the white South African community were almost completely severed.[18] Very few of them had ever visited Europe or were in communication with anyone living there. However, it should be remembered – especially in view of the unfavourable

---

kaner gehang". Remarking further upon such thinking, Scholtz provides the background against which such an idea could have taken root among the early Afrikaners: "Ander volke kon reeds aan die einde van die agtiende eeu van hierdie aweregse vertolking van die Bybel ontslae raak. Vanweë die isolasie waarin hy verkeer het, het die Afrikaner hierdie ewolusie nie meegemaak nie en is die skadelike opvatting sodanig aanvaar dat daar vandag nog duisende Afrikaners is wat daaraan glo."
Theal (*History and Ethnography of South Africa before 1795,* iii, pp. 306–307) maintains that the feeling of superiority towards the Blackman was further strengthened in the everyday contact they had with them. "Observation and experience" he said, and personal dealings with the "wild Hottentots", "savage Bushmen" and "barbarous Xhosa", "had taught them [the Afrikaners] that these races who did nothing for the world's good were inferior to their own, and they did not, and could not, set the same value upon the life of one of them as upon the life of a civilised white man".

18. Hartz, *The Founding of New Societies,* p. 187; Theal, *History and Ethnography of South Africa before 1795,* iii, pp. 285–286.

comparisons between them and various African tribes which had been made by certain travellers[19] – they belonged to one of the most intelligent races in the world, and if intelligence in every branch of knowledge was not apparent, it was because the faculties were dormant and not because they were wanting.[20] Sheer distance and the dangers and discomfort of the voyage to Europe were not the only cause of this separation. Within two years of their emancipation, the free burghers were protesting to Van Riebeeck that "instead of being helped, we are oppressed". In the first decade of the eighteenth century there was vigorous protest against the administration of W. A. van der Stel. In the 1770's 'patriots' of the south-western Cape signed a petition and sent delegates to protest to the States-General, and in 1795 the trekboers of Graaff-Reinet and Swellendam had declared their districts to be independent of the Company. These were merely the highlights in a relationship which was always essentially disharmonious. The Dutch East India Company, having had no intention of forming a colony, had no interest in the grievances of its colonists. First and foremost were its shareholders – if people chose to settle at the Cape it was not going to cost the Company anything. Such an outlook did nothing to encourage the loyality and affection of the colonists to the Company and went far to build up a spirit of independence in the new Colony which they had made their home.

Although some 500 miles separated the agriculturalists in the south-west and the extreme pastoralists in the interior, differences between them should not be overaccentuated. Essentially they formed a single people. They worshipped in the same church and spoke the same language, their own Afrikaans, and, above all, they shared the same colonial environment which had shaped them all.[21] The differences between those living in the established areas in and about Cape Town and those who lived in the wilds near the border under the cover of an ox-wagon or mud house were, in fact, due to the temporary differences in economic well-being and political stability. The more

---

19. This was continually harped on by Barrow and Percival throughout their works, while the ultra-critical J. W. D. Moodie in his *Ten Years in South Africa,* i, pp. 169–170, went to great lengths to indicate that actually the Boers were not anything as refined as even the Hottentots. *Vide infra,* Chapt. VI.
20. Malherbe, *Education in South Africa,* p. 47.
21. Scholtz, *Politieke Denke,* i, pp. 418–420; *C.H.B.E.,* viii, p. 167.

outspoken critics of the Afrikaners certainly thought of them as being one people. Percival, for instance, had considered there was little difference in the personality of the farmers near Cape Town and the graziers of the interior districts: "The same unsocial and selfish character is conspicuous in both."[22] As far as Barrow was concerned the grazier inhabitants of Graaff-Reinet, for instance, were simply the *least* advanced or, the *most* indolent.[23] Nor was it that the inhabitants of Cape Town were really any better, it was just that they were not quite *as bad*. To such persons it was a question of degree.

In the Hollander Pallandt's opinion it was the interior which was "the principal point, the fountain of the Colony's happiness and which consequently deserves all possible notice and attention".[24] When the British arrived the burghers of the interior districts were in a state of insurrection against the authority of the Company, immediately drawing attention to themselves as a trouble spot, particularly since those districts were indispensable to the Colony for its supply of meat.[25] An even greater problem area, however, was the frontier where friction with the Xhosas in the past had erupted into warfare, which point alone was enough to make the frontier the chief problem area of the Colony. To the British, who had conquered the Cape in 1795, the greatest contributory factor to the situation as it existed was the overall weakness of the administration of the Dutch East India Company, whose glaring inconsistency was the indiscriminate granting of farms to colonists on the one hand, and the weakness of the government which had been unable to check this expansion on the other. As a result there had been no proper management of relations between European and Xhosa. As far as the English were concerned, this state of affairs had led to the colonists assuming an aggressive disposition towards both the natives and the Government and it was this that constituted the frontier problem.

Contact between the White- and Blackman had commenced in 1652 the moment Van Riebeeck set foot on African soil. It will be remembered that he had been instructed to establish a refreshment station where supplying the needs of passing vessels was to have been

22. Percival, *An Account of the Cape of Good Hope,* p. 204.
23. Barrow, *Travels,* ii, p. 401.
24. Pallandt, *General Remarks on the Cape of Good Hope,* p. 11.
25. Neumark, *The South African Frontier,* pp. 48–56.

achieved in a manner which would carefully maintain friendly relations with the natives. Such a state of affairs could only exist as long as the two parties did not offend each other. In reality, though, and as far as the Hottentots were concerned, such a relationship could only be maintained as long as no attempt was made at colonising the Cape. To begin with all went well. The Hottentots, while they had never actually welcomed the appearance of the Europeans, had none-theless not been ill-disposed towards them. The reason for this is plain. While Van Riebeeck and his party confined themselves to the original limits of the settlement, both could live in relative peace as there were no grounds for hostilities, neither party feeling his interests to be threatened. (For the sake of peace the Company had been prepared to ignore any losses incurred through Hottentot thieving.) However, the decision of the Company to adopt a policy of colonisation with the emancipation of the free burghers altered the relationship as this meant that farms were granted beyond the limits of the settlement. With the adoption of this policy the Cape immediately assumed the status of a colony. This resulted in the Hottentots instinctively feeling insecure and their relationship with the officials, now turned colonists, rapidly deteriorated. Petty thieving increased and the free burghers, who now had a personal stake in the losses, demanded redress from Van Riebeeck and threatened action themselves if the authorities did not do so.

The significance of the first outbreak of hostilities between the Europeans and Hottentots is to be found in the ensuing peace of 1660 for it was this 'treaty' which shaped future White and Black contact.[26]

26. The description of the state of affairs created by this first outbreak is well outlined in the *C.H.B.E.*, viii, pp. 124–125. Utilising the *Dagverhaal* (III, 300 sqq.) it is stated: "[After the peace] the Natives made valiant and pathetic efforts to regain their rights to the grazing lands now occupied by the whites, "standing upon it, that we (the Dutch) had gradually been taking more and more of their land, which had been theirs since the beginning of time . . . Asking also, whether, if they had come to Holland, they would have been permitted to do the like." The Commander replied that if their lands were restored, there would not be enough grazing for both nations. Whereupon the Hottentots retorted, "Have we then no cause to prevent you from getting more cattle? The more you have, the more lands you occupy. And to say that the land is not big enough for us both, who should by right give way, the rightful owner or the foreign invader?" Plainly disconcerted by such logic, the Commander, in accordance with the ideas of his time and the universal practice of colonising peoples, could only adduce the right of conquest. In the end the Hottentots had to accept the situation and promise to cease their molestations."

An expanding colony, which European interests called for, meant that Hottentot land would, by right of conquest, become European land. It was further apparent that as time went by, the colonists and their children's children would, as their herds increased, require more and more of the land hitherto occupied by the aborigines. The clash between white and black pastoralist societies over the issue of good grazing land had, within the first years of the Colony, already assumed recognisable proportions and it was clear that it would preoccupy the European throughout the ensuing centuries.

By 1795 the expansion of the Colony by the trekboer, his spirit having then been infected with something of the *wanderlust* (also, the economic demands placed upon a grazier were few), had resulted in the Colony sprawling over the extensive area of almost 158 000 square miles – extending nearly to the Orange River in the north and the Fish River in the east. This meant that the more advanced colonists now resided as far away as 500 miles from Cape Town – a journey of forty days by wagon. The Hottentots and Bushmen, having provided little resistance to the advance of the colonists, had not seriously retarded expansion and those who had not retreated were found to be in the employ of the colonists, no longer possessing lands of their own. Their tribal system almost entirely disintegrated, the Hottentots of the eastern half of the Colony were for the most part either vagrants or miserably paid farm labourers. Conversely, the collision with the powerful and southerly migrating Xhosa nation during the second half of the eighteenth century provided the frontiersmen with their first major barrier to further expansion which was so effective that it was only circumscribed by the Great Trek. The sacking of the European occupied Zuurveld during the opening years of the nineteenth century well illustrates the severity of this collision, especially as it threatened the continued existence of the Colony as a White settlement. This had great significance as it forced the government of the day, for the first time in the history of the Colony, to fully investigate the frontier situation and provide a solution. This fell to the British who had again occupied the Colony in 1806.

The problem governing the frontier was deeply rooted. Governors who might have wished to enquire into the existing state of affairs were frustrated by having to rely upon persons who either did not know the facts or whose accounts were untrustworthy. Into the first category fell those "who might suppose themselves qualified to answer" but were not in a position to offer judgment, for although they might have been born at the Cape, they had no first-hand knowledge of the frontier. The second category numbered those who, although they held government positions and therefore had the opportunity of making on-the-spot observations, because of a common failing of wishing to represent "their own conduct in [a] very favourable point of view", tempered their accounts with a "bias, which self-interest, connexions, or enmities, will so frequently produce", thus rendering questionable the validity of their researches.[27] According to Collins, the man despatched by the colonial authorities to investigate the state of the frontier in 1808, this lack of communication between the Government and the frontiersmen had been responsible for "a great portion of the miseries that have fallen to the lot of the Aborigines and Colonists".[28] It went deeper than this, however. The administration of the Dutch East India Company, considered "ill-contrived, and badly executed",[29] was held to be responsible for the entire situation which had led to the frontier hostilities, for it was found that the habits of the colonists of increasing their holdings of land could be attributed to the lack of a "regular exercise of control".[30] This, maintained the influential Commissioners of Enquiry in 1825, had given rise to the colonists encroaching upon "lands occupied by the native Tribes",[31] recognised by all as the basis of friction between European and Aborigine. Van Riebeeck, by having granted lands belonging to the Hottentots,[32] had created a precedent which had become the norm – a state of affairs which was bound to

27. C.O. 48/6, "Col. Collins' Report on the Frontier Districts", 1809, f. 35.
28. *Ibid.*, f. 34.
29. Anon., *An Account of the Colony of the Cape of Good Hope with a view to the Information of Emigrants*, p. 39.
30. C.O. 48/76, "Report of the Commissioners of Inquiry at the Cape of Good Hope, dated 25th May 1825", f. 56. It is interesting to note that in 1831 the view was expressed that the oppression which the Hottentots experienced at the hands of the Boers was "chiefly owing to [the] absence of those warlike propensities which characterises most uncivilised tribes, and the little energy which the Hottentots displayed among themselves". (C.O. 48/144, "Missionary Institutions at the Cape of Good Hope", dated Colonial Office, 15 Oct. 1831, f. 23: encl. to Cole to Goderich, 10 May 1831.)
31. C.O. 48/76, "Report of the Commissioners of Inquiry at the Cape of Good Hope, dated 25th May 1825", f. 56.
32. Philanthropists spoke of what they called the "Van Riebeeck Principle",

continue until either the colonists no longer required additional land or they were forcibly prevented from acquiring it.

Sparrman had believed that the belligerent attitude of the Bushmen towards the colonists had been assumed in order to "withstand the encroachments" of the latter;[33] Collins more or less reiterated this view when he concluded that as far as the "actual commencement" of hostilities had been concerned, there did not appear to be "any distinct cause", except that there had been mistrust on the part of the Bushmen and this they had been quick to manifest towards the colonists "from the moment of their approach".[34] What had proved unfortunate was that the first colonists to reside on the frontier[35] had shown themselves "destitute of the qualifications necessary to remove these unfavourable impressions" from the minds of the Bushmen.[36] What Collins judged to have been responsible for sparking off actual hostilities, as opposed to a mere "dislike arising from original impressions", had been "the imprudence of an individual".[37] Collins recalled a time when the relationship between the colonists and the Bushmen (on the Tak River) had been one of peaceful co-existence and instanced early recollections of certain colonists who had settled on their side of the river some sixty years previous. Even though the Bushmen had shown active animosity towards the Namaquas – "a timid people possessing cattle"[38] – relations with the colonists had been so friendly that Bushmen even returned stray cattle belonging to the Colony.[39] And so it had continued until a servant of a colonist carried off the wife of a Bushman. Seeking revenge, the Bushman murdered the servant and to retaliate the colonists called up a commando. Hottentots in the employ of the farmers sided with the Bushmen and this resulted in armed collision. The peace of the past was shattered.

In the absence of military protection, the commando system –

---

whereby it was held that Van Riebeeck had calculated the number of White casualties which would be required to ensure a victory in any collision with the Hottentots over any particular piece of land. If the price was "reasonable", then agitation for expansion was instigated.

33. Sparrman, *A Voyage to the Cape of Good Hope,* ii, p. 142.
34. C.O. 48/6, "Col. Collins' Report on the Frontier Districts", 1809, f. 38.
35. In this case the colonists of Camdeboo.
36. C.O. 48/6, "Col. Collins' Report on the Frontier Districts", 1809, f. 38.
37. *Ibid.,* f. 37.
38. C.O. 48/2, Collins to Caledon, 30 May 1808, f. 10.
39. *Ibid.,* ff. 10–11.

mounted bodies of armed Boers called out to retaliate against the raids of Bushmen, Hottentots and Bantu and used for the purpose of tracing stolen cattle – became an integral part of frontier life and something which drew strong condemnation because of abuses allegedly perpetrated under its auspices. Collins, on referring to the actions of these military expeditions, claimed that they had "disgraced the name of Christian".[40] Abuse of the commando system during the seventeenth and eighteenth centuries was thought to have been widespread by all Englishmen who commented upon the state of affairs on the frontier during the rule of the Dutch East India Company[41] – hence it became known as the commando "system" – "system" having ominous overtones. The concensus of English opinion was as follows: In the face of constant thieving from Bushmen and on finding it impossible to draw them into their employ as servants (like the Hottentots), the more distant and turbulent Boers represented the Bushmen to the authorities in far-off Cape Town as "unfit to live".[42] The implication is clear. Owing to a necessity to expand territorially and the accompanying requirement for labour, the Boers reported the state of affairs to the Cape Government as critical so that a commando could be mustered. Under these circumstances a "system of desultory warfare" was pursued which satisfied the need not only for land but also for labour.[43] Besides serving as a defence, therefore, the commando fulfilled a further two-fold purpose and became a profitable expedition. The main problem was the absence of government control. Collins was certainly of this opinion and again referred to the ignorance of government which had resulted in the reports of "interested parties" being too credulously received and from which stemmed an "unrestrained licence"[44] for "unlimited commandoes"[45] being granted to the colonists in the prosecution of their war against the Bushmen.[46] This state of affairs was seen as giving

---

40. C.O. 48/6, "Col. Collins' Report on the Frontier Districts", 1809, f. 39.
41. *All* Englishmen from Barrow onwards were in agreement on this point. Successive and various governors as well as the British Government also held this view. *Vide infra,* Chapt. III.
42. C.O. 48/6, "Col. Collins' Report on the Frontier Districts", 1809, f. 39.
43. C.O. 48/76, "Report of the Commissioners of Inquiry at the Cape of Good Hope, dated 25th May 1825", f. 56.
44. *Ibid.,* f. 57.
45. C.O. 48/6, "Col. Collins' Report on the Frontier Districts", 1809, f. 39.
46. Other than proclaiming the Fish River as a boundary between White and Black and decreeing a policy of non-intercourse, the Company had done

rise to the Boer attitude which "confidently hoped" that the Bushmen would be exterminated.[47] Little wonder the Commissioners of Enquiry in 1825 described the commando system as having been "most fatal in its effect" upon the Bushman population.[48]

The circumstances leading to the collision with the Bantu at the Fish River during the last decades of the eighteenth century had hardly differed and again the findings of the Commissioners of Enquiry indicated that the onus for the hostilities lay with the colonists.[49] It was not that the Colony should not have expanded in the first place as some had argued,[50] declaring that any difficulties the Boers encountered were of their own making, but rather that the spark which had flared into warfare had been occasioned by the Boers ineffectually protecting their cattle – "committed to the Charge of a few ill-paid Hottentot Herdsmen" – and, in short, holding out the "strongest temptation" to the Xhosa to commit theft.[51] Again the Boers called out commandos: "reprisals were indiscriminately made . . . and as they did not limit themselves to the recovery of the Cattle stolen, but captured large Herds on which the subsistence of the Caffres depended, they [the Boers] drew on the Colony the hostility of the Tribes whose incursions were attended with general devastation of the Frontier Provinces."[52] Peace was restored to the frontier in 1792 and a "friendly understanding established" but by 1799 tension on the frontier had again stretched to breaking point and eventually erupted in the Xhosa and Hottentot uprising of that year – once

---

nothing to regulate race relations on the frontier. As for control over the commandos, all that was required was that the government in Cape Town be notified when a commando had been called out.

47. C.O. 48/6, "Col. Collins' Report on the Frontier Districts", 1809, f. 40.
48. C.O. 48/76, "Report of the Commissioners of Inquiry at the Cape of Good Hope, dated 25th May 1825", f. 58. In his report, Collins stated that he had met the leader of a commando party who had claimed that within a period of six years the men under his control had either captured or killed 3 200 Bushmen. Another leader maintained that his parties had caused the destruction of some 2 700 Bushmen. (C.O. 48/6, "Col. Collins' Report on the Frontier Districts", 1809, f. 40.)
49. The point needs to be made that only the Hottentots and Bushmen can be considered as the aborigines of the Cape (defined by the Fish River). The Xhosas, like the Afrikaners, were not indigenous to the Colony.
50. Such as the *Commercial Advertiser,* vide infra, Chapt. VIII.
51. C.O. 48/76, "Report of the Commissioners of Inquiry at the Cape of Good Hope, dated 25th May 1825", f. 57.
52. *Ibid.*

more triggered off by a "renewal of the outrages before complained of".[53] The Commissioners of Enquiry had considered that the root of the problem rested with the local authorities' inability to assert themselves as a government in the face of the commandos which, under the jurisdiction of the local commandant, represented the interests of the colonists. Thus a situation came into existence where the authority of the commandos was greater than that of the local functionary representing the Cape Government, for without military backing the local authorities were helpless. Under such circumstances Barrow had stated "the boor, indeed, is above all law"[54] and as a body they had been able to resist the measures of "restraint and conciliation" which had been the policy of government towards the frontier.[55] Summing up the situation on the frontier, Pallandt judged it to be "an evil which could not be remedied owing to the lack of means".[56]

Collins' report on the state of the frontier in 1809 is of infinite importance as it marks the rise of a more locally orientated English opinion of the Afrikaner. Virtually all travellers to the Cape referred to the impressions created by the "celebrated author", John Barrow. Many of them, such as Percival (1801) and Fisher (1816), and Philip, Pringle and Moodie of an even later period, laid great store on his work claiming: "What Mr. Barrow says, speaking of the farmers of the Cape, is perfectly true";[57] others, however, adopted the opposite view. Collins, Lichtenstein (1812), Burchell (1822–1824), the Commissioners of Enquiry (1825) and others paved the way for a revised outlook on the Boers when it was held that their condition was not nearly as degraded as had been alleged previously, nor was their general treatment of the Blackman anything as severe. While accepting that Barrow and others who supported his views might have provided some truth, their own researches had found that the attitude of the Boers towards the Blackman and their own overall condition had greatly improved since the British had first occupied

53. C.O. 48/76, "Report of the Commissioners of Inquiry at the Cape of Good Hope, dated 25th May 1825", f. 58.
54. Barrow, *Travels,* ii, p. 407.
55. C.O. 48/76, "Report of the Commissioners of Inquiry at the Cape of Good Hope, dated 25th May 1825", f. 59.
56. Pallandt, *General Remarks on the Cape of Good Hope,* p. 12.
57. R. B. Fisher, *The Importance of the Cape of Good Hope as a Colony to Great Britain,* p. 27.

the Colony, and while the reported atrocities committed under cover of the commandos were totally condemned by this more locally orientated school of thought, they did not assume the same attitude towards the Blackman on the frontier – as is illustrated by Collins' tough recommendations that the Xhosas should be cleared from the Zuurveld, which recommendations were carried out in 1812 by Cradock.

Collins asserted that unless a traveller did not have "the most distant expectation of having any personal interest in the matter which he details", his statements could not be relied upon. Clearly, he implied that Barrow was not qualified to provide the "candid and impartial" account of the conditions within the Colony which he had so strongly claimed to have done. The highly respected William J. Burchell[58] wrote: "I am convinced that many incorrect and absurd things, which have been written about this colony," (referring as he was in particular to John Barrow) "would never have been said, had the writers been sufficiently acquainted with the language to converse with every class of its inhabitants".[59] He was of the opinion that to gain a balanced view of the Colony all classes of its inhabitants needed to be mingled with, not only the "better part of society". As a point of interest it is worth noting that Barrow was most certainly class-bound and had only an imperfect knowledge of the Cape Dutch language, while Percival could not understand it at all.

As important as these observations undoubtedly are, there was a far greater and more embracing barrier which separated a certain class of English travellers from the colonists – something which was bound into the structure of upper class English society, something which plainly prejudiced them against the colonists and was responsible for much of the contempt and disdain with which they kept themselves aloof from the Afrikaners. In 1806 a soldier, Sir Robert Wilson, commenting upon English behaviour at the Cape, pointed to the probable reason for this bias. He wrote that "the man not the title" was the object of consideration at the Cape and that all Whitemen were considered to be equal.[60] Certainly these principles

58. William J. Burchell visited the Cape Colony during 1810–1812. His chief work on South Africa (mainly botanical in content) was *Travels in the Interior of Southern Africa.*
59. Burchell, *Travels in the Interior of Southern Africa,* ii, pp. 15–16.
60. Br. Mus., ADD. MSS. 30097, vol. 3, 1805–1806, "Journal of Sir Robert Wilson", 3 Jan. 1805, f. 52.

of equality held by the colonists must have been a source of irritation to any English lady or gentleman of worth. Mentzel had remarked that the people of the Cape were not given to ceremonious treatment; in fact, "they are blunt and outspoken, and hate all show and affectation".[61] Little wonder Wilson was able to promise his countrymen that their "self-importance would never be exposed", neither would their vanity "be gratified by servile obsequiousness".[62]

It would be a mistake to make too great a point of "British superiority" but nonetheless, it would seem to have been a very frequent feature in English/Cape Dutch relationships during the first years of British involvement when High Toryism was much in evidence in the personality of British civil servants. In 1822 Bird had the following to say: "An Englishman, from the Orkneys to New South Wales, is the same unbending creature. He accommodates himself, with difficulty, to the manners of other countries; and nothing can be right or proper, that is not English, and to which he is unaccustomed",[63] while in 1834 Howison had remarked much the same:

> "Unhappily the British do not possess the art of conciliating those people whom they bring under their subjection; because, considering themselves superior as a nation and as individuals to all other inhabitants of the earth, they never have intercourse with foreigners without allowing them to perceive how thoroughly they despise them. Whenever they observe manners or modes of thinking different from their own, they pronounce sentence of condemnation against those who have adopted them; and, wrapped in a supercilious self-complacency, weigh and measure their fellow-creatures by an imagined standard, and undervalue them in proportion as they fall short of it."[64]

More pertinent to the turn of the century, the fashionable Lady Anne Barnard, with words of "a little parade . . . suits the Dutch and procures respect from their stupid heads",[65] well illustrates how she scoffed at the Dutch in Cape Town. What must she have thought of

---

61. Mentzel, *Description of the Cape of Good Hope,* ii, p. 106.
62. Br. Mus., ADD. MSS. 30097, vol. 3, 1805–1806, "Journal of Sir Robert Wilson", 3 Jan. 1805, f. 52.
63. W. W. Bird, *State of the Cape of Good Hope, in 1822,* p. 154.
64. J. Howison, *European Colonies, in various parts of the World, viewed in their Social, Moral, and Physical Condition,* i, p. 324.
65. Br. Mus., ADD. MSS. 37308, Wellesley Papers (Series II), vol. XXXVI, Lady Anne Barnard, 23 Sept. 1799, f. 258.

the more primitive frontier Boers when they visited the town?

Percival had bitterly complained that the British, who had brought prosperity to the Colony, did not receive the "civility and attention" they deserved. Percival is an excellent example of one who expected a great deal more of Cape Town than its 5 000 Europeans could offer. That it possessed a small town mentality was to be expected, for a small town it was, and that it was not a flourishing cultural centre and that its inhabitants assumed the personality of their environment should neither have been reason for wonderment nor basis for criticism. Barrow, Percival and others who visited the Colony must have been acutely aware of the shortcomings of Cape society in comparison with the sophisticated society of metropolitan London. Such differences inevitably created social barriers. Distrust and suspicion was the reaction of the Cape Dutch towards the English, while the English came to look down upon everything that was Cape Dutch with disdain.

In a society where fine manners and studied courtesy were out of place and tended to hinder rather than encourage intimacy,[66] Wilson advised that an Englishman who had perhaps been "rendered too nice by the comforts of his own country" should remember that neither Rome nor London had been built in a day.[67] In his opinion it would be a mistake for the British to attempt to radically alter or revolutionise the structure of Cape society and he advised that the English who proceeded there should remember that "any contemptuous treatment of these honest people, now fellow subjects, on account of their simplicity of habits and principles of equality would be far from honourable to their own feelings or advantageous to the interests of their country".[68] His words do not appear to have been out of place.

Collins maintained that "from some unaccountable cause" Barrow had "exerted all his ingenuity to exhibit the African Farmers in the most unfavourable point of view", and because of his "eloquent declaration" his opinions had been regarded as "incontrovertible altho' his statements respecting them are extremely incorrect".[69] Re-

66. Mentzel, *Description of the Cape of Good Hope,* ii, pp. 105–106.
67. Br. Mus., ADD. MSS. 30097, vol. 3, 1805–1806, "Journal of Sir Robert Wilson", 3 Jan. 1805, f. 66.
68. *Ibid.,* ff. 52–53.
69. C.O. 48/2, Collins to Caledon, 30 May 1808, f. 16.

ferring to the "exaggerated accounts" of Barrow, Collins stated in 1809:

> "Had that gentleman confined himself to the districts of Graaff Reinet, which I had not then seen, in observing the wanton cruelties that had been committed against the Bosjesmans, and had he simply mentioned instances of misconduct without degrading the inhabitants of a whole country below the lowest of the human race, I should not have ventured to protest against his decrees; but when he included the farmers of the whole frontier in the first class, and those of the remaining districts in the other, I could not allow so unfair a judgement to pass unnoticed."[70]

Burchell had been of the same mind when he had stated "I cannot allow the unfavourable qualities of an individual, to be adopted as the *general character* of the Dutch colonists, any more than I could admit selected examples of individual worthiness, to be taken as specimens of the whole colony". He added: "of the latter, I know many: of the former, I wish I knew none".[71] In 1830 Saxe Bannister remarked that Barrow's reputation "rendered his errors important" and took him to task for "failing to notice the *exceptions* to the character which he applies to the boors".[72] Sparrman, too, was of the opinion that although atrocities had without doubt been committed against the Blackman, the idea that such was the *general* behaviour of the colonists appeared preposterous to him. He held that the majority of the colonists were very much against abusing the natives "lest the vengeance of heaven should, for all these crimes, fall upon their land and their posterity".[73]

Lichtenstein considered it totally unfair of Barrow to have compared the African colonists to the English "day-labourers", the conditions within the Colony and those in England being so totally different, and felt justified in remarking: "I was led almost daily to ask myself whether these were really the same African colonists which the celebrated Mr. Barrow represented as barbarians, as such no more than half savages".[74] Wilson referred to the "heavy denunciation"

---

70. C.O. 48/6, "Col. Collins' Report on the Frontier Districts", 1809, f. 41.
71. Burchell, *Travels in the Interior of Southern Africa,* ii, pp. 69–70.
72. S. Bannister, *Humane Policy,* pp. 12, 186.
73. Sparrman, *A Voyage to the Cape of Good Hope,* ii, p. 144.
74. Lichtenstein, *Travels in Southern Africa,* p. 48.

which had been brought against the colonists of the Cape, "as if virtue here were more rare, or vice more licentious, than in any other European territory", and estimated that

> "Censors of natural morals, should be well acquainted with the state and manners of society in the several polite nations of the world before they publish their remarks upon any particular country, so that the scale by which they measure public worth or depravity may be regulated upon an equal and intelligible principle. Some writers artfully advance the interests of their own works by insinuations which move the passions whilst they pretend to rebuke levity and immorality. But the visitors of the Cape will find that its inhabitants afford no more matter for reproach and reproof than all civilized societies . . ."[75]

An altogether different impression of the Colony is obtained from writers such as Burchell and Wilson. Of Cape Town the latter had remarked "nothing offends the gaze",[76] while Burchell wrote "nothing can be neater, or more pleasant, than the appearance which this town presents"[77] and after his first day in the Colony was able to muse: "Gratified by everything I had met with, when I retired to rest, a train of pleasing reflections and anticipations long kept me from sleep."[78] Clearly, these writers created a different feeling towards the Colony and its white inhabitants. From the following extract the attitude Burchell adopted towards the inhabitants of Cape Town and their daily customs can be seen as quite contrary to that of Barrow: "the inhabitants frequently walk or sit [on their verandahs], in the cool of the evening and often at other times, to enjoy the air, or to converse with passing friends".[79] From Wilson's writing, too, a more tolerant and generous attitude can be deduced:

75. Br. Mus., ADD. MSS. 30097, vol. 3, "Journal of Sir Robert Wilson", 3 Jan. 1805, f. 62.
76. *Ibid.*, f. 49.
77. Burchell, *Travels in the Interior of Southern Africa,* i, p. 53.
78. *Ibid.*, p. 15.
79. *Ibid.*, p. 53.
Mentzel (*Description of the Cape of Good Hope,* ii, pp. 113–114) describes this activity in the following terms: "The whole population then gathers on the stoeps, or merely in front of the houses, and neighbours exchange reminiscences or just gossip away the evening. This form of amusement is cheap and pleasant; groups of people sometimes sit on their stoeps on hot summer evenings till midnight. Temporary sojourners from passing ships, whose acquaintance the members of the family have made, are welcome to a corner of the stoep." *Cf.* the account of daily life, *supra,* pp. 8–11.

"The men in Cape Town generally employ their mornings by attendance at their sales or upon shipping concerns and in the superintendence of their neighbouring farms. They dine about two then repose and in the evening resort to the society house where they smoke, play backgammon, cards, billiards and talk over their affairs. The younger men who have leisure are more gallant in their occupation and they are not destitute of resources to pass their time pleasantly. Their manners are unexceptionable. They are cheerful companions . . ."[80]

Probably the emphasis between tolerance and intolerance cannot be better illustrated than by comparing the attitudes of the *Quarterly Review* and William Burchell on the simple question of Boer hospitality. As has already been shown,[81] the *Quarterly Review* spoke of it as the "savage virtue of hospitality" whereas Burchell was inclined to think of it in terms of "every Christian-like colonist, opening his door to the hungry and benighted traveller".[82]

A further example of this more moderate attitude towards the colonists is found in Burchell's description of the living conditions of the interior Boers, itself worthy of comparison with Barrow's above:

"The situation of the house was bleak and exposed, and exhibited but little display of art or cultivation around it. At the back, extended a wild flat, bounded by high rocky mountains. One large room, having a mud floor, and a single glazed window, showing, by its broken pains, proofs of the scarcity of glass, constituted the principal part of the house. At one end were the bedrooms; and a door through the back wall, opened into the kitchen. Hanging from the rafters of the thatched roof, was seen a hetrogenous assemblage of domestic utensils and stores. The other end was filled by a very wide and deep fireplace, exactly resembling that of an English farm-house; and a large iron cauldron of boiling soap was standing over the fire . . . A few chairs and benches, with a large family dining table, were ranged in order round the room. On a shelf lay a variety of articles, with a large Bible . . . A black slave woman and a Hottentot girl assisted in the domestic duties; while the more laborious work of the farm was performed by a man-slave and a few Hottentots. The daughters were three good-tempered women . . ."[83] ". . .

---

80. Br. Mus., ADD. MSS. 30097, vol. 3, "Journal of Sir Robert Wilson", 3 Jan. 1805, f. 63.
81. *Vide supra,* p. 22.
82. Burchell, *Travels in the Interior of Southern Africa,* i, p. 102.
83. *Ibid.,* ii, pp. 142–143.

I now for the first time, had an opportunity of witnessing the old colonial custom, of *washing feet* after supper."[84]

Before attempting to arrive at some kind of objective picture of the Afrikaners as they were during the period 1795–1806, the comments of the psychologist I. D. MacCrone are worth quoting. "Generalizations", he says, "... are often very misleading as a way of describing the facts. This is true particularly where so much of the direct evidence available is derived from the writings of Travellers who paid flying visits to the frontier districts and whose observations were coloured by a background of experience very different from that of the people with whom they came into contact or whose conditions of life they described. Under such circumstances there is always the tendency to pay special attention to the unusual or striking, but superficial aspects, while neglecting or overlooking the realities of the situation."[85]

It is necessary to appreciate that during the period under discussion isolation, not only from Cape Town but also from the world beyond, had led to the interior farmer developing a strong sense of individualism and conservatism, and because the society which he had evolved was a non-monetary society, his wealth being counted in heads of cattle and sheep, he showed little of what is ordinarily thought of as ambition. The interior Boers, then, were hardly an intellectual group for, as Scholtz has remarked, that they could read and write "het van hom egter nog geen intellektueel ontwikkelde mens gemaak nie".[86] On the other hand again, as Lady Anne Barnard and many others pointed out, that they were lacking in an intellectual awareness lay entirely in the fact that "education had been wanting".[87] The condition of and differences between the Afrikaners living in fine residences in the south-west and those who inhabited mud houses on the border were, as Walker correctly argues, due only to temporary differences in environment and he further points out that as soon as circumstances allowed, the interior Boers started to erect more suitable dwellings which were comparable with those nearer

84. Burchell, *Travels in the Interior of Southern Africa,* ii, p. 87. No doubt Burchell appreciated more fully than Barrow had that there was a scarcity of water in the Colony and it had to be kept in buckets.
85. I. D. MacCrone, *Race Attitudes in South Africa,* pp. 110–111.
86. Scholtz, *Politieke Denke,* i, p. 178.
87. *South Africa a Century Ago, Letters of Lady Anne Barnard,* pp. 184–185.

Cape Town.[88] The remarks passed by Barrow and others respecting the "paucity of ideas" among the interior colonists should, as Theal suggested, be seen in its proper perspective. Obviously the Boers were not well informed as to world events simply because that knowledge was not readily available to them but how surprised an English traveller would no doubt have been, says Theal, had an old Boer rattled off at length detailed accounts of the Old Testament heroes:

> "On subjects like these the grazier could talk freely enough, because they came within his range of experience. He was living under such skies as those under which Abraham lived, his occupation was the same, he understood the imagery of the Hebrew writers more perfectly than anyone in Europe could understand it for it spoke to him of his daily life. He had heard the continuous roll of thunder which was as the voice of the Lord upon many waters, and he had seen the afrighted antelopes drop their young as they fled before the storm, when the great trees came down with a crash and the lightning divided like flames of fire . . . When he spoke of these things he could be eloquent enough, but they were not subjects for conversation with casual visitors."[89]

To the old frontiersman his church played an important role in his life, as is illustrated by the tedious journeys he would undertake to have his children christened and to attend *nagmaal*. Not only was his church important for the services it performed, however, but it was a constant reminder of his European origin. In particular, his religion gave him instruction as to the shape his relationship with the Blackman should take – a relationship which favoured the Afrikaner but which tended at times to show the weaknesses inherent in mankind when acting beyond the limits of constituted law. When taking into account the disadvantages experienced by the Cape Colony because of its isolation and environment it is also necessary to listen to 'the other side' and, as Hartz has said, even if the strictures of British travellers are discounted on the assumption that they were moved by bias, Dutch and German assessments cannot be entirely ignored.

O. F. Mentzel, who was a German, deplored the ignorance and dullness of the Afrikaner frontiersmen, found that they had a "kind of secret hatred towards the Europeans", and feared that without a

---

88. *C.H.B.E.*, viii, pp. 167–168.
89. Theal, *History and Ethnography of South Africa before 1795*, iii, pp. 301–302.

continuous infusion of fresh European blood they would "degenerate and become uncivilised".[90] After touring the interior in 1768, J. W. Cloppenburg, who was the Company's official next in rank to the Governor, expressed similar views. And in 1803 Lichtenstein had had the following to say of the burghers of Graaff-Reinet:

> "Selfishness, lawlessness, hardiness, intolerance, and a thirst for revenge, are the reigning vices of their character, which will perhaps hardly be thought atoned by a disposition to be easily satisfied, by a spirit of economy yet united with unbounded hospitality, a firm adherence to truth, and a great respect for religion. But what is most to be deprecated in the character of some of them, is the harshness with which they treat their slaves and Hottentots, and in others, the bitterness and irreconcilable animosity with which they carry on their differences among each other."[91]

By 1806, when Britain made her second occupation of the Cape, there were two dominant opinions voiced on the Afrikaner – opinions which still held good at the end of the century and quite probably will still hold good at the end of the twentieth century. These two opinions, directly in opposition to one another, were epitomised by the remarks of two men: Barrow and De Mist. The first maintained that the Afrikaners "will never become civilized until they are ruled with a rod of iron";[92] while the second judged: "Give no credit to Mr. Barrow nor the enemies of the inhabitants. They have their faults, but these are more than compensated by good qualities. Through lenity . . . they may be conducted to any good."[93] Whose opinion had been the more sound time and experience alone would tell.

---

90. Quoted by Hartz, *The Founding of New Societies,* p. 190.
91. Lichtenstein, *Travels in Southern Africa,* p. 464.
92. Barrow, *Travels,* ii, pp. 136–137.
93. Theal, *History of South Africa since 1795,* i, p. 150.

CHAPTER THREE

A Pattern Develops
1795–1820

When considering the official attitude of Great Britain towards the Afrikaners of the Cape Colony in 1795, it should be realised that the situation which greeted the British left much to be desired if a good start was to be made in their relationship with the colonists. Although the tiny European population of Dutch, French and German origin formed a closely-knit society it was, nonetheless, divided into three broad eco-political groups which meant that the coming of the British to the Colony would be viewed by each group in the light of its own particular interests.

Firstly, there was the merchant and official class residing in and about Cape Town. These 6 261 Europeans, found to be living comfortably in well estabished homes, were Orangeman and because of their so-called 'colonial mentality' – a dependence upon government employment and passing trade – did not resist the Colony falling to the British.[1] However, the second group, which comprised the 7 256 farmers of the well established agricultural districts of Stellenbosch, were politically opposed to the Prince of Orange and therefore, as can be expected, did not welcome the British in the Colony. These burghers, who some years earlier had been behind the Cape Patriot movement, would no doubt have preferred the Cape falling into French hands – a feeling maintained by some to have been general throughout the Colony.[2] The districts of Swellendam and Graaff-

---

1. It will be remembered that during the 1740's the English were officially welcomed as allies, but it was the fact that they bought up the surplus produce that chiefly endeared them to the Cape merchants.
2. G.H. 1/1, Halloran to Liverpool, 25 Sept. 1810, memorandum, "Cape of Good Hope" by W. B. Halloran, D.D., f. 811.

Reinet made up the third group and were strongly republican and pro-Holland, yet dissatisfied with the Company's administration. Found to be living in primitive circumstances, these 8 229 burghers were in rebellion against the Company authorities, declaring themselves independent from the Company the very week before the British landed.

Outside the ranks of Cape Town society, then, the British were not popular. In spite of an oath of allegiance to the British Crown, Craig told Dundas "nearly every man in the colony is our enemy",[3] while even within the capital certain Dutchmen had asserted: "as long as Holland remained a Nation, they could not feel contentment under any other Government".[4] As far as the burghers of the interior districts were concerned, the coming of the British could not possibly have been more inopportunely timed. If nothing else, the actions of these men – burghers who owed neither political, economic nor ideological allegiance to the British Empire – left no doubt in British minds whatsoever that there was a great deal more to the Cape Colony than fresh vegetables, water and meat.

To understand the official British attitude towards the Cape Dutch it is necessary to consider what had drawn the British to the Colony in the first place as this directly affected their future relationship with and opinion of the colonists. During the latter half of the eighteenth century Clive and Hastings had already been busy laying the foundations of what was to become the modern British Empire, this time embracing the East, so that with the collape of the old British Empire, marked by the Secession of the Thirteen American Colonies which caused Great Britain the loss of her monopolist position in the North Atlantic trade triangle in the face of a rising United States, the Cape of Good Hope suddenly found herself brought directly into the new sphere of British interests. While the Cape had been occupied by the Netherlands, a country which had been strong enough to maintain an independent position in European politics yet sufficiently weak to exert little or no pressure on British interests in the East, all was well as far as Great Britain was concerned. However, the designs of Napoleon upset this balance and so the Cape was temporarily occupied by Great Britain in 1795 to meet this threat. The return to normal brought about by the peace

3. *Recs. of the Cape Colony,* i, Craig to Dundas, 22 Sept. 1795, p. 156.
4. C.O. 48/11, Cradock to Liverpool, 31 Dec. 1811, f. 2.

with France in 1801, which temporarily ended the French threat, is shown by *The Times* of 3 October advocating that the Cape again be made a free port which, for all commercial purposes, had always been the object of Britain. By 1806, however, *The Observer* of 20 April reported a significant change in British policy: "The Cape of Good Hope, we hear, is to be the grand military depot for the supply of our Asiatic possessions". And so South Africa's fate was sealed. For within the commercial basis of the modern British Empire – a system embracing London, India and South America – the Cape's role was to be one of vital strategic importance.

British involvement in 1795, then, had been no more than a political manoeuvre, a temporary measure taken to thwart the French occupying the settlement and thus protect British interests in the East for, as it had been warned: "what was a feather in the hands of Holland will become a sword in the hands of the French".[5] There was no idea of permanency in their action and while in a state of war in Europe, the last thing British statesmen desired was the need to undertake the internal reconstruction of the Cape Colony; still less, however, did they wish to sit calmly by and permit sprouting independent republics to take root in the interior of the Colony which were more in sympathy with French principles than with Great Britain.

The experience of the war with the American Colonies fought by the colonists in the name of liberty and inspired by revolutionary France, determined that overall British policy towards the Cape, as in all colonies acquired during the Napoleonic Wars, although it would be conciliatory, would be firm and the form of government autocratic,[6] and until the Cape Colony was formally ceded to her in 1814 when the threat of Napoleon had been finally checked, the British approach continued to be conservative and one of non-expansion and economy. One thing is certain, the British were hardly in the mood to deal sympathetically with the "Jacobine Mania" which Barrow vowed was aimed at the "subversion of all order"[7] and which was reported to be running rife throughout the Colony.[8]

---

5. *Recs. of the Cape Colony,* i, Blankett to Napean, 25 Jan. 1795, p. 26.
6. C. R. Kotze, *Owerheidsbeleid Teenoor die Afrikaners, 1806–1820,* pp. 46–47.
7. Barrow, *Travels,* i, pp. 52–53.
8. *Recs. of the Cape Colony,* i, "Memorandum on the Condition of the Colony", by F. Kersteins, p. 168.

No doubt it was at the bottom of the political upheaval experienced in the interior[9] and under such circumstances the British could hardly be expected to show tolerance towards the Afrikaners.

To the British, the uprising in the interior represented their first important crisis. That there had been a collision of interests between the Dutch East India Company and the farmers of the interior and that the Dutch East India Company had been forced to succumb was of relatively minor importance. More critical, was the evidence of French and Batavian flirtations with the colonists. This was something which could not be tolerated and investigation showed that the "troublesome and dangerous"[10] state of affairs in Graaff-Reinet and Swellendam would remain "more or less troublesome and difficult to manage and control" as long as Britain remained at war with France".[11] (Britain could spare few troops for the Cape whilst involved in a major European war.) However, the most significant outcome of the insurrection was that it brought the British (particularly Barrow, who had been despatched with Bresler to pacify the malcontents), face to face with the cardinal issue in the affairs of the Cape Colony – the relationship between the Boers and Xhosas on the eastern frontier.

In 1800, on reflecting upon the overall mood of the interior Boers, Dundas revealed much of what was passing through official minds when he wrote:

> "Considering the extent of country over which the latter [the inhabitants of Graaff Reinet] are dispersed, the rude and uncultivated state in which they have hitherto lived, and the wild notions of independence which prevail among them, I am afraid that any attempt to introduce civilisation and a strict administration of Justice, will be slow in their progress, and likely, if not proceeded upon with caution and management, rather to create a spirit of resistance, or a disposition to migrate still further from the seat of Government, than to answer the beneficial views in which they might be undertaken. In fact, it appears to me, that the proper system of policy to observe towards these persons would be to interfere as little as possible in their domestic concerns and interior economy, and to consider them rather as distant tribes dependent upon H.M. Government, than as subjects necessarily amenable to all the laws and regulations estab-

9. Barrow, *Travels*, i, pp. 52–53.
10. C.O. 49/9, Dundas to Gen. Dundas, 6 Aug. 1800, f. 310.
11. C.O. 49/9, Dundas to Macartney, 26 Jan. 1798, f. 142.

lished within the immediate precincts of that Government. The mutual advantages arising from mutual barter and commercial intercourse ought to be the great link of connection between them and us, and by a strict adherence to good faith and justice in all the relations which may result from such intercourse, joined to an efficient protection and occasional act of kindness on the part of Government, I conceive we shall more effectively ensure to ourselves their attachment, and the benefit to be derived from it, and to them a state of gradually improving comfort and civilisation, than by any hasty attempt to substitute our laws and customs to the institutions and habits, however imperfect and barbarous in some respects, under which they have hitherto lived."[12]

Such an appraisal of the colonial situation, the condition of the interior Boers and the proper policy to be adopted towards them brings to the fore a basic attitude or policy — anglicisation. This policy has seldom been properly represented as it is taken to mean that the British simply wished to force their language upon the Afrikaners, with the latter resisting on grounds of a love for their own *taal*. Yet this conveys little of what was really envisaged. Of course, the question of language was important,[13] but in itself language must be regarded as no more than the necessary mechanism for implementing that change which was aimed at, and which was often referred to as the raising of the "level of civilisation" of a nation. Language was the tool of the ideological imperialist and formed part of the British desire to civilise the world.[14]

The policy of anglicisation can best be understood by showing what it was expected to produce. Through its implementation the attachment of the Afrikaners to the English system, understood in its broadest possible context, would be won. In this manner Britain would obtain the political security she required in South Africa. Parallel to this was the raising of the level of civilisation, or the

---

12. C.O. 49/9, Dundas to Yonge, 28 July 1800, ff. 284–287.
13. *C.H.B.E.*, vi (Canada and Newfoundland), p. 194.
14. F. A. van Jaarsveld in his work, *The Afrikaner's Interpretation of South African History*, p. 3, develops the idea of how most nations at one or another time take upon themselves the concept of a "calling" — that is, having been chosen to perform some task to the world for the sake of the world. Referring to the Anglo-Saxon race, Joseph Chamberlain is reported to have said: "[it] is infallibly destined to be the predominant force in the history and civilization of the world".

"manners and morals"[15] of the Afrikaners to that enjoyed by the English themselves. In other words, through an endearment to British institutions it was hoped that the allegiance of the Afrikaners would be secured for Great Britain, and through the establishment of schools, churches, a rule of law and the creation of a more settled way of life (particularly on the frontier), progress towards a more ordered society could be made. Thus, through anglicisation the problems facing the Colony on its frontiers would largely cease to exist or otherwise effectively be solved. Yonge spoke of anglicisation in 1795, as did Milner just over a hundred years later. Language only has significance inasmuch as it holds sentimental or emotional value and it conveys the all-important question of national or group identity. If anglicisation was rejected it was certainly not done on grounds of the Afrikaners not caring for the English language; but rather, of what association with that language meant and because of the importance of an independent language to political assertion.

The policy of anglicisation which culminated in the adoption of the English language, to the exclusion of Dutch, in government offices in 1824 and the courts of the Colony in 1828 is usually attributed to Somerset; however, it also formed part of the British state of mind in 1795, especially after Barrow had provided the officials at the Castle with his account of frontier society. His findings left no doubt in Engish minds as to what the problems facing the Colony were and where the fault lay and that any solution was to be found in the raising of the level of civilisation of the colonists. This is not meant to imply that Great Britain came to the Cape with a missionary zeal wishing to transform the Colony. It did not. Nevertheless, anglicisation should be regarded as the logical development of the adopted policy of conciliation, and after the Cape had become an integral part of the Empire in 1814 Somerset was more freely able to implement those British ideas and British institutions which would come to have an increasing influence upon the Colony. Yonge had said: "It is desirable to knit and tie this colony to the Mother Country as much as possible",[16] while Caledon had been in full agreement with Grenville on the necessity of augmenting a vigorous

---

15. C.O. 49/12, Goulburn to Somerset, 10 April 1821, f. 203.
16. Quoted by *C.H.B.E.*, viii, p. 191. See also, *Recs. of the Cape Colony*, iii, Yonge to Dundas, pp. 28–30, 37–41, 86–100, 356–358.

consolidating and anglicising policy at the Cape.[17]

The need for improvement was felt particularly on the frontier. The concensus of British opinion was that the weakness of those regions was to be found in the character of the Boers living contiguous to the Xhosa. "There can be no doubt" wrote the philanthropically minded Dundas in 1800, "that the origin [of the Hottentot and Xhosa uprising] is in a great degree to be attributed to the cruel and oppressive treatment of the Hottentots, Cafres and natives by the white inhabitants".[18] (On an earlier occasion Dundas had spoken of the Boers as "the strongest compound of cruelty, of treachery and cunning, and possessing most of the bad qualities with few very few of the good ones, of the human mind".[19]) Because of this state of affairs any peaceful solution to the frontier difficulties would need to be initiated by the Europeans, which, to the British, meant that the society of the Boers would need to be altered in such a way as to make an amicable arrangement possible with their native neighbours.

In 1818 Cradock wrote the following to Liverpool: "it appears necessary to alter the whole system in that [interior] part of this territory . . . It is required to concentrate on population for the advantage of society and defence and fix the pursuits of the inhabitants upon agriculture, rather than pasture alone, which at present leads to a roving life and it is the source of their present weakness and occasioned misconduct".[20] General Dundas hit the nail squarely on the head when, speaking of the administrative difficulties of governing the Cape, he referred to it as "this too extensive colony".[21] Hobart was in agreement and criticised the loan farm system for being responsible for the Colony expanding at a rate too rapid for the size of its population, pinpointing it as the main obstacle in the way of the "increasing prosperity" of the Colony.[22] Collins, too, shared this view and emphasised the need for achieving a concentration of population on the frontier for, besides the advantage of greater security which a large number of colonists would bring, the

---

17. Quoted by *C.H.B.E.*, viii, p. 203. See also, *Recs. of the Cape Colony,* vi, Alexander to Stewart, 2 July 1807, pp. 164–166.
18. C.O. 49/9, Dundas to Yonge, 28 July 1800, f. 284.
19. *Recs. of the Cape Colony,* iii, Dundas to Yonge, 24 Feb. 1800, p. 58.
20. C.O. 48/14, Cradock to Liverpool, 10 June 1812, ff. 44–45.
21. *Recs. of the Cape Colony,* ii, Gen. Dundas to Ross, 10 Aug. 1799, pp. 462–463.
22. C.O. 49/9, Hobart to Gen. Dundas, 1 May 1801, ff. 379–380.

society itself would be more settled. Through establishing a more fixed, agriculturally embedded society the need for the so-called Boer "land hunger" would not exist or, at least, not to the same extent as in the past. However, the solution to the frontier problem (as far as *White* complicity was concerned) lay in removing the cause rather than simply attempting to prevent excursions across the frontier. At the heart of the matter lay what Pallandt had described as the frontier Boers' attitude towards both the Government and the natives – an attitude or philosophy which had denied the natives having rights to the land and, because of the administrative weaknesses of the country, had given rise to what he had called "... this freedom, this spirit of independence and false liberty".[23] Therefore, to the British way of thinking, if a change in the personality of the frontier colonists could be achieved, then peace with the Xhosas could be established and, by "kind treatment and instruction, with [the natives receiving] a fair portion of their own land",[24] this peace could be maintained.

All Englishmen agreed that atrocities *had* occurred against the Blackman in the distant districts[25] and it was commonly conceded that this ill-treatment had been facilitated, as it were, by the absence of government control. It will be remembered that Collins and others had not disagreed with Barrow on grounds of *whether* atrocities had, in fact, taken place or not, but rather because Barrow had created the impression that such abuse characterised the manner in which the Boers *generally* had treated the Blackman. In 1809 Collins felt that he could report an overall change in the attitude of the frontiersmen towards the natives. In fact, he claimed that he had observed nothing in them which indicated that "implacable hatred which they are generally supposed to feel"[26] towards the aborigines and found that the colonists at that time "exerted themselves with as much zeal to acquire the friendship of the Bosjesmans, as they had before done

---

23. *Vide supra,* p. 18.
24. Remark of Barrow as quoted by C. Lloyd, *Mr. Barrow of the Admiralty,* p. 68.
25. That this was the case can hardly be considered as grounds for singling out the Afrikaners for special condemnation as cruel or oppressive in view of the fact that this was the experience throughout the world where the European came into contact with the aborigine.
26. C.O. 48/2, Collins to Caledon, 30 May 1808, f. 15.

to blot them from Creation".[27] He explained the reason for this:

> "The journey undertaken by Mr. Barrow at the desire of My Lord Macartney *seems to have opened the eyes of the inhabitants* [italics added] of the district to the criminality of their conduct. They had never before harboured a thought that any Government would condemn their proceedings, but on the contrary they conceived that their exertions in this unjust cause were the most certain means of recommending them to favour . . ."[28]

After the shambles of 1806 when the Zuurveld had been overrun, the Fourth Frontier War in 1812 witnessed some 20 000 Xhosas expelled from that region. This led to the implementation of Collins' recommendations that a partially fortified border be erected patrolled by troops and burghers and that magistrates be appointed at the new centres of Cradock and Grahamstown. For the first time in the history of the Colony a government had taken the initiative and established a rule of law. Under such influences a somewhat different picture of the old Cape Boer began to emerge.

Cradock maintained that in spite of the ill-conduct of the colonists during the past towards the Bushmen — "and great I fear it was" — perfect peace existed between the races. "Indeed" he continued, "I have every reason to hope that, of late years oppression and misconduct have much ceased, and that the pains that have been taken to create new principles and benevolent proceedings, have not been thrown away."[29] The report of the 'Black' Circuit Court of 1812 went a long way to provide the concrete evidence required to substantiate the feeling that race relations had vastly improved — all of which added to Bathurst's "most lively satisfaction".[30]

Not everyone, however, shared Bathurst's pleasure regarding the state of the Colony. From the time George Schmidt had initiated missionary work amongst the Hottentots in 1737 it had become apparent that the treatment the Hottentots received from the colonists, and their relationship with them, would always be a bone of contention and philanthropists would have a good deal to say about the matter. Accordingly, at a time when race relations were reported by Cape officials to have improved, in 1809 the London Missionary

27. C.O. 48/6, "Col. Collins' Report on the Frontier Districts", 1809, f. 41.
28. *Ibid.*
29. C.O. 48/14, Cradock to Liverpool, 10 June 1812, ff. 43–44.
30. C.O. 49/10, Bathurst to Cradock, 23 Dec. 1813, f. 253.

Society missionary, van der Kemp, upset the colonial apple cart by complaining to his Society that atrocities not only continued to be committed by the Boers but also that they were committed with impunity, thus casting suspicion upon the integrity of the Colonial Government.

> "Indeed" claimed Read, who succeeded van der Kemp in 1811, "the complaints [against the Boers] are become so numerous we can no longer pinch our consciences. There are of late many Hottentots missing, but we fear little will be done, as those who are accused as their murderers, are not arrested. Some of the falsely called Christian Boors are accused of 8 or 9 murders – Many of our poor people have also lost their children . . ."[31]

It was the old story all over again. Boer abuse of Hottentots, with children taken as servants or slaves. Allegations were also brought against the landdrost of the district, Cuyler, under whose jurisdiction the crimes were supposedly perpetrated. Of Cuyler, Read had this to say: "[He] who was unfortunately appointed to investigate the matter has married one of these Farmers Daughters, of course shutting his ears to the poor Hottentots."[32] With a hint of spiritual blackmail, the missionary pleaded: "If God should be pleased to incline the Government to give an impartial attention to the business, which is our daily prayer, then would the most happy effects follow for the poor Hottentots."[33]

Refuse the Colonial Office could not and its response was straightforward: "the immediate adoption of the most effectual measures to [ensure] the exemplary punishment of such atrocious crimes" would be undertaken and every effort would be made to shield "the injured natives from the barbarity of their oppressors in future".[34] Clearly the British Government had little faith in the Afrikaner in so far as his dealings with the Blackman were concerned – had not Barrow provided abundant proof of the Boer character? In addition, the

---

31. C.O. 48/13, "Extracts from the Letters and Journals of the Missionary James Read, relating to the murders of numbers of Hottentots", f. 119: encl. to C.O. 48/13, Wilberforce to Percival, 5 Aug. 1811. Published in 1809 as No. 20, *Transactions of the Missionary Society at London.*
32. *Ibid.*
33. *Ibid.*
34. C.O. 49/10, Liverpool to Cradock, 9 Aug. 1811, f. 163.

honour of the Colonial British Government was at stake. The policy of the Home Government towards the frontier had, from the first, been one of non-intervention and of maintaining peace with the least possible expenditure — even if it proved detrimental to the safety of the colonists on the frontier — rather that than plunge the whole Colony into a state of war.[35] The basic problem to be faced on the frontier, or rather the main responsibility of government was to keep the peace, which in practice involved the garrisoning of the frontier — a costly undertaking. Both the Dutch and early British administrators, for reasons of economy, had neglected this duty — the failure of which, no doubt, stemmed from the fact that the interior was of little value to either governments, and to the British their troops could be better employed elsewhere. Only when it became imperative that force be resorted to would it be sanctioned[36] for, as Liverpool told Cradock on another occasion:

> "It will be material however that you should distinctly ascertain that the aggressions by the Caffres are *not* measures of retaliation and that they are not justified in some measure by the conduct of the Dutch settlers who reside contiguous to their frontier."[37]

Therefore any reported misconduct of the Boers towards the natives could not be left uninvestigated — "even should the Dutch settlers have shown no disposition to molest them".[38]

As a group the missionaries had always received a cool reception from the officials at the Castle since the British ruling class until 1830 was Tory and the Tory outlook was still of the eighteenth century, thus sharing the conservatism of the Afrikaners. Yonge had from the first regarded the motives of the missionaries as somewhat 'Jacobine'; de Mist had simply looked upon them as trouble-makers; while in 1801 Hobart had advised: "all persons of this description should in like manner be attended to with great circumspection".[39] In 1812 the judges of the Circuit Commission had condemned the missionary institutions (except those of the Moravians) for teaching what was

---

35. Kotzé, *Owerheidsbeleid*, p. 75.
36. *Ibid.*, p. 74.
37. C.O. 49/10, Liverpool to Cradock, 20 Dec. 1811, f. 170.
38. *Ibid.*, f. 171.
39. C.O. 49/9, Hobart to Gen. Dundas, 1 May 1801, f. 381.

thought to be "overstrained principles of liberty",[40] and had even gone as far as to recommend that the L.M.S. station at Bethelsdorp be disbanded or at least have its activities curtailed.[41]

Read's accusations were far from conclusive[42] yet, as a result of the bad publicity which the missionaries later secured in Britain for the 'Black' Circuit, together with the condemnatory remarks in the press based on Barrow's *Travels,*[43] these accusations went a long way to establish in the British middle class mind an incorrect conception of Boer brutality for, as Manning has pointed out, "Pious folk in England naturally believed what they were told by the missionaries, whom they were zealous enough to send out to convert the Hottentots and Kaffers" no matter what lengths the Cape governors might have gone to to refute the missionary tales.[44]

Cuyler pointed out that three alleged "horid murders" had in fact taken place a full six years before Read had compiled his report, and then they had occurred when the Colony had been in a state of war. This, of course, meant that these were not murders but more correctly, war casualties – a circumstance, maintained Cuyler, which had been known to the missionary, "altho' Mr. Read's letter very artfully wishes to put it upon the world as a recent transaction".[45] Querying whether the atrocities had *ever* occurred, Cuyler enquired why it had been that *if* these crimes had taken place the missionary had not reported the matter to the landdrost – "Mr. Read's unbounded duty as a Christian" – instead of having it "published at home".[46] Pointing out further shortcomings in Read's testimony, Cuyler continued: "That article respecting the slave woman of Botha, I perfectly remember she had run away from her master who I sent for on the occasion and found the matter on enquiring,

---

40. C.O. 48/19, "Report of the Circuit Commission, 14 Nov. 1812", f. 102: encl. to C.O. 48/17, Cradock to Bathurst, 11 Aug. 1813.
41. *Ibid.,* ff. 102–105.
42. Kotzé (*Owerheidsbeleid,* pp. 57–63) enters into this entire question with relish, showing the shortcomings of the philanthropist movement in general.
43. *Vide infra,* pp. 66–67.
44. H. T. Manning, *British Colonial Government after the American Revolution, 1782–1820,* p. 405.
45. C.O. 48/13, Cuyler to Caledon, 25 Oct. 1810, f. 20: encl. to C.O. 48/13, Cradock to Liverpool, 27 Jan. 1812.
46. *Ibid.,* f. 21.

different to what is stated by the missionaries."[47] On further investigation Judge Truter was able to impress upon Cradock that the accusations were without foundation and to Cradock's relief he was able to assure Liverpool that a "great exaggeration . . . has been bestowed upon the entire representation".[48] In 1814, similar unproven allegations were represented by the missionary John Campbell and in despair all Cradock could do was shake his head and state "so much misrepresentation seems constantly to attend this subject . . ."[49]

It goes without saying that the allegations brought about by van der Kemp and Read were not the first such attacks on the colonial character, nor were they by any means to be the last. There were many cases involving allegations brought against either the colonists or the Colonial Government. No doubt it is an exaggeration to say that unless an author was able to discover 'fresh evidence' of atrocities, or he wholeheartedly agreed with those reported by earlier writers, his work would be considered as inferior, yet this is the impression gained when reading certain of the publications.[50] Possibly the most striking example of such a case is R. B. Fisher (author of *The Importance of the Cape of Good Hope as a Colony to Great Britain* which was published in London in 1816 and considered by the *Quarterly Review* to be an utterly ridiculous piece of work[51]) who, in the same year, published a paper addressed to William Wilberforce and among other absurdities maintained that "bodies of no less than 13 infants [Hottentots and slaves . . . had been found] lying exposed on the beach, and no inquiry made".[52] No wonder Somerset, like his predecessor, Cradock, could only shake his head and remark: "From a perusal of the very extraordinary work Mr. Fisher has put forth, I can conceive that some mischievous individuals have from mere wantonness imposed upon a credulous and

47. C.O. 48/13, Cuyler to Caledon, 25 Oct. 1810, f. 22: encl. to C.O. 48/13, Cradock to Liverpool, 27 Jan. 1812.
48. C.O. 48/14, Cradock to Liverpool, 24 June 1812, f. 81.
49. C.O. 48/22, Cradock to Bathurst, 14 Feb. 1814, f. 47.
50. This was, in fact, claimed to be the case by W. B. Boyce in his work *Notes on South African Affairs from 1834–1838*, p. ii.
51. *Quarterly Review*, July 1819, pp. 206–207.
52. "Memorandum addressed to William Wilberforce, Esq. M.P.", by R. B. Fisher, 1 Aug. 1816. In this extraordinary representation to the anti-slavery leader some of the most outlandish remarks ever passed on the Cape are to be found.

weak mind, probably without supposing that their inventions would be published to the world in a manner Mr. Fisher has thought proper to bring them into notice."[53]

However, despite the barrage of criticism the Cape Government remained firm, convinced that "whatever may have been the misconduct, and the impunity permitted, in the interior of the Colony [in the past], the same cannot happen again, from the energy that has been given of late years to the course of justice and the establishment of regular Circuits to take immediate cognizance of all offences".[54]

What the English in official circles in Cape Town thought of the Boers and their treatment of the natives, both past and present, was crystallised by Cuyler in 1810 when he slammed Read's accusations:

> "I have no hesitation in believing", he conceded, "that some years ago, particularly under the first Dutch Government's time and perhaps of a latter date, barbarous cruelties were committed in the distant districts from the capital, and perhaps they were as much the fault of the Government as of the people who committed them, for in those days I fancy little or any notice were taken of acts of this kind by the subordinate officers of the Government in the interior, and consequently scarcely an example made of murder or any sort of check put to the illtreatment of the Hottentots. The inhabitants probably seeing things going on this way, concluded themselves at liberty to do almost as they pleased, many of them not knowing the laws or perhaps the meaning of *Justice* not unnatural to a people grown up and kept in ignorance, and who had no control set over their passions but that such should happen at the present time under the present Government and passed with impunity appears almost impossible . . ."[55]

The general improvement in race relations the Circuit judges "confidently attributed" to the fact that landdrosts had been impressed that "the maintenance of *equal Right* and *equal protection* to all classes of society formed the basis of H.M. Government" and, in fact, that this formed "the chief point of their duties".[56] In 1813, after his tour of inspection of the Colony, Cradock could write to Bathurst

53. C.O. 48/33, Somerset to Bathurst, 19 May 1817, f. 176.
54. C.O. 48/14, Cradock to Liverpool, 24 June 1812, f. 81.
55. C.O. 48/13, Cuyler to Caledon, 25 Oct. 1810, ff. 22–23: encl. to C.O. 48/13, Cradock to Liverpool, 27 Jan. 1812.
56. C.O. 48/19, "Report of the Circuit Commission, 14 Nov. 1812", f. 68: encl. to C.O. 48/19, Cradock to Bathurst, 11 Aug. 1813.

in London: "with confidence I may assure H.M. Government the greatest progress is evident in religion, education and all those moral principles which will establish the good order and prosperity of a country."[57] In fact, so impressed was he by the condition of the Colony that the following appeared in the Government Gazette:

> "His Excellency cannot be more anxious to express his unfeigned sentiments of approbation, upon the good order, the apparent kindness, and general conciliation of all classes of inhabitants to each other, and while he has witnessed the example of proper authority, exercised by the Superior Magistrates, and all other persons in power, he has had the correspondent satisfaction to observe the respect and subordination, shown by the lower orders, and the due conformity to the laws and regulations. The main principle of all Governments, 'protection and obedience' throughout every rank, seemed to be understood, and has produced these happy consequences. His Excellency with heartfelt gratification, reflects upon the success of the Paternal Orders of H.M. Ministrators to the successive Colonial Governments; and it is to the progress of Religion, Education, and Moral Instruction, in evident increase, he attributes the power to make the present sincere –, that he has not met with one complaint, nor has he discovered one instance of cruelty, oppression, or prevailing misconduct . . ."[58]

Referring to the Afrikaners as a *whole,* following his tour of inspection in 1817, Somerset drew a strong contrast with the earlier picture painted of the Boers:

> "I dwell with particular pleasure on this remark of industry of the [Dutch] settlers, because from previous reading and from hearing the contrary opinions of many who had travelled through this country without making allowance for the peculiarity of climate and the nature of the avocations of a peasantry, whose wants do not call them to constant agricultural labours, I was not prepared to meet, as I have done throughout an energetic, hardy and active race of men, courteous to each other and hospitable to strangers far beyond what our habits induce us to expect."[59]

---

57. C.O. 48/22, Cradock to Bathurst, 12 Jan. 1814, f. 3.
58. *The Cape Town Gazette and African Advertiser,* 8 Jan. 1814.
59. C.O. 48/33, Somerset to Bathurst, 24 April 1817, f. 118. *Cf.* Somerset's remarks on the colonists when he referred to the Slagter's Nek incident. *Vide infra,* pp. 64–65.

The coming of the British administration had resulted in the introduction of a rule of law. Of course, it did not render abuse of the Blackman impossible, but it did mean that it could not happen with impunity. Nevertheless, although the missionaries were often, and indeed generally, over-credulous in believing the tales the Hottentots brought against their white masters, their evidence cannot be summarily dismissed. For instance, although the 'Black' Circuit on the whole exonerated the Boers as a people,[60] the charges had been difficult to prove since they had covered many years and a wide area, and persuading a servant to give evidence against his *baas* was difficult as there could easily have been domestic repercussions. However, official reaction to the outcome of the circuit courts was one of satisfaction and rightly, too, for violence there would always be, especially within the rough environment of a frontier but what had been established beyond reasonable doubt was that the Boers as a group could not justly be labelled cruel or oppressive in their dealings with the Blackman.

To British observers in 1815 the incident known as Slagter's Nek afforded living proof that there continued to exist a strong die-hard element on the distant frontier. Somerset correctly attributed the "unpleasant disturbance" to a reaction by the frontiersmen to the influx of British principles as implemented by the circuit courts and introduced, he considered, to check "the wanton and atrocious conduct of the ignorant and half savage Boors *of the frontier* [italics added] towards their slaves and the Hottentots in their service".[61] This harsh judgement, more reminiscent of byegone days than 1815, was no doubt directed to the small minority of frontier colonists who favoured rebellion and whom Kotzé refers to as the "swakkere" type of Afrikaner.[62] Also, it was uttered before his tour of inspection in 1817. He had been absolutely correct in his assumption that the attitude of the ringleader, Bezuidenhout, had stemmed from his total rejection of the laws which had placed bounds upon him and which

---

60. The "Black" Circuit of 1812 had investigated 17 charges of murder, only one of which ended in a conviction for assault, two cases were postponed and three referred to the High Court in Cape Town; of fifteen charges of violence brought against the colonists, seven were found guilty and two cases were held over for lack of evidence.
61. C.O. 48/29, Somerset to Bathurst, 11 Dec. 1815, f. 257.
62. Kotzé, *Owerheidsbeleid,* pp. 89–90.

tended to raise the Blackman to the same level as himself, a White-man:

> "It does not appear . . . that they had any grounds for complaint . . . but accustomed to consider the Hottentot as an inferior species, only preserved for their use, or to be destroyed as they plundered their flocks or herds, or lurked about for these purposes – they are extremely impatient of the restraint the British regulations have put upon them . . . this is the feeling which pervades not only those who have committed themselves in the present business . . . but is very general."[63]

Bathurst, the Secretary of State in London, regarded the incident with concern as he felt that the episode contained the identical elements which had characterised the earlier insurrections of the Boers – a challenge extended to the authority of the Government. He therefore congratulated Somerset on his decisive action as it forestalled the Colony being "exposed to all the evils which it formerly experienced".[64] Unfortunately, in Somerset's opinion, there was no simple solution to the problem since the whole incident had revolved around the use of the Hottentots Corps in the arrest of the rebels. "I should wish", advocated Somerset, "gradually to bring these people [the Boers] to other habits and other feelings and I am convinced that this is not to be done by maintaining among them, to overawe them, a garrison against which from long habit their prejudices are excited; were the frontier garrison purely British troops, they would mix and associate with the Boors and gradually form them to their manners – this can never be the case with Hottentots, for independent of the great distinction between Christian and heathen (which they look upon all Hottentots to be) the difference between black and white it will take much time to do away in the feelings of this people . . ."[65]

The incident blew over but again in 1818 further mention was made of these same "turbulent men" who, it was reported, had established themselves in Ghoup and Nieuwveld, "there removed from the eye of the Magistrate".[66] Again Pallandt's remarks come to mind

63. C.O. 48/29, Somerset to Bathurst, 11 Dec. 1815, f. 257.
64. C.O. 49/10, Bathurst to Somerset, 10 Feb. 1816, f. 328.
65. C.O. 48/29, Somerset to Bathurst, 11 Dec. 1815, f. 257.
66. C.O. 48/37, Somerset to Bathurst, 28 Dec. 1818, f. 306.

respecting the mistaken ideas of freedom held by this element of the colonial inhabitants.

Whatever overall progress might have been achieved in the field of race relations in the Colony or whatever clouds might have appeared on the horizon of the future, not a great deal of interest was shown in the affairs of the Afrikaners in Great Britain. Prior to 1815 the relationship between Great Britain and the Cape Colony had been on a war footing with the Cape being regarded as a garrison which could reinforce India in the event of an emergency. The close of the Napoleonic Wars meant that the usefulness of the Colony would need to be re-appraised. The Liverpool government (1812–1827), straddled with post-war economic recession, argued that in spite of there being no French threat the Cape was still worth maintaining owing to its important position on the trade routes of the Empire and the price to be paid for keeping order in the interior of the Colony was well justified. Thus, the Cape was still regarded in terms of its geographic position and therefore no particular interest was shown in the non-British colonists. South Africa received little attention in the British parliament other than the occasional remark passed in connection with the general affairs of the Empire and the first debate on the Colony came as late as 1819 when the question of colonising the eastern frontier was discussed.

This state of indifference was reflected in the British press which showed itself equally disinterested in the affairs and inhabitants of the Cape. In 1812 the influential *Quarterly Review*,[67] on referring to the Cape of Good Hope, remarked: "Of the Dutch colonists we shall say little . . ." and by and large kept within the limits of the pattern set by Barrow, and perpetuated by van der Kemp and Read, labelling them a "lazy, revengeful, cruel people".[68] *The Times* had even less to say about the Cape colonists. What interested this newspaper, once the settlement had been secured in 1795, was the number of British vessels successfully rounding the Cape, besides mentioning the "benefit of a pure air" to convalescents.[69] Slight interest was shown in the "frequently troublesome" colonists residing in the

67. *The Atlas,* 15 Oct. 1826, states that the *Quarterly Review* had double the circulation (12 000) of its closest rival, the *Edinburgh Review,* and that its readers were the most influential and that "it may be regarded as the organ of their political sentiments".
68. *Quarterly Review,* Dec. 1812, p. 391.
69. *The Times,* 18 Sept. 1799.

interior, though at one point there was talk of the Boers – "a hardy race inhabiting part of the interior" – being impressed into H.M. fighting forces.[70] In 1804, on the return of the Cape to the Dutch and the realisation that the Colony had proved "a drain upon Great Britain [financially] instead of a benefit",[71] *The Times* lost all interest in the Colony. Even with the establishment of a Cape press in 1824, this important newspaper did not directly concern itself again with the affairs of the Colony until the middle of the century, although it did report on the recall of Somerset. The other major newspaper of the period, *The Observer,* showed comparable interest. Some prominence was given to Barrow's publication in 1802 and the "deplorable situation" outlined in an earlier chapter was briefly mentioned but after 1810 this newspaper also turned its back on the Cape Colony, and it was not until the 1850's that it and the press in general showed anything like an active interest in the affairs of what had then become South Africa.

In 1819, however, the plan to settle 6 000 British immigrants on the frontier of the distant Cape of Good Hope aroused much public curiosity in this hitherto little heard of possession,[72] as is illustrated by the appearance on the British market of no less than six publications dealing with the Colony specifically from an emigrant's point of view.[73] Whatever might have been thought of the Afrikaners, the consensus of opinion was that "an emigrant . . . with the superior intelligence and activity of a European . . . would be enabled to thrive on the spot which has afforded no more than a mere maintenance to one who has pursued no other than the usual Cape system of management".[74] But a more concise and significant description of the Cape Colony, also written specifically for the benefit of intending

70. *The Times,* 4 Nov. 1800.
71. *Ibid.,* 3 Feb. 1804.
72. H. E. Hockly, *The Story of the British Settlers in 1820 in South Africa,* p. 27.
73. Anon., *Considerations on the means of affording an improved and correct system of colonisation in the British Territories of Southern Africa.*
William J. Burchell, *Hints on Emigration to the Cape of Good Hope.*
G. Ross, *The Cape of Good Hope Calendar, and Agriculturalist's Guide.*
Anon., *An Account of the Cape of Good Hope, with a view to the information of Emigrants.*
Anon., *A Guide to the Cape of Good Hope, describing its geographical situation, climate, etc.*
John Wilson, *An Emigrant's Guide to the Cape of Good Hope.*
74. Burchell, *Hints on Emigration to the Cape of Good Hope,* p. 10.

emigrants, appeared in the *Quarterly Review* in an unprecedented forty-three page article[75] written, it can be assumed, by none other than John Barrow himself.[76]

It is surprising to learn from this journal that the Cape "has always maintained a favourable hold on the public opinion", a state of affairs which stemmed from the reported excellence of its climate, the fertility of the soil and "the respectable appearance of every class of its inhabitants".[77] This regard for the Cape and its suitability for colonisation, said the *Quarterly Review,* was amply demonstrated when the plan to send settlers there was "hailed with applause by every part of the House" and by the vast crowds which thronged Downing Street in order to await the decision of the Colonial Office on individual applications. The article therefore, it was claimed, had been undertaken to moderate the "gross mistakes and the exaggerations" and "unreasonable expectations" which had arisen from the six newly published works.[78] Without wishing to "throw a damp" upon the proceedings, the *Quarterly Review* (or John Barrow, if preferred) wrote:

> "We entreat our readers to believe that we come to the discussion of this interesting subject with many advantages; we happen to have some local knowledge of the country, and we have before us every thing, we believe, that has been written on it. In the absence, therefore, of such a work as we are deploring, a few observations from us may not, perhaps, be altogether without their value."[79]

One by one the demerits of the relevant publications were brought to light: shortcomings which dealt with the economic strength and climate of the Colony, and the general prospects awaiting the emigrant, rather than with the Afrikaner inhabitants. Of Fisher it was

---

75. *Quarterly Review,* July 1819, pp. 203–246.
76. This is based on the fact that Barrow was considered the leading authority on the Cape in Britain, together with his contributing (with one exception) more than anyone else to the *Quarterly Review.* Also the *Commercial Advertiser,* 31 Aug. 1825, specifically refers to Barrow's contributions to the *Quarterly Review* in connection with articles published on the Cape. Besides this, the style of the article is distinctly that of John Barrow.
77. *Quarterly Review,* July 1819, p. 205.
78. *Ibid.,* p. 206.
79. *Ibid.*

said: "Scarcely a page occurs in which there is not some gross absurdity, some ludicrous blunder, or some false information".[80] The anonymous writer of *Considerations on the means* . . . had been "misled" by Fisher; Burchell, because of the "scanty portion of actual information" he provided, was thought of as being of only slight value to the emigrant; while Ross's publication was found to be inaccurate when dealing with the various aspects of the Colony's economy. *An Emigrant's Guide* by John Wilson and the anonymous *Guide to the Cape of Good Hope* received very little credit, indeed: "The two 'Guides', we fear, will prove but *blind guides* to those who put their trust in them."[81] Actually, it must be admitted that the reliability of these books was indeed dubious when such information as "cotton wool is produced from the backs of sheep" was provided![82] The anonymous work, *An Account of the Cape of Good Hope, with a view to the Information of Emigrants* was regarded as the most reliable of the books under review. Drawing from the earlier works of Barrow, Le Vaillant, Lichtenstein, Campbell and Latrobe, the author of this book pointed out that the works to which he had referred cost ten guineas while his publication would cost the emigrant only six shillings and sixpence – no small consideration. The *Quarterly Review* added that the writer "has availed himself with judgement of these authors' labours"[83] and it is not surprising that the picture presented of the Afrikaners followed very closely the impression created some twenty years earlier. Examples of Boer atrocities were again brought up and generally it was found that their manners were "revolting to Englishmen"[84] and predictably they were described as being quarrelsome and perverse.[85]

In 1819, some twenty years after Barrow had first introduced the Cape Dutch people to the British reading public, he again, through the circulation of the influential *Quarterly Review,* was largely responsible for preparing the Settlers for what they could expect in the Cape Colony, not least of which was what they could expect from the Afrikaners. His descriptions in 1819 followed very closely those which appeared in his *Travels* although there were some differences.

---

80. *Quarterly Review,* July 1819, p. 207.
81. *Ibid.,* p. 211.
82. Anon., *A Guide to the Cape of Good Hope,* p. 17.
83. *Quarterly Review,* July 1819, p. 211.
84. Anon., *An Account of the Colony of the Cape of Good Hope,* p. 122.
85. *Ibid.,* p. 118.

The prospective Settlers were told by Barrow that the farmers living within thirty miles of Cape Town (those of Stellenbosch, Drakenstein and Paarlberg) lived in affluent circumstances on large establishments – "their houses spacious and respectable, and wearing the appearance of substantial comfort".[86] Actually, there was not much to discredit these colonists with. The quality of their grapes was good and although the wine and brandy had a distinctive *Caap-smaak* it was easy to grow accustomed to the flavour. These colonists, like the inhabitants of Cape Town itself (whom Barrow did not mention on this occasion), were thought of by all "as a very distinct race" compared to those living in the interior of the Colony.[87]

As in the old days the corn farmers of the Swartland and more distant parts of Stellenbosch were still looked upon as being a class below the wine farmers, evidence of this being found in the quality of their houses. Furthermore, they were described as being "unskilled agriculturalists", having no knowledge of crop rotation or the provisioning of dry foods to meet the contingency of drought, a neglect which had in the past led to cattle perishing in great numbers. Their methods of ploughing, sowing and reaping remained haphazard, while there was a great demand for irrigation. In this appraisal of the corn farmers Barrow revealed a far more moderate tone than exercised in 1797 when he described these same farmers as the "most miserable of the agricultural class" and he showed himself in an even more generous vein with this surprising statement that "in few parts of the world is finer wheat produced than at the Cape".[88] However, he still held fast to his earlier opinions of the Cape Dutch whom he had criticised for not showing a greater spirit of expirement and improvement – a state of mind which he held to be still "very general among them" – yet at the same time conceding that new circumstances were forcing them to change their ideas.

> "The truth is", he wrote, "these farmers, possessing all the necessaries of life, gave themselves little or no concern about raising produce for which there was no demand; it was enough for their fathers, and, according to their own principle, for themselves, to supply the quota required by their rulers; beyond that no object existed to stimulate their exertion. Since our acquisition of the

86. *Quarterly Review,* July 1819, p. 216.
87. Anon., *An Account of the Colony of the Cape of Good Hope,* p. 126.
88. *Quarterly Review,* July 1819, p. 219.

> colony, however, and the abolition of public granaries, the demand for exportable produce has increased; which, together with the diminution of the number of slaves, has contributed to create in such of the old proprietors, as reside within reasonable distance of the capital, a degree of activity unknown under their former rulers."[89]

The cattle farmers, or *vee-boers,* of whom Barrow had formerly been most critical, had also improved in some respects as it was reported that something of this same spirit of industry had managed to rub off on them though, of course, the effects were not so marked – but then, "a suggestion of this kind leading to a deviation from the good old rule of doing exactly what *vader* had done before him, would be lost on the Cape boor".[90] Needless to say, the old frontier Boers continued to occupy a prominent place in the general description of the colonists but for good reason, as it would be among these colonists that the British emigrants would be settled. The *Quarterly Review* briefly sketched the background of these men, describing them as a kind of society moulded by environment, the old system of land tenure having caused these colonists to scatter themselves deep into the interior where they lived a life of splendid isolation. "Thus removed from the seat of authority, and placed where no one was near enough to see, much less control his actions, the Vee-boor lorded it over the kraal of Hottentots, with the undisputed power of a feudal chief, from whose tyranny they had no appeal."[91]

Politically, the old picture of the frontier Boer was outlined. The rebellion in 1795 (and 1799) which had shown "extreme rashness and folly to rise upon the British government" was represented as being no more than a Boer reaction against the protection afforded to the "oppressed Hottentot race".[92] It must have been a relief for intending settlers to read that the crisis had been resolved by the establishment of a garrison at Algoa Bay designed "to keep the refractory boors in awe, prevent their quarrels with the Caffres, and, if possible, put a stop to their mutual depredations".[93]

It is necessary to detail at least one description of the frontier Boers whom the Settlers would meet:

---

89. *Quarterly Review,* July 1819, p. 220.
90. *Ibid.,* p. 223.
91. *Ibid.,* p. 221.
92. *Ibid.,* pp. 221, 223.
93. *Ibid.,* p. 222.

"The interior of the Vee-boor's establishment is as slovenly as its exterior accompaniments: a clay floor, in the pits of which are splashes of sour milk or mud; a roof open to the thatch; a square hole or two in the wall for windows, without glass; an old rug or blanket, or a wattled partition, separating the sleeping apartment, are leading features of his hovel. A large chest, which serves as a table at home or a seat in his wagon when he travels; a few ricketty stools with bottoms of the thongs of sheep skins; a bedstead or two of the same fashion and material; an iron pot and a few dishes; a musket of tremendous size, and a large horn to contain his gunpowder, constitute nearly the whole inventory of his furniture — yet this man is probably the owner of five or six hundred head of cattle, and four or five thousand sheep . . . Though there may be some excuses for the Vee-boor neither ploughing, nor planting vineyards, beyond the demands of his own consumption, there is none whatever for his slovenly habits, his total neglect of the decencies of life, and, above all, his inhuman and frequently dishonest conduct towards the Hottentots in his employ. Insulated as he is, and wholly removed from the benefit of a church or market, it would be unreasonable to expect from him the manners of polished society, or the dress and furniture which the carpenter and tailor could supply; but cleanliness is always within reach, and it might be naturally supposed that self-gratification would induce a sufficient degree of domestic industry to supply himself with the common conveniences of a household; — not so: he prefers seeking them at a distance, and at an expense of toil and suffering far beyond their worth. The great distance from the Cape, the rough and rugged roads, the rivers frequently unfordable, render the whole value of his waggon load of the lightest articles of produce, by the time they reach the market, scarcely equal to the expenses of the journey; but the wandering life of two or three months suits his habits, and if he carries to the capital enough butter, soap, ostrich feathers, and leopard skins, to purchase in return a little coffee, brandy, and gunpowder, the purpose of his journey and his life is answered . . . This picture, in which the reader may be assured there is nothing of caricature, may be taken as a general representation, though there are many exceptions to it: several of the farmers, who live at a distance, have carried with them the more polished manners of the Cape; and almost all of them are friendly and hospitable to strangers."[94]

To the intending Settlers the question of the natives, both within the Colony and upon its borders, must have rested uneasily upon their

---

94. *Quarterly Review,* July 1819, pp. 224–226.

minds. What could they expect on first contact with the Blackman? In 1809 the Hottentots had been represented as "intelligent, active, faithful and brave"[95] and had been described by travellers as a timid race. In 1819, the *Quarterly Review* wrote: "We sincerely hope that this good-humoured and tractable race will meet with every encouragement from the new settlers."[96] Despite the fact that the Boers were held to have misrepresented the Hottentots as the "most brutal and filthy of the human race", persons "held synonimous with everything nauseous and disgusting", experience in the mission fields had shown them to be quite the opposite.[97] As such, then, there was no cause for alarm as far as the Hottentots were concerned, for although they had been "robbed" and "swindled" of their cattle and territory by the old colonists, they were suitable as farm labour where their use was potentially immense.[98]

The "absurdly called Caffres, or infidels" were represented as a mild and peaceable race who, although they had "given way to the encroachments of the Dutch", had nonetheless "resisted all the attempts to enslave them" – unlike the Hottentots.[99] The circumstances which had led to the Xhosas invading the Colony during 1818–1819 had been rectified, considered the *Quarterly Review;* however, if the Xhosa character had undergone a change for the worse, it was "unquestionably . . . owing to their connexion with the Dutch boors, near the frontiers".[1] All the same, Barrow wrote, "we are pretty sure that the Caffres will give the colonists little further molestation."[2]

While the *Quarterly Review* might have dispelled any ideas that Albany was a land flowing with milk and honey, the prospects facing the 1820 British Settlers still looked good. With industry the Colony could be developed and although the frontier Boers were considered to be a somewhat narrow-minded and ultra-conservative people they were, nonetheless, friendly and anyhow, it was highly probable that finding themselves "hemmed in on every side, and his old habits broken in upon, the boor . . . will . . . betake himself beyond the

95. *Quarterly Review,* Aug. 1809, p. 91.
96. *Ibid.,* July 1819, p. 226.
97. *Ibid.,* pp. 226–229.
98. *Ibid.,* p. 226.
99. *Ibid.,* p. 230.
1. *Ibid.*
2. *Ibid.,* p. 231.

Snowy Mountains"[3] – a highly significant remark when viewed in terms of the events of 1836. In any event, the Settlers would arrive in parties and establish themselves in their own little England communities. As for the native problem, this had been the doings of the Afrikaners and as far as Barrow could see: "From the Hottentots nothing whatever is to be apprehended [by the English Settlers]; they are living quietly with the farmers, or at the several missions. The Bosjesmen are some hundred miles removed from the new settlers, and the Caffres are not very likely to attack people who never offended them, and who possess nothing that can tempt them to hostilities."[4]

The planting of a sizeable body of 6 000 Englishmen at the Cape Colony was of the greatest importance for until their arrival there had been no resident English population there to speak of. Until that time, opinion of the Afrikaner in Great Britain had been virtually non-existent and such opinion as there was had been confined to those who were directly involved in the affairs of the Colony and had taken the trouble to read upon the subject. With the 1820 Settlers a new state of affairs was created. Obviously there would always be the official class, the Cape would always have a garrison, travellers would continue to come and go, while missionaries would pursue their labours among the natives and submit their reports to London; however, now the Cape had obtained its English connection and people in Great Britain would be inclined to take a more direct interest in the affairs of the Colony. Above all, from now on Englishmen would be sharing the same environment as that of the Afrikaner, particularly respecting contact with the Blackman, and this would have tremendous influence upon what Englishmen so placed would have to say about the Afrikaners.

---

3. *Quarterly Review,* July 1819, p. 243.
4. *Ibid.,* p. 236.

CHAPTER FOUR

British Settlers and Boers
1820–1828

> "We have seldom seen in writing a good description of Colonial life . . . to which we can refer for a manly view of the character and pursuits of Colonists. Your travellers are sometimes tolerably correct respecting the height of a mountain or the course of a river; but of the domestic, daily, inwards life habits, and mode of thought of a whole people, what a mass of ill-balanced misrepresentations do most of their REMARKS, NOTES, TOURS, JOURNALS, VISITS, DESCRIPTIONS, and STATEMENTS exhibit. Superficial, restless, and impatient, you see these gentry running to and fro over the outside of this world as earnestly as if something important depended upon their speed – jumping over the fences of private and personal affairs – bouncing into every open door, and prying through the windows of decent retirement with an impudent face of curiosity, and after all producing nothing which a man of ordinary reflection could not have told them, or invented for them, without quitting his own parlour . . . The truth is, a country can be faithfully described by none but its own inhabitants. They alone have a due degree of interest in it. They alone know its real character; and their accounts, by showing their own disposition and ability, let you at once into the mind and heart of a people among whom they dwell."[1]

Compared to what they actually experienced in their new-found Albany, the impression the British Settlers had gained of the Cape Colony in 1819 prior to their leaving England had not been altogether accurate.[2] Despite the encouraging reports regarding the frontier relationship with the powerful Xhosas, the natives were not

---

1. *Commercial Advertiser,* 10 March 1824.
2. See, for instance, *Commercial Advertiser,* 4 Feb. 1824.

as peaceable as the *Quarterly Review* had made them out to be. Neither, for that matter, did practical experience show the Hottentots to be the admirable labour force they had been represented as, considered at best by the Settlers to be of poor quality. Likewise, the description of the Afrikaners was found to be wanting. The accounts upon which the Settlers had had to rely had portrayed them as they had been some 20 years earlier when Barrow had travelled among them, although some concessions had been allowed. Their opinions had been coloured by their informants not, or not sufficiently, having taken into account those changes represented to have taken place in the colonists by the colonial authorities and the favourable aspects which had emerged from the 'Black' Circuit – certainly most pertinent to the character of the Afrikaners. Of the various publications which had appeared in 1819 for the benefit of the Settlers, including John Barrow's account in the *Quarterly Review,* not one had been inclined to mention the more generous and realistic concessions allowed by Cradock and Somerset on the manner in which the Boers had 'settled down' under the British administration and how, in fact, this had also effected a great improvement in the Boer relationship with the Blackman – instead, the relationship as it had existed during the previous century had been outlined. All that had been allowed was that the agriculturalists of the Colony had been moved to greater activity, while it was more readily conceded that the colonists were the product of their environment. In short, the advantageous effects of the British administration noted by Collins, Cuyler and the circuit judges had been most inadequately reported and generally the colonist of 1820 had been depicted as the old colonist of 1795.

In the relationship which developed between the British Settlers and the Afrikaners a new element in the opinion-making process becomes strikingly evident namely, the personal involvement of a non-official group of Englishmen in the every-day affairs of the Colony. These men, sharing the same environment as the Afrikaners, demonstrated none of the scorn and superciliousness which had marked earlier traveller literature, and while it was to be expected that the two races would not readily mix, the impression gained is that the English accepted the Afrikaners were different from themselves without insinuating that because of such a difference there was something radically wrong with the Cape Dutch. Compared to the earlier contact made by the Tories with the Afrikaners, the 1820 Settlers exercised far greater tolerance. While Pringle had thought of the Boers as "uncultivated" they were by no means disagreeable neighbours, and along a somewhat lighter vein, they were found to be "exceedingly shrewd" at bargain making – "too sharp sometimes even for cautious Scotchmen"![3] "On the whole" he judged, "their demeanour towards us, whom they might be supposed naturally to regard with exceeding jealousy, if not dislike, was far more friendly and obliging than could, under all the circumstances, have been anticipated".[4] Of course, there were still harsh descriptions of the base mode of life and slovenly household management of the more distant frontier Boers as Barrow had depicted in 1819. For instance, Rose did not hesitate to write in 1829 that he considered a "perfect specimen of a boor" to be "phlegmatic, indifferent, a large lump of apathy, whose hat scarcely ever left his head, or the pipe his mouth".[5] Neither did Thompson refrain from speaking of the "cruel unchristian prejudices" of a certain section of the Afrikaners,[6] nor T. Phillips feel restrained to state that the past treatment of the Blackman by the Dutch colonists "must strike every reflecting mind to have been erroneous", the consequence of which, it was found, had "driven the Caffres to desperate retaliation".[7] What was significant, however, was the perspective in which these events were placed. In keeping with the finding of the Commissioners of Enquiry in 1824/25, there no doubt existed in the minds of the Settlers as a group the belief that the Dutch *had* treated the Bushmen and Hottentots most severely; but this, it was felt, had all happened a long time ago and under very different circumstances. Any such irregularities, when instanced, were quite specifically reported to have originated in an individual or minority group without in any way implying that such practices were general.

Seeing that the *Quarterly Review* and the various publications on the Cape Colony which had been reviewed by that journal had provided the Settlers with their first description of the Afrikaner character and colonial life, the Settlers would naturally compare what they

3. Thomas Pringle, *African Sketches,* pp. 169–170.
4. *Ibid.,* p. 170.
5. C. Rose, *Four Years in Southern Africa,* p. 252.
6. George Thompson, *Travels and Adventures in Southern Africa,* i, p. 200.
7. T. Phillips, *Scenes and Occurrences in Albany and Caffer-land. South Africa,* p. xi.

had read with their own experiences. Thompson did, for one, and from his eight years in the Colony considered that a true description of the Afrikaners lay somewhere between Barrow's "somewhat overcharged picture" of 1797 and that of Lichtenstein who had contradicted Barrow "without just cause".[8] Both had taken the "two extremes" whereas Thompson claimed that the Afrikaners were "neither generally so brutal as they appear in the pages of Barrow nor so refined as represented by Lichtenstein".[9] The general concensus of opinion among the Settlers was that *many* of the back-country Boers *were* as "savage, indolent and unprincipled" as Barrow had depicted them to be and, in fact, Thompson contended that even in the year 1827 *some* of them had not yet much improved. However, generally the cattle farmers of the Cape were found to have "many good and pleasing qualities" and were thought to be of superior standing to their counterparts in many other colonies, particularly those of the Americas. It could not be escaped, said Thompson, that the disagreeable characteristics of the Boers could be ascribed to their environment – disadvantages emanating from their dispersion and isolation, their not having had the moral restraint which religious instruction brought, and generally their living under a system of government which favoured the "unrighteous aggression against the native tribes".[10]

The work of George Thompson in particular did much to create a more favourable impression of the Afrikaners than that of Barrow and others. Because of his "plain and unaffected account" the well-balanced journal, *The Atlas,* referred to Thompson's work as "the completest book on the subject", containing "the best and most rational account of the important Colony of the Cape".[11] As already mentioned above, Thompson was of the opinion that the Cape Dutch colonists had been too severely judged by earlier travellers who had been "apt to generalise hastily". It was all a matter of perspective, he maintained, and to illustrate this provided examples to show how,

---

8. Thompson, *Travels,* ii, pp. 113–114.
9. *Ibid.,* pp. 114–115.
10. *Ibid.,* p. 115.
11. *The Atlas,* 6 May 1827, p. 283.
John Philip, too, in his well known *Researches in South Africa* (ii, p. 42), wrote of Thompson that his "well-known integrity is a sufficient voucher for all the statements he gives".

with incomplete knowledge of the colonists, a traveller could easily be misled into obtaining an unbalanced impression.

On reading the following examples it will be more easily understood how it was possible to arrive at conclusions similar to those those of Barrow in his *Travels* even during the 1820's:

> "On my return from the Cango, in 1822, I arrived at the house of a rich corn and wine boor, not 100 miles from Cape Town, who had been recently married, and who, in honour of the happy occasion, had that day given a grand ball . . . I was most hospitably welcomed. The dancing, which had commenced before our arrival, was continued till past mid-night, and the female part of the company conducted themselves with great propriety and decorum; but the gentlemen had evidently been indulging far too freely in the bottle, and were much more noisy and riotous, than pleasant or entertaining. About one o'clock in the morning the company sat down to a splendid and luxurious supper; after which the wine again circulated profusely among the male guests, and those who were disposed to sobriety were absolutely compelled to drink by the the more boisterous of the party, who also began to play off rude practical jokes such as exploding squibs and crackers among the dancers, etc. Wearied out by a long ride the preceeding day, and with a surfeit of this rough horseplay, I stole off, with one or two of my fellow-travellers, about five o'clock in the morning, and took refuge in an outhouse, in hopes of there getting a little repose before we continued our journey. But we reckoned 'without our hosts;' for, as soon as our absence was discovered, a numerous party of the Bacchanals sallied forth in search of us, and dragged us by main force back to the hall. A second time we made our escape – but in vain. Our resistance only provoked these riotous fellows to more mischievous persecution. They got hold of an old cannon which happened to be about the place, loaded it with powder, and stuffed it to the muzzle with wet straw, and then fired it into the room where we were just sinking into sleep, – breaking with the concussion all the windows to shivers, and very nearly shaking down the roof about our ears. Finding it useless to contend with madmen, we returned to the party; who continued their *vrolykheid* (as they call it) without intermission till morning, when we were allowed to depart, glad to escape from such boisterous hospitality."[12]

---

12. Thompson, *Travels,* ii, pp. 118–120.

And again:

> "Mr. P., a friend of mine, travelling into the interior, was riding past a farm-house, near the Zonderend River, when he was furiously assaulted by about a score of dogs belonging to the place, in consequence of which he was thrown from his horse, and his thigh-bone broken. The boor, a young man of the name Vanderwalt, came to the door, and seeing the accident, stood gazing at a distance, without offering to assist the gentleman who was lying on the ground, until he was called forward, and requested of him to help him into the house. Mr. P. then asked him to send off a messenger instantly for the district surgeon at the village of Caledon, about three hours distant. Vanderwalt replied that he had no one who could be spared, except a slave who was at work in the field, and whom, with some hesitation, he agreed to send for. After waiting, however, about an hour, no slave appeared; the young fellow sitting all the while, quietly smoking his pipe, besides the agonized traveller. At length the latter demanded whether he meant to send anyone or not, or, if his slave was not at hand, why he did not ride off for the doctor himself? To this the farmer, taking the pipe from his mouth, replied with great *sang-froid*, 'Jaa Mynheer, ik kan zelvers ryden – als Mynheer zal my daarom ordentelyk betaling.' 'Yes, Sir, I can ride myself, if you will pay me handsomely.' Finding himself at the fellow's mercy, Mr. P. suppressed his indignation at his unfeeling avarice, paid him what he demanded, (about four times the hire of a man and horse for the distance,) and Vanderwalt rode off for the doctor."[13]

Vulgar, and quite in keeping with Barrow's earlier descriptions,[14] a certain class of the country farmers certainly were, attested Thompson; however, he pointed out that by selecting "a few striking scenes or characters" as illustrations of the general state of manners among the people whom they visited, a picture either "favourable or otherwise" could be created by a traveller according to his "temper, talents, taste or extent of observation".[15] By virtue of his long residence and of having visited every district in the Colony and having mingled familiarly with all classes of the colonists, Thompson stated that he did not hesitate to "characterise [the Cape Colonists] gene-

---

13. Thompson, *Travels*, ii, pp. 121–122.
14. It will be remembered that Thompson (*supra* p. 78) stated that there was a section of the Afrikaner population which had not changed at all since the time Barrow first described them.
15. Thompson, *Travels*, ii, p. 121.

rally as a shrewd, prudent, persevering, good-humoured, hospitable, and responsible class of men".[16] That there were among them individuals undeserving of all or any of these epithets was no more discreditable to the Cape Dutch as a people than the existence of a "few swindlers or ruffiians among English farmers, to the body of our respectable yeomanry".[17]

Once more the benefit of Thompson's relatively long experience in the Colony is obvious in his writing:

> "Notwithstanding the evil influence of slavery, and of their rancorous hostilities with the Bushmen and Caffers, they [the Boers] are not *generally* a depraved or inhuman race of men. Neither are they so indolent as they have generally been represented. Many of the farms that have been for any length of time occupied upon a secure tenure, exhibit proofs of a prudent, persevering industry, not unworthy of their Batavian progenitors. In the interior districts, where less agricultural enterprise is visible, it is to be considered that the great, I might say, the only source of profit, hitherto, has been the breeding of sheep and cattle, which necessarily induces habits somewhat unsettled and averse to steady labour; and, besides this, on the Caffer frontier, the colonists have been so frequently driven from their dwellings, that it is only since the Keiskamma became the boundary, that they have really begun to consider themselves as secure and permanent occupants of their farms. But wherever they have been settled for any considerable time, in favourable situations, their industry is, generally speaking, not less apparent than in the Sneeuwberg, – which pleased Mr. Barrow so much, that he was led to regard the inhabitants of that district as a class of colonists superior to the rest of their countrymen."[18]

Two years after the *Quarterly Review's* publication of Barrow's 'revised' account of the Colony for the benefit of would-be immigrants this same journal published a further article, a book review, dealing with the Cape Colony. The book in question,[19] itself insignificant, is important inasmuch as the remarks passed on it reveals a changing attitude towards the Afrikaners held by this important journal. Actually, the author of this review, whom we can accept was

---

16. Thompson, *Travels,* ii, pp. 121–122.
17. *Ibid.,* p. 122.
18. *Ibid.,* pp. 125–126.
19. Anon., *Notes on the Cape of Good Hope, made during an Excursion in that Colony in the Year 1820.*

not Barrow — or if so, a very different Barrow — did not say much at all. What he did was to show the inaccuracies of some of the more outlandish remarks passed upon the Colony and the Afrikaner inhabitants of Cape Town and agree with the more moderate profile given of the interior Boers, adding: "the Dutch boors in fact are not now what they were a quarter of a century ago, when Barrow travelled among them", and explaining the grounds for this somewhat mystical transformation, he continued:

> "Barrow was the first Englishman they [the interior Boers] had seen; he visited them in an official character, and when they were in a state of rebellion against the government; and equally without religious instruction and legal restraint. Since that time, however, many English regiments have been among them; and they have fought together against the common enemy, the Kaffers. Churches have been erected, and ministers appointed to perform divine service. A committee of members of the Court of Justice makes an annual circuit, and they are become good and loyal subjects . . ."[20]

A far cry from Barrow's earlier description of the Afrikaners in 1797 and 1798 which had been presented to the British reading public and intending settlers in 1819!

"Four years ago" remarked the infant *South African Commercial Advertiser,* in one of its first editions, "the advantages of the Cape Colony were held forth by ignorant and interested pamphleteers to the admiration of the world, in terms equally overstrained and delusive".[21] The British Settlers to South Africa in 1820 had learnt the hard way. Frustrated and disillusioned as they were by the realities which they had had to contend with — not the least of which had been the reported peaceful character of the Xhosas and the industry of the Hottentots — and removed as they were from Great Britain and without the means to return, they had had no option but to succeed and establish themselves within their new environment. The importance of the 1820 Settlers cannot be overstressed in so far as the arrival of so large a body of people made a concentrated settlement on the frontier possible for the first time and this fact, plus their undeniable enterprise, led to the development of the eastern province as a whole. For the purposes of this study their settlement is of even

20. *Quarterly Review,* July 1821, p. 459.
21. *Commercial Advertiser,* 4 Feb. 1824.

greater significance since prior to 1820 the permanent British element in the Colony had been small, no more than a few hundred, and confined to Cape Town and its immediate environs. After 1820, however, the settlement of some 4 000 Englishmen within the same environment as the Boers in the interior districts of the Colony meant that henceforward there would be a far greater contact and intermingling between the two groups. Under these circumstances the future promised that English opinion of the Afrikaner within the Colony would be more complex than before and it is not surprising to find two distinct schools of thought springing up. One was personified by the Cape Town based *Commercial Advertiser,* established in 1824, and distinguishable by its philanthropic attitudes and interest in missionary work, the other by the *Graham's Town Journal,* situated near the frontier and established at the end of 1831 when the interests of the English (and Afrikaner) colonists were no longer reflected by the Cape Town press. However, until 1828 when the far-reaching effects of the Hottentot Ordinance became a colonial issue, the *Commercial Advertiser* broadly represented Settler sentiments and from the pages of this newspaper can be seen what it was hoped the future would hold for those people, 6 000 miles from home, and what form their relationship with the Afrikaners took.

Not surprisingly, the *Commercial Advertiser* looked to the Cape Colony becoming more British in character following the introduction of British institutions to the Colony and the overall anglicisation of its Afrikaner inhabitants.[22] From the outset it defended the Afrikaners against the "old system" of government, accusing it of having been autocratic and top-heavy.[23] Although, in this instance, the *Commercial Advertiser* was particularly referring to the administration of the Dutch East India Company, it will be recalled that despite the Cape Colony having been permanently ceded to Britain in 1814, the autocratic form of government was maintained since it was held that it was better suited to the Afrikaner personality than more liberal institutions.

The withholding of "liberty" and the supplementing of "tyranny" was a most unhealthy state of affairs and the *Commercial Advertiser*

---

22. This is apparent from the following letters to the editor, *Commercial Advertiser:* "Britannicus", 17 March 1824; "A Subscriber" (Graaff-Reinet), 21 April 1824; "A Parent" (Uitenhage), 28 April 1824.
23. *Commercial Advertiser,* 27 Feb. 1830.

saw the only answer as being the introduction of what it termed a "new system" which would rest on a system of government by the people themselves. "Remove these natural and wholesome stimulants [liberty]", it wrote, "which not only excite but strengthen, and substitute authority and fear, the principle of weakness and indifference, and you shall soon perceive every division of Society stricken with sloth and poverty".[24] The struggle for the freedom of the press in the Colony against the autocratic Somerset was typical of what was understood as the "old system". What was now called for was the introduction of a legislative assembly. However, for this to become a reality the Cape Colonists would need to show themselves worthy of and capable of maintaining such an institution. Obviously, the Cape Colony would need to develop. Communications would need to be improved, agriculture expanded, the benefits of schooling and the influence of the church more generally made felt, an increased awareness in the maintenance of law and order would need to take place, and generally a peaceful relationship between the various population groups of the Colony would need to be established and consolidated[25] – all of which would be taken by the British Government as an indication of readiness on the part of the colonists to handle their own internal affairs.

For this to come about the co-operation of the Afrikaners was needed since the English were too few in number to effect such a development alone. Herein lies the basic (ulterior) motive behind the *Commercial Advertiser's* attitude towards the Afrikaners, which of course goes a long way to explaining its attitudes towards people such as Barrow until approximately 1832 when the split in the Colony, as manifested by the appearance of the *Graham's Town Journal*, took place.

The English, with the advantage of their European background, would provide the Colony with its leadership and thus give the impetus for development which until then had been absent. By publishing its columns in Dutch as well as in English, the *Commercial Advertiser* reckoned a good start had been made especially as the venture, it was said, had been undertaken "solely for their accom-

---

24. *Commercial Advertiser,* 3 Jan. 1829.
25. An integral part of the "new system" was the elevation and integration of the Non-Whites of the Colony with the European colonists. *Vide infra,* Chapt. VI.

modation and instruction".[26] Further, it was essential that the barriers which separated Englishman and Afrikaner, and the differences which kept White and Black apart within the Colony, be broken down so that a spirit of unity could be created. What this amounted to was the awakening of an awareness of the similarities existing amongst the two white population groups while minimising or overlooking differences in their national attitudes;

> "Are we not men of one blood," called Fairbairn, the *Commercial Advertiser's* editor, "members of one community — subjects of one sovereign — followers of one faith? Our country — our character — our interests are one. Let us do away with all narrow-minded party prejudices, combinations and coteries; and cordially unite our efforts in promoting great and good objects, whether they originate from Dutch or English."[27]

To achieve this worthwhile goal, two vital steps were necessary. First the Cape Dutch would need to be converted to the English way of thinking. As one correspondent worded it, it was necessary that education in its broadest form, and through the medium of the English language, be sown upon the "soil of ignorance and barbarism" of the Afrikaner youth.[28] Second, and of equal importance, the English colonial press would need to gain the confidence of the Afrikaners in order to get close enough to them to be able to exert influence upon them.

Before the *Commercial Advertiser* could hope to achieve results in unifying the colonists in any common cause, it needed to define precisely what its views were on three points: first, on Barrow's *Travels,* the Dutch translation of which was "generally read throughout the colony"; second, the views expressed by the *Quarterly Review*[29] whereby the Afrikaners had been "persuaded that all Englishmen regard them with the same uncandid and contemptuous feelings"; and third, recent traveller literature which had "imitated Barrow's worst faults without any capacity to emulate his excellencies" — all of which, but particularly the work of Barrow, it was reported, "sticks in the stomachs of the [Dutch] Cape Colonists"[30]

---

26. *Commercial Advertiser,* 17 March 1824.
27. *Ibid.* See also, 7 Dec. 1831.
28. *Ibid.,* "A Parent", 28 April 1824.
29. *Quarterly Review,* July 1819, pp. 203–246; *Vide supra,* Chapt. III.
30. *Commercial Advertiser,* 5 May 1824.

The *Commercial Advertiser* pursued the only course it could and adopted a protective attitude towards the Afrikaner colonists:

> "It is, no doubt, a certain and humiliating fact that civilized man, when withdrawn from the control of improved society, sinks, in general, much more readily to the level of the savage, than the latter rises to this level, when brought from the woods and forests to enjoy social intercourse with people of humane and polished habits. A thousand complicated levers are requisite to elevate the barbarian to the rank of civilization; but you have merely to withdraw these levers to throw him back to his former state of brutal and sensual existence. What is true of the individual is equally true of bodies and communities of men. To establish a flourishing Colony, therefore, in the midst of savage tribes, it is not merely requisite to transplant thither a few hundred or thousand families of civilized people, and as soon as they have taken root to abandon them to nature and themselves; but the '*Plantation*' . . . must be fenced, and sheltered, and unremittingly watered, and weeded, and pruned, and new-grafted, — and we must 'dig about it and dung it', and watch over it with unsleeping diligence, if we wish to reap a return deserving of our regard or worthy of the stock it was derived from. — If we act otherwise, and neglect the duty of good husbandmen, what can we expect but that our 'Plantation' will either pine away in sickly and dwarfish degeneracy, or, on a soil of greater fertility, shoot up in wild and wasteful luxuriance, undistinguished for any profitable quality from the native thickets around it."[31]

It was clear what had happened to the Afrikaners in the past. In keeping with the shortcomings of all European nations who colonised, the Dutch had shown themselves "too eager after commercial gains, and too careless of the moral and intellectual improvement of the inhabitants they placed in them".[32] The purely mercantile manner in which they had treated the Cape as no more than an outpost or half-way house had been responsible for stifling the development of both the Colony and the colonists. Without the necessary government encouragement or "good husbandry", the colonists had increasingly adopted the characteristics of their primitive environment. Even the "better policy" of Great Britain since 1795 could not "speedily restore a heartful and vigorous progression", although by 1824 the *Com-*

31. *Commercial Advertiser,* 4 Feb. 1824.
32. *Ibid.*

mercial Advertiser could claim: "We have much improved our manners since that time."[33]

The *Commercial Advertiser* accused the English travellers in general of having adopted a 'take-walk-make-book' mentality and defended the Colony as follows: "Our situation and circumstances are in many respects so very different from those of the old and long-improved nations of Europe, that any strict comparison with *them* [as opposed to other colonies] must be often unfair and entirely fallacious."[34] Of course this was true and what Fairbairn of the *Commercial Advertiser* intensely resented was the "flippant tone" assumed by those whom he classed as the "common heard of English Travellers"[35] — persons who had so glibly "filled their journals with angry and insulting declamations about the poverty and ignorance, sloth and vulgarity of the inhabitants".[36] Referring to the "revolting account" of Barrow[37] — on another occasion his work was spoken of as "fairy-land descriptions"[38] — the *Commercial Advertiser* accused him of breeding contempt, stating it to be no easy matter restraining its indignation when a man of Barrow's stature was seen "sitting calmly down at his desk and, addressing himself to the vulgar passions of his countrymen, recommend that a people should be ruled *'with a rod of iron'*, because he has discovered some instance of depravity amongst them, and because they do not eat, drink and sleep, and manage *their* affairs as he would have them do".[39] "Barrow", it was judged, "is evidently a man who takes strong and hasty views of things — who forms his opinions rapidly, and adheres to them pertinaciously",[40] and it was considered incredible that Barrow had not been aware of the fact that "the character and habits of men are formed by the institutions under which they have been reared".[41] As for the primitive living conditions of the Boers in the interior, the *Commercial Advertiser* was quite convinced that their domestic habits could be

---

33. *Commercial Advertiser,* 4 Feb. 1824.
34. *Ibid.*
35. *Ibid.,* 5 May 1824.
36. *Ibid.,* 4 Feb. 1824.
37. *Ibid.,* 5 May 1824.
38. *Ibid.,* 25 Nov. 1829.
39. *Ibid.,* 17 March 1824.
40. *Ibid.,* 5 May 1824.
41. *Ibid.,* 17 March 1824.

ascribed to poverty, while Barrow, on the other hand, had put it down to their "indolence and wilful destitution".[42]

Barrow's ill-judged statements could easily be accounted for. He had visited the Colony at a particularly inopportune time. "Some of them", stated the *Commercial Advertiser* of the interior Boers, "were in arms against the English Government; others were submissive only from fear of interests; many were dissatisfied; all were jealous or ill at ease."[43] Furthermore, because of Barrow's high office he had hardly been in the position to meet the Boers on equal terms which had made it "scarcely possible" for him to form a correct estimate of their character. Presenting for its readers what it considered to be a more fair description of daily life in the interior[44] – obviously a complimentary picture – the *Commercial Advertiser* appealed for unity between the English and Afrikaners, claiming that Barrow had lately, in the *Quarterly Review* (or so they *supposed* it to be him) retracted many of his earlier charges against the colonial character.[45] In any event, it was impressed upon the Afrikaner readers of the newspaper that such sentiments did in no way reflect the attitude of the Government, nor did "practical men" attach much importance to them.[46] In 1824/25 the relationship between the English and Afrikaners was thought, in fact, to constitute a most regrettable state of affairs. As a result of the early travellers' accounts of the Afrikaners the two 'nations' had kept to themselves which had tended "to keep alive national distinctions and jealousies, and retard that cordial and complete amalgamation of the Dutch and English Colonists". The *Commercial Advertiser* therefore undertook to "defend . . . every class of our fellow colonists that may be unjustly or ungenerously aspersed".[47]

While there is evidence to suggest that the relationship between the English and Afrikaners in Albany was quite amicable,[48] it is nonetheless a fact that the English and Dutch continued to regard each

---

42. *Commercial Advertiser,* 6 Feb. 1830.
43. *Ibid.,* 5 May 1824.
44. *Ibid.,* "A Vee Boer of the Sneuwberg, in 1823" (from an unpublished journal). The journal referred to was Thompson's *Travels,* published in 1827.
45. *Commercial Advertiser,* 31 Aug. 1825, referring to the article in the *Quarterly Review,* July 1821. *Vide supra,* pp. 81–82.
46. *Commercial Advertiser,* 31 Aug. 1825.
47. *Ibid.,* 5 May 1824.
48. H. E. Hockly, *The Story of the British Settlers of 1820 in South Africa,* pp. 173–177.

other as separate groups and although circumstances brought them into contact, they did not easily *mix*. From the *Commercial Advertiser,* however, it seems that the Settlers felt that they should at least meet and a letter from Grahamstown in 1826 referred to an event which had afforded the English of the town "much pleasure" when an Afrikaner's horse had won the local turf racing cup since it was thought "likely to induce our *Dutch-Brother Colonists* to visit us on other occasions and thereby to lay the foundation of that union of effort and sentiment so much desired by every well wisher to the country".[49] A regular correspondent to the newspaper, "Agricola", suggested that agricultural societies and fairs be established in order to further the interests of agriculture and commerce in order to lead "the respectable farmers of both nations into a more close and friendly intercourse rendering them at once mutual instruction and emulous competitors in the race of improvement",[50] – an idea which received support and was, in fact, implemented some years later.

Comparison between the English and Dutch by the English themselves was to be expected. "Agricola", on commenting upon the "laudable anxiety"[51] which the *Commercial Advertiser* showed in the development of the interior of the Colony, had the following to say after a tour of the districts of Albany, Somerset and Graaff-Reinet: "The old Colonists had more property, prudence and experience – the new settlers more enterprise and intelligence".[52] He found Graaff-Reinet to be "considerably in advance" of the two English districts; "but," he added, "what Graham's Town and Albany in general have chiefly to depend upon for future prosperity is the superior enterprise of the inhabitants. In whatever else the British Settlers may be behind the older colonists, they unquestionably far surpass them in the spirit of enterprise; and this quality, in my apprehension, will more than compensate for all the other disadvantages of their situation".[53] "Agricloa" enlarged still further:

> "I speak of the spirit of enterprise directed by European intelligence, opposed to hereditary apathy increased by narrow and

49. *Commercial Advertiser,* 31 May 1826.
50. *Ibid.,* "Agricola", 21 Sept. 1825.
51. *Ibid.,* "Agricola", 14 Sept. 1825.
52. *Ibid.,* "Agricola", 21 Sept. 1825.
53. *Ibid.,* "Agricola", 14 Sept. 1825.

timid views. And yet while I speak thus favourably of the superior enterprise of the British Settlers, I mean no unfair or unfriendly insinuation against the character of the Dutch Colonists. On the contrary, I think them to be in general a very respectable class of men, and *much superior*, in some points, to what they have been represented by *hasty* observers. There is something solid, and substantial, and prudent in the character of the African Boor, which is not unworthy of his Belgic origin, and not frequently to be found, I conceive, among the Back Settlers of most other Colonies. In occupying a country so different from his own, he has, in many things, so judiciously adapted himself to the circumstances of his new situation, as to leave nothing to improve on. He has done much – and it is not wonderful that he has left much still to do. He became accustomed to his situation, and ceased to contrast the position he had gained with the one he had left at home. His standard of excellence became lowered to what he saw best around him. He built a house of three apartments – planted a few vines and fruit trees, ploughed a patch of corn-land, increased his herds of big-horned cattle and big-tailed sheep – and then sat still. A new race from Europe obtain all the advantages of his experience, without the long drudgery he endured to gain it. They start from the point he has reached, to emulate the improvements they have lately left behind. But the Dutch and the British Colonist have each something to learn from each other. The one is more prudent and experienced; but at the same time too timid and careful of small matters to attempt novel improvements:– the other is more enterprising and intelligent, but also somewhat rash and imprudent. They would do well to sink every sort of reciprocal jealousy or dislike – learn to estimate each other candidly – and imitate what on either side is most worthy of imitation."[54]

From the start the relationship between the British and Afrikaners within the Colony had not been marked by any spontaneity respecting co-operation or intercourse when in 1795 the Afrikaner colonists came into contact with the high-minded Tory mentality of the first British occupation. This is not meant to imply that there was no co-operation between them – there was. However, effecting unity would be difficult and the question arises as to how realistic, under the circumstances, the hopes or ambitions of the *Commercial Advertiser* were in this respect. In 1795, when the Cape had been first occupied by the British, there had been little or no inclination on the

54. *Commercial Advertiser,* "Agricola", 14 Sept. 1825.

part of the English residents to accept Dutch institutions which ran contrary to British traditions and which, considered *The Times,* afforded "a sorry specimen of the degree of liberty" at the Cape.[55] So bad was the state of affairs considered that in 1810 W. B. Halloran had written that the English were "exposed to individual imposition and insult and subjected to the operation of Arbitrary Laws, and ministered in the most summary way".[56] What proved a particular stumbling block, then, was the Dutch system of jurisprudence which frequently was in opposition to English law and practice and which was the "subject of daily unpleasant conversation" between the English and Cape Dutch.[57] Differences such as this formed the basis of the English/Afrikaner estrangement, in addition to which, in the opinion of W. W. Bird writing in 1822, (and others[58]) there was the old story that an Englishman "accommodates himself with difficulty, to the manners of other countries; and nothing can be right or proper, that is not English, and to which he is unaccustomed".[59] Obviously differences in traditions or national attitudes would retard intercourse and prohibit integration.

From thc Afrikaner side, too, the alien British had by no means been popular outside the ranks of Orange society in Cape Town and were thought of with suspicion – so much so, in fact, that Wilson had thought it would be necessary to take steps to convince the Afrikaners that they were not freebooters.[60] Possibly the underlying feeling of the Dutch towards the English was that they were thought of as "foreigners and conquerors".[61]

Barrow had originally attributed any reluctance on the part of the Cape Dutch to coming forward and mixing with the English to the manner which a "vanquished people" always felt towards their conquerors;[62] yet, while this might have been true there was more to the matter than this as the lack of intercourse rested largely upon the differences in class existing within society at the Cape than upon

---

55. *The Times,* 11 Jan. 1802.
56. G. H. 1/1, Halloran to Liverpool, 25 Sept. 1810, f. 812.
57. C.O. 48/17, Cradock to Bathurst, 2 Oct. 1813, f. 124.
58. *Vide* Kotzé, *Owerheidsbeleid,* p. 55; *vide supra,* pp. 7–8, 40–42.
59. Bird, *State of the Cape of Good Hope in 1822,* p. 154.
60. Br. Mus., ADD. MSS. 30097, vol. 3, "Journal of Sir Robert Wilson", 3 Jan. 1805, f. 100.
61. C.O. 48/40, Ellis to Goulburn, 19 Oct. 1819, f. 316.
62. Barrow, *Travels,* i, p. 51.

any clearcut division of race. This accounts for the situation which developed at Cape Town where, similar to the British experience in French Quebec, the upper classes mixed freely with the English and fell into the sphere of Lady Anne Barnard's social evenings at the Castle, while the other classes remained aloof. Nonetheless, in 1807 Caledon had been pleased to report on the "respect towards the British nation", claiming it to be the "prevailing sentiment" of the Cape Dutch.[63] Cradock, four years later, held the same view and attributed the reckless actions of the malcontents in the past to the expectation that the Cape would be returned to is former rulers[64] – no an entirely unrealistic hope. However, once it became known that this was not to be the case, it seems that those persons began to adopt certain English habits.[65] As for assimilation, that was far too premature at this stage, for even as late as 1835 it was remarked that only among the merchant class of Cape Town was there any real intercourse.[66]

After 1820, where the colonists shared common interests and where their dependence upon each other became pronounced, they drew closer to each other and co-operated to the extent that it could even have been mistaken for real and lasting unity. Examples of this are the agitation against Somerset which had united "cautious Settlers, radical pressmen and liberal Dutch-speaking colonists",[67] the Anti-Convict agitation of the 1840's and even the Hottentots Ordinance of 1828 – on this issue the Colony was divided into two main camps, one of which was composed of Settlers *and* Afrikaners. However, in spite of the fact that the Commissioners of Enquiry in 1823 could report that the "British settlers are so intermixed with those of the Dutch colonists" and that many of the English mechanical and labouring classes were rapidly entering the employ of the more wealthy Afri-

---

63. C.O. 48/1, Caledon to Windham, 30 May 1807, f. 52.
64. C.O. 48/11, Cradock to Liverpool, 31 Dec. 1811, ff. 8–9.
65. C.O. 48/38, undated, anonymous treatise, "Observations on the Cape of Good Hope", f. 313.
66. J. W. D. Moodie, *Ten Years in South Africa,* i, p. 31. It is only possible to guess at what Lloyd in his work *Mr. Barrow of the Admiralty* (pp. 183–184) meant, when on referring to Barrow's Afrikaner wife, he said: "She is a shadowy figure in his life, her chief talent being the drawing of botanical specimens . . ." It would be very interesting indeed to know whether Barrow and his Cape wife shared a happy life together.
67. *C.H.B.E.,* viii, p. 262.

kaner farmers,[68] under stress the flaws in the binding which might have drawn them together, and the more deep-seated differences which separated them, rose to the surface. The remarks of "Philo-Africanus" in the *Commercial Advertiser* show clearly the bitter feelings of at least a section of the English at that time. Entering upon a question which this correspondent maintained no one had been prepared to answer, he asked why farms in the Neutral Territory had ben granted exclusively to the Boers and why they had been granted so much land compared to what they, the English, had received. In this affair, which rested squarely between the Settlers and the Colonial Government, the writer reflected what must have been a deeply ingrained hostility towards the Afrikaners, and in answer to his own question he wrote: The Boers had lately submitted two memorials written "in their own gibberish" to the Commander of the Frontier and the Governor wherein their "many virtues" were enumerated. Was it not remarkable, he demanded, that these very colonists who had signed the petition – to the man – had been allocated the coveted land to which he was referring? Then followed the rub: "It is also somewhat remarkable, that so many of those persons who have been seized with this sudden fit of loyalty and affection [towards the Governor], should have been particularly distinguished by a very opposite feeling for the British Government a few years back" when (referring to Slagter's Nek) "some of their less fortunate companions made a rather awkward exit from the world!"[69]

If nothing had occurred in the colonial life to accentuate the differences between its various groups, the *Commercial Advertiser* might have achieved some results from the stand it took on Barrow and other commentators, for it can be supposed that, having a common environment, the English and Afrikaners would have drawn closer together to the point of their ultimately becoming a single people. However, seeing that issues *did* develop within the Colony, notably the Hottentot question and promulgation of the 50th Ordinance in 1828, all that the *Commercial Advertiser* could realistically have hoped to do was to placate the Afrikaners and try to convince them that not all Englishmen thought as Barrow had. A further hindrance to the *Commercial Advertiser's* campaign was the increasing problem of English exclusiveness. The Settlers were deve-

68. C.O. 48/76, Bigge and Colebrook to Bathurst, 25 Sept. 1823, ff. 4, 6.
69. *Commercial Advertiser*, "Philo-Africanus", 22 Feb. 1826.

loping a marked degree of pride in their achievements and the contributions they had made to the development of the Colony at the virtual exclusion of Afrikaner participation.[70] One correspondent, who contemplated a further scheme to bring British settlers to the Cape, spoke of the "real English feeling" that such people would meet in the Colony – again without mentioning the Afrikaners.[71] All that could be said of the Afrikaner was well illustrated by Pringle himself who urged that it was "solicitous to keep upon friendly terms" with them.[72] A further impression gained from the *Commercial Advertiser* is that the English held themselves to be of a higher moral calibre than the Boers, something blatantly suggested by "A Traveller" in the colonial press: "The Settlers brought a beginning of Liberty to South Africa," meaning that the natives of the Cape had lately received a fair deal from the Whiteman as opposed to the treatment they had received at the hands of the Boers in the past.[73]

That the Afrikaners were thoroughly separate from the English, although living in close proximity to each other is emphasised in the comments of someone who had just returned from a visit to the predominantly English district of Albany. "At Cape Town" he wrote, "our society is so mixed by being composed by Dutch and English, that it is quite natural for both parties not to feel quite so much at ease with each other, as when habits and customs are alike."[74] Bird, it will be remembered, had also made mention of the differences in habits stating that because of there not being an "amalgamation of habits" there was little actual association between the English and Afrikaners "as is usual with individuals of a common stock".[75]

During the 1820's people in Great Britain came to accept that the treatment the Blackman received in the Cape Colony had improved.[76] The findings of the Commissioners of Enquiry to the Colony, published in 1825, added weight to the growing impression that the abuses of the past, which had formerly been such a powerful

---

70. One obtains this feeling particularly from a letter singed "A Settler", *Commercial Advertiser,* 17 Dec. 1828.
71. *Commercial Advertiser,* "A Settler", 20 Dec. 1828.
72. Pringle, *African Sketches,* p. 169.
73. *Commercial Advertiser,* "A Traveller", 18 March 1829.
74. *Ibid.,* Anonymous letter, 18 Nov. 1828.
75. Bird, *State of the Cape of Good Hope, in 1822,* p. 164.
76. Philip, *Researches,* p. xvi.

influence in the shaping of English opinion of the Afrikaners, in fact had had their roots in the weakness of the Dutch East India Company's administration, and that the presence of British government was responsible for the improved state of affairs in the Colony. Of course, some attributed the improvement in colonial character to the "peaceable and intelligent character" of the English Settlers placed on the frontier which meant that the natives were "no longer insulted, robbed, and shot as in the time of the Dutch"[77] but perhaps this was just too partisan a view. However, there definitely had been a change for the better since the British occupied the Colony as a report in *The Times* must have shown when it published an account of a Boer being executed for the murder of a slave.[78]

Socially, too, a much more agreeable picture was emerging. A correspondent to the *Manchester Guardian* spoke highly of the valuable assistance which the Boers had given the British immigrants;[79] Phillips, Rose and others all commented on the wonderful hospitality they had received from the Afrikaners; and Thompson, on referring to the exceedingly kind treatment he had experienced with a certain Schalk Burger, said: "where such men are found in the walks of common life, the mass of the community, we may feel assured, cannot be altogether so brutal and degraded, as some English writers have too unqualifiedly represented them".[80] And although the Afrikaners might have been thought of by Phillips as "distant and reserved, and at first their approach appears cold",[81] the British reading public were nonetheless led to believe that the Boers with whom the Settlers had come into contact, while they might have been "uncultivated", were by no means disagreeable neighbours.[82]

On the other hand, however, while the *Commercial Advertiser* might have been perfectly justified in crying out against the past misrepresentation of the Afrikaner character and despite most colonial accounts stressing the marked improvement of his personality, the rising influence of philanthropists, such as Philip, on those responsible for policy in Great Britain was something to be reckoned with and

77. *Blackwood's Edinburgh Magazine,* July 1828, p. 33.
78. *The Times,* 7 Feb. 1823.
79. *Manchester Guardian,* 16 June 1821.
80. Thompson, *Travels,* ii, p. 145.
81. Phillips, *Scenes and Occurrences in Albany and Caffer-land,* p. 20.
82. Pringle, *African Sketches,* pp. 169–170.

in consequence certain basic reservations respecting the Afrikaner persisted. The *Quarterly Review,* described by the *Commercial Advertiser* as a journal which had "always professed narrow principles" and which wielded "very great" influence in Britain, gave a cool reception to the call made by the Cape press for greater freedom for its colonists.[83] Cautioning the British Government not to grant legislative assemblies to *any* of their colonies as it would cost both trouble to themselves and inconvenience to their subjects, the *Quarterly Review* made the following observations on the Cape:

> "The Cape of Good Hope, too, with its fifty-five thousand white inhabitants, scattered over a surface of about 500 by 300 miles, is petitioning for a Legislative Assembly – that is to say, the English part of the population, which does not amount to more than about two thousand, or rather, the two hundred out of these two thousand who may be established in Cape Town – nay properly speaking, it is a part only of these two hundred who are calling out for a House of Representatives. The Dutch inhabitants are perfectly satisfied to be governed by an Officer appointed by the Crown. We happen to know that the most respectable natives of the Colony of the Cape of Good Hope are of the opinion, that the state of their small society, which is very much connected with ties of relationship, is not at all suited for the boon we have bestowed on them by the introduction of that institution which we value so highly – Trial by Jury, and in some places it is next to impossible, to collect a sufficient number of qualified persons to form a jury . . ."[84]

In reply to the *Quarterly Review,* the *Commercial Advertiser* was quick to draw attention to the incorrect population statistics. It was shown that the Colony contained some 134 000 persons, of whom 100 000 were free and the rest slave, while 7 000 colonists could boast British parentage. Then it was pointed out that the petition for a supreme court, trial by jury, a free press, and the petition for a legislative assembly in 1827 had been signed by more than 1 500 people, of whom a fair proportion had been Afrikaners. The petition in 1828 for an assembly had been even more marked by the co-operation between the English and Afrikaners as it was stated that for every one Englishman who had signed there had been three Afrikaners. The *Commercial Advertiser* also refuted the contention that

83. *Commercial Advertiser,* 1 Aug. 1829; 5 Aug. 1829.
84. *Quarterly Review,* June 1829, p. 75.

problems had been encountered in finding suitably qualified persons to act on juries, as did it maintain that the Colony could quite easily cope with a system involving political representation.[85] As for the Afrikaners, the *Commercial Advertiser* claimed that the development which the Colony had experienced since the coming of the Settlers in 1820 had also much affected the personality of the older colonists. Their political unreadiness, which had been epitomised in their well known attitude of "the Government knows best, Sir, what is good for the people",[86] was becoming a thing of the past as, too, was the conservatism of the Boers, as manifested in the customs of following "without thought or reflection, the customs of their forefathers, resisting, with unreasonable obstinacy, all changes, however clearly shown to be for their advantage",[87] and while the *Commercial Advertiser* still spoke of the "caution which distinguishes the conduct of our farmers",[88] as early as 1826 it had maintained that the inhabitants were beginning to perceive the advantages which could be reaped from the introduction of such liberal institutions as a free press.[89] New innovations were being accepted and the state of affairs was "daily improving" thus promising greater progress for the Colony in the future.[90] "By being educated in the same schools, imbued with the same moral, religious, and political principles, by inter-marriages, and by daily intercourse in the ordinary affairs of life, the Colonists have become, or are rapidly becoming, one People"[91] and therefore, as far as the *Commercial Advertiser* was concerned, the old argument that the Afrikaners were insufficiently reconciled to the supremacy of Britain to be entrusted with the enjoyment of such a political privilege as the granting of a legislative assembly had "lost all weight".[92] As far as the *Commercial Advertiser* was concerned the Afrikaners created no problem:

> "They are chiefly of European extraction, and in their person and habits differ very little from their ancestors, whom, in their religion, morals, and general character also as private indivi-

85. *Commercial Advertiser,* 1 Aug. 1829; 5 Aug. 1829; 21 Aug. 1830.
86. *Ibid.,* 15 March 1826.
87. *Ibid.,* 19 Sept. 1829.
88. *Ibid.*
89. *Ibid.,* 8 Feb. 1826.
90. *Ibid.,* 16 Sept. 1829.
91. *Ibid.,* 21 Aug. 1830.
92. *Ibid.,* 7 June 1826.

duals, they very closely resemble. They are mighty hunters, and extensive breeders of cattle, sheep, goats, and horses, of which they possess a very superior breed. They raise considerable quantities of excellent wheat, and five or six kinds of improveable wine. They engage eagerly in trade and foreign commerce, from which they are beginning to derive considerable profits and other advantages. They build commodious and substantial houses, which they fit up with excellent furniture, and every imagineable comfort and convenience within their reach. They are particularly strict in their marriage contracts and ceremonies, baptise their infants, are careful to educate their children to the utmost of their means and abilities; they believe in the Apostle's Creed, and keep the Ten Commandments as well as any people we have known."[93]

However, although such assurances made pleasant reading, the more substantial writings of John Philip[94] claimed greater attention in official circles in Britain when it came to determining whether or not political power should be granted to the Cape Colonists, the overwhelming majority of whom were Afrikaners. How would they utilise the power they received if a legislative assembly was granted to them? A thought at the back of British minds was that perhaps the Afrikaners would again attempt to challenge the authority of the Crown as they had done in 1795, 1802 and again in 1815, and of tremendous importance was the question of the kind of treatment the Hottentots would receive if the colonists were granted the political power they sought.

Precisely these questions came up for debate in parliament in 1830 when Lord Milton placed before the House the petition for a representative government which had been received from the "British Settlers and others" at the Cape.[95] The grounds upon which the Secretary of State, Sir George Murray, had little difficulty in persuading the House of the impolicy of granting such a request underline the reservations held about the Afrikaners and leave little to the imagination as to what parliamentarians thought of them.

First, the petition had come only from a portion of the Colony and from that portion, too, in which slavery did not exist. This, he considered, made a big difference since there was no country where slavery existed in which the expediency of introducing a representa-

---

93. *Commercial Advertiser,* 3 Jan. 1829.

94. *Vide infra,* pp. 106–110.

95. *Hansard,* New Series, XXIV, Commons 24 May 1830, cols. 1005–1014.

tive legislature might not be most seriously doubted. Second, the state of the Colony needed to be taken into account with reference to the size of its population and the extent of its development. The population of the Cape being so small and scattered meant that it could hardly take advantage of the privileges and powers of representation. Of paramount importance, however, was the fact that the British Government was unwilling to grant representation to the white colonists when they were divided into Afrikaner and British camps (and where the British were in the minority) as this would mean that the legislature would be divided into two distinct parties, one Afrikaner and the other English. Under these circumstances very good reasons would need to be submitted before the petition of the colonists could be met. Then there was the question of the Hottentots, which perhaps best of all indicates what was thought of the Afrikaners. In reply to the comments of the Secretary of State, Dr. Lushington maintained that political representation would seriously jeopardise the "best interests" of the Colony and unless the innovation could guarantee the improvement of the treatment received by the slaves and Hottentots, he would resist the measure. In fact, he would do so until he saw in the colonists "a disposition of the strong to protect the weak", and as far as he was concerned, granting a legislative assembly would not produce these effects. On referring to the present condition of the Hottentots, the details of whose "oppression" he preferred not to enter into – though he did remark upon the "miserable condition in which the Hottentot population was kept" – Lushington maintained that if he were to elaborate, he was certain that the House would view the petition with "indignation and abhorrance".

In short, the Cape Colony would not be granted a legislative assembly owing to the imbalance in the composition of its white colonists, where the Afrikaners were in the majority and whose political past cast suspicion on their future actions if given a free hand. Furthermore, as long as the Hottentots were thought of as being oppressed, Great Britain would be morally bound to withhold political power from their 'oppressors'. This point, the treatment of the Hottentots, was to play a major role in the future affairs of the Cape Colony, and ultimately was largely responsible for the division of South Africa between what has often been referred to as the 'colonial south' and the 'republican north'.

CHAPTER FIVE

Against the System
1828–1831

> "The sufferings of the natives under the Dutch government, have been fully depicted by MR. BARROW, but it did not begin to be suspected in England, till lately, how little their condition has been improved by the change of masters they experienced when the English took possession of the Cape. It seems to have been too easily taken for granted, that because we could declaim against Dutch inhumanity, and because the natives in the first instance viewed our conquest of the colony as a deliverance, that all their early expectations had been realised, and that their oppressions had passed away with the power of their former masters. Such were the impressions, at least under which I arrived at the Cape of Good Hope in 1819, and such were the feelings I endeavoured to cherish, till I could no longer retain them . . ."[1]

The promulgation of the 50th (or Hottentot) Ordinance of 1828 in the Cape Colony, designed for "improving the condition of the Hottentots and other free persons of colour", should be regarded as the coming of age of the philanthropic incursion into South Africa. At a time when abolitionists in Great Britain had gained considerable support and the influence of the philanthropists in general was fast approaching its zenith, this ordinance, together with the publication of John Philip's *Researches in South Africa* in the same year (an extract of which appears above) drew such a reaction from the Cape Colonists that it completely shattered all hope for colonial unity.

The main point around which the controversy raged was the status

1. Philip, *Researches*, i, p. xvi.

the Hottentot[2] should occupy within white colonial society. The application of the 50th Ordinance divided Englishmen within the Colony between east and west, while the gulf between the English and the Afrikaners widened further and the Colony witnessed the coming into being of a "Colonial" party on the one hand, supported mainly by the farming community of the eastern province, and on the other a small but highly vocal pro-philanthropist "Anti-Colonial" party which was located in Cape Town.[3] When, therefore, in 1829, the *Commercial Advertiser* had set about repudiating the remarks passed by the *Quarterly Review* on the subject of political representation for the Colony, the colonists had, in fact, already become divided. Such a state of affairs, of course, put paid to any hopes of a legislative assembly based upon colonial solidarity, especially as the split had been brought about on the crucial question of proper treatment of the Hottentots.

In view of the immediate commotion Philip's publication caused in the Cape Colony, it is perhaps surprising to learn that his *Researches* received little attention in Great Britain.[4] There were two reasons for this. First, in 1828 the British public was content to limit its interest in philanthropy to the abolition of slavery and had not yet extended its concern to the actual improvement of the treatment of the Blackman, whether he was slave or nominally free. Second, the importance of colonies was still regarded dubiously which meant that the British people were not really interested in the affairs of the colonies. Using *The Times* as a pointer to illustrate the interest the British public showed in the Cape Colony, it becomes apparent that although the *Commercial Advertiser* was quite regularly referred to (particularly during the confrontation with Somerset) actually it (*The Times*)

---

2. The term "Hottentot" can be misleading. In 1800 the 'coloured people' of the Colony comprised, besides a handful of Bushmen, a widely scattered population of 'free men', loosely known as 'Hottentots', and roughly equal in number to the slaves of foreign origin and were mainly concentrated in the extreme west. Even at that date the Hottentots were a much mixed people, perhaps predominantly Hottentot in origin, but including strains of Bushmen, Malay, Negro and European. In colour they ranged from brown or black to nearly white.
3. A. L. Harington, *The Graham's Town Journal and the Great Trek, 1834–1843*, pp. 59–60.
4. *C.H.B.E.*, viii, p. 294. *The Atlas*, 27 April 1828, gave notice that Philip's *Researches* had been received from its publishers for review, yet did not review it.

could not have been concerned less about the Afrikaners, while not a great deal more interest was shown directly in the affairs of the Hottentots. Fortunately for Philip, however, his appeal to the British public was not of great importance. Turning his attention directly to those in power he made it his business to make his case felt. Although his work was far from accurate[5] and has been much overrated, it had the desired effect of prompting the British Government to action.[6] Its appeal, like that of Read and van der Kemp some 15 or 16 years earlier, was irresistable to philanthropic sympathisers like the Secretary of State.[7]

There can be no doubt that the lot of the Hottentots was hard. Deprived of their old grazing lands, they had also lost whatever wealth they had ever had in cattle, they had no "reserves", and were too poor to buy land, even if they had not been legally debarred from acquiring it. "Untaught, hardly even deemed worthy of employment",[8] the majority of them drifted into a state of servile dependence upon the colonial farmers and having no recognised status, they came to be considered a lesser breed without the law.[9]

However, any movement aimed at elevating the Hottentots to rank beside the white colonists would naturally draw a reaction from the Afrikaners for, irrespective of the Afrikaner beliefs regarding the inborn status and destiny of the coloured peoples, their degree of prosperity depended largely on Hottentot labour. Besides this, the Afrikaners feared that a change in the status of the Hottentots would jeopardize the security they had come to take for granted. Of course, such reservations were not confined to the Afrikaner ranks alone. The Colonial Office, for instance, had replied to Philip's assertion that inequality in the sight of the law was the worst possible evil, by

---

5. Despite what W. M. Macmillan in his work *Bantu, Boer and Briton,* p. 19, has termed as Philip's "unimpeachable evidence", a detailed investigation of the accuracy or inaccuracy of Philip's statements, including those in his *Researches,* is of sufficient scope to warrant an independent study.
6. E. A. Walker, *A History of South Africa,* pp. 176–177.
7. Despite the fact that the Hottentot Ordinance in 1828 was passed in Cape Town by Governor Bourke while Philip was in England (where and when he published his *Researches*) philanthropists regarded this controversial legislation as the fruits of Philip's labours. Philip was also thought of as the champion of the Blackman in South Africa.
8. *C.H.B.E.,* viii, p. 282.
9. Macmillan *Bantu, Boer and Briton,* p. 6; *C.H.B.E.*, viii, pp. 279–288.

saying that "such laws are universal".[10] Judge Menzies, on referring to a query from the Colonial Office in 1829 on the possibility of introducing "principles of justice and law" to the Cape Colony, had agreed that of course this was most desirable, but added: "I take the liberty of stating my decided conviction of the impolicy of adopting any measures having a tendency to make the Law of England in all respects the law of this colony . . ."[11] The point he was stressing was that the Cape Colony was not England owing to the composition of its population with its "slaves, and semi-civilised barbarians, or wholly uncivilised savages", and therefore should not be treated as such simply to be in keeping with the "abstract principles of the British Constitution".[12] Such misgivings had also been voiced two decades earlier in 1812, when the judges of the circuit court had suggested that ". . . those authors who have endeavoured to make the world believe the many fine dreams they have written on the happiness of man in his natural state of simplicity, should live for a little while among those men of nature in order to form a just estimation of their own works".[13] In 1812, on reflecting upon the important question of what would be the most effective guiding principle or policy to adopt towards the Hottentots, the circuit court judges had referred to the results obtained by the missionary institutions. Concerning the Moravian Brethren and the London Missionary Society, they wrote:

> "The principle adopted there [at the Moravian station Genadendal] by the teachers seems to be, to encourage those people to industry, order and subordination, and to practise those social virtues, as essential religious duties, the beneficial effects of this instruction are visible in walking through this little Hottentot village; every family has a dwelling and a garden; he cultivates his piece of ground, from whence he derives food and nourishment, and a degree of cleanliness reigns in all those little houses, which is not natural to that people; their religious meetings are zealously attended, and the doctrine preached to them, which bears the marks of simplicity, seems to be heard with attention . . . The other of those missionary institutions, namely Bethels-

10. C.O. 48/127, Comments in margin, Philip to Colonial Office, 3 Dec. 1828, f. 393.
11. C.O. 48/133, Menzies to Hay, 18 Feb. 1829, f. 168.
12. C.O. 48/133, Menzies to Stephen, 16 Feb. 1829, f. 250: encl. to C.O. 48/133, Menzies to Hay, 18 Feb. 1829.
13. C.O. 48/19, "Report of the Circuit Commission, dated 14 Nov. 1812", f. 114: encl. to C.O. 48/17, Cradock to Bathurst, 11 Aug. 1813.

dorp [of the London Missionary Society] is very far from being compared thereto; nothing of what is good in the former, is here to be perceived, the founder of the same, the late Mr. van der Kemp established such an overstrained principle of liberty as the ground work, that the natural state of barbarism appears there to supercede civilisation and social order; the former commission already remarked the same in their ample record . . . Laziness and idleness and consequently dirt and filth grow here in perfection and inimical partiality against the inhabitants reigns in such a manner that not only the Hottentots belonging to the institutions, are to be induced to hue themselves to the inhabitants but even frequently the other Hottentots are drawn away from the service of the farmers and reduced to increase the number of the idle and lazy, and especially when they possess any cattle, which are then swallowed up at the institution among the general mass, and must serve for the support of the others, who have already spent theirs – It is certainly not to be denied, but that some of the Bethelsdorp Hottentots in former times suffered injuries from some of the farmers . . . but at the same time it is not less true, that there are many Hottentots at Bethelsdorp who have a considerable part in plundering, robbing, setting fire to the places, and even murdering the inhabitants; and as the Hottentots as well as the missionaries, who at present exercise the immediate control over them, do not wish to see those things brought to light . . ."[14]

While the 50th Ordinance had virtually elevated the Hottentots[15] to the level of the European colonists it had, nonetheless, failed to achieve full legal equality for them. Maintaining that such a state of affairs was "contrary to the principles of the British Constitution",

---

14. C.O. 48/19, "Report of the Circuit Commission, dated 14 Nov. 1812", ff. 101–104: encl. to C.O. 48/17, Cradock to Bathurst, 11 Aug. 1813. See also, C.O. 48/144, "Missionary Institutions at the Cape of Good Hope", dated Colonial Office 15 Oct. 1831, ff. 24–25: encl. to C.O. 48/144, Cole to Goderich, 10 May 1831.
15. In 1808 Dundas introduced the first control to regularise the relationship between Hottentot farm labourers and their white masters by making registration of service contracts between them compulsory. Acting upon Collins' recommendations, Caledon proclaimed in 1809 what has been called the "Magna Carta of the Hottentots". In the face of Hottentot vagrancy and the possibility of Boer abuse of their servants, this measure purported to protect both parties. For the farmer, all Hottentots were to have fixed places of abode and were contracted for service for a period of one year. In the event of the Hottentot moving to another district, which he was entitled to do unless bound by a contract, he had to obtain a "pass" from the local landdrost or face arrest as a vagrant. Wages were to be paid to the Hottentots and payments in kind were to be witnessed;

Philip added: "by putting the Natives under the same laws as the colonists, whether Dutch or English, the British Government will teach the former to respect themselves and thus forcing the colonists to respect them, a foundation will be laid for the amalgamation and the elevation of both classes".[16] On another occasion he spoke his mind more forcefully: ". . . it is equally unnecessary for me to say that not only the mass of the White population, but many influential individuals in this Colony are yet to be taught that the Hottentots are, in all matters of right, to be treated exactly on the same footing as themselves".[17]

Philip holds a place in the history of South Africa for a number of reasons but most particularly he is remembered for the part he played in the agitation for improved conditions for the Hottentots, which bore fruit in the Hottentot Ordinance, and for the rumpus it caused in the Colony, which in turn precipitated the rift between the colonists in the east and those in the west. When he returned to the Colony in 1829, after having published his *Researches* in Britain, public outcry was at its height, particularly as it was maintained by the colonists in the east that the clause in the ordinance which had abolished the pass system had now resulted in the Hottentots turning vagrant. This elevation of the Hottentots to their new position in colonial society provided the foundations of what the *Commercial Advertiser* had often referred to as the "new system" and because of Philip's implication in it he became "the personal embodiment of everything they [the Afrikaners] so bitterly resented".[18]

In the preface to his *Researches* Philip had stated "my object . . .

---

liquor was not to rank as a necessity of life nor wages; no claims of personal service were to be laid against the servant in respect of debt and anything due to the employer beyond the value of the servant's wage, was to be recoverable only by ordinary process of law. In 1812, Cradock introduced the so-called "apprenticeship system". Under this system Hottentot children were to be bound from their 8th to 18th years to any farmer who had supported them in their infancy and, with the exception of certain amendments made by Somerset in 1819, this remained the law of the land until the 15th Ordinance of 1828 which completely removed compulsory service of the Hottentots from the statute book. Furthermore, they became legally entitled to purchase or possess land and the abuses attendant on the apprenticeship system were also rectified.

16. C.O. 48/127, Philip to Colonial Office, 3 Dec. 1828, ff. 393–394.
17. C.O. 48/144, Philip to Sec. to Government, 4 March 1831, f. 173
18. Macmillan, *Bantu, Boer and Briton,* p. 21.

has not been to expose men, but measures"[19] and therefore, although he charged the frontier farmers with cruelty and oppression of the Griquas and other tribes bordering the Colony, he did not have as much to say about the Afrikaners directly as might perhaps have been expected. Nonetheless, the Afrikaners themselves formed a large part of the system of which he was critical and therefore it is necessary to understand the basis of Philip's criticism and the mould into which the Afrikaners fell under his pen.

It must be realised that the basis of the criticism brought against the Afrikaners in 1795 by Barrow differed greatly from that brought by Philip in 1828. During the earlier period the Afrikaners, particularly the frontiersmen, were condemned for the open abuses with which they allegedly treated the natives; during the second period, when it can be accepted that this kind of treatment was the exception rather than the rule, the Afrikaners were criticised for the part they played in the "system", the *status quo* in the relationship between White and Black wherein, for example, emphasis was placed on the lack of equality the Hottentots suffered under the colonial law. What Collins and company had refuted were Barrow's remarks on the Afrikaners being indolent, abusive to the natives, etc., and not the master-servant relationship which is what distinguishes Philip's criticism from that of the earlier period.

Commencing the philanthropic assault against the "system" or, the colonial way of life, Philip had mused: "It is painful to reflect that the history of South Africa, a country which has been so long colonized from Europe, and by men professing that faith which teaches us that 'God hath made of one blood all nations of men, for to dwell on all the face of the earth,' should furnish no points of relief to the dark shades of a picture which exhibits the inhabitants of the eastern and western shores of this continent, as the wretched victims of European avarice and cruelty"[20] – a point of view later strongly endorsed by the Aborogines Protection Society and the broad mass of British travellers to the Cape Colony during the late 1820's and 1830's such as Rose, Bannister, Wright, Kay, Pringle and Moodie. The movement for which Philip, and philanthropists in general, were to win considerable support in the United Kingdom during the 1830's, and which was to continue until the mid-1840's, recreated the belief

19. Philip, *Researches,* p. xiii.
20. *Ibid.,* p. xxxii.

in Britain that the coming of the Whiteman in 1652 had been to the detriment of the native population — once again the "rightful owners".

> "In the beginning of the last century", wrote the powerful Aborigines Protection Society, "the European colony in Africa was confined to within a few miles of Cape Town. From that period it has advanced, till it now includes more square miles than are to be found in England, Scotland, and Ireland; and with regard to the natives of [a] great part of this immense region, it is stated, 'any traveller who may have visited the interior of this colony little more than twenty years ago, may now stand on the heights of Albany, or in the midst of a district of 42,000 square miles on the north side of Graaff Reinet, and ask the question, Where are the aboriginal inhabitants of this district which I saw here on my former visit to this country? without any one being able to inform him where he is to look for them to find them'."[21]

Certainly a most pertinent question, and Philip's main attack was directed at the British Government, both home and colonial, for continuing a system created by the earlier Dutch authorities. As can be expected, at the heart of the matter lay the question of the territorial expansion of the Colony upon which had been based the foundations of a system wherein the "very existence" of the natives had come to be regarded as "subservient to the interest of the boors".[22] In the beginning, he explained, contact between the Europeans and Hottentots had been conducted in a most amicable spirit until the point when the colonists had increased in number and had come to feel more secure in their new numerical strength. From here developed the pattern of encroachment upon the lands of the natives. He noted with interest the manner in which this expansion had taken place. While in some instances it is "pretended" that land was purchased from the Hottentots,[23] asserted Philip, the colonists simply advanced completely disregarding the earlier claims to the land by

---

21. *Report of the Parliamentary Select Committee on Aboriginal Tribes (British Settlements)*, Reprinted, with comments by the Aboriginal Protection Society, p. 29.
22. Philip, *Researches*, i, p. 18.
23. The missionaries strongly contended that the natives did not really sell the lands which they occupied, since it was argued that it could be questioned whether the natives understood the meaning of the term purchase, equating it more with the granting to the colonists the joint use of their springs and lands.

the Hottentots. Under these circumstances "the Hottentots gradually and insensibly ebbed with their flocks and herds from the vicinity of Table Bay and the Cape Peninsula . . .",[24] and as a result, the relationship between the two parties came to be marked with disputes. The Hottentots, with what little property they still had, were either forced into the service of the Boers – "itself worse than slavery" – or they were forced to occupy the most barren and uninviting parts of the country. At length the natives, "who had for a long time suffered with exemplary patience the injuries inflicted upon them, finding no retreat could protect them from the cruelties of their oppressors, sought resources of annoyance from the desperate condition to which they were reduced; and the colonists smarting under the reaction of the accumulated evils they had heaped upon them during the space of 70 years, and which could no longer be endured, formed the project of making the colonial government a party to assisting to enslave or exterminate all that remained of the original inhabitants".[25]

Briefly, then, Philip's contention was that the lot of the natives had not changed to any marked extent since 1795 and he based this upon two points. First, the commando system, with its accompanying element of territorial expansion and the "most atrocious cruelty towards the poor Bushmen", had not stopped for in the past 32 years, he maintained, some 30 commandos had taken the field; and commenting generally on the state of the Bushmen[26] – and the Hottentots may be included – Philip summed up the lot of the natives in South Africa as follows:

> "Whatever may be said, on a comparative view of English and Dutch humanity, it is evident that the mass of evil brought upon the wretched Bushmen is greater under the English government than under the Dutch. Forcibly dispossessed of their country, or, at least, the only valuable parts of it, and of the game on which they subsisted, were the conduct of the colonists towards them ever so mild, little would remain for them but starvation; but as the colonists are solely intent upon their slavery or their destruction, the distribution of the former through their country must

24. Philip, *Researches,* i, p. 17.
25. *Ibid.,* p. 41.
26. Often during the earlier part of the nineteenth century travellers and missionaries did not distinguish, or did not do so accurately, between the Bushmen and Hottentots. Thompson (*infra,* p. 109), for instance, referred to the Bushmen as being cattle owners when, in all probability, he was referring to the Hottentots.

give them, almost without the aid of commandoes, tenfold greater facilities. Besides the commando system, which has been revived, the Bushmen that escaped were treated as outlaws, and either driven from their native soil, or seized by the farmers. The whole of their country to the north-east, (the only fertile part,) from the former borders to the great Orange river, has been measured out by the colonial government to the new proprietors; and every Bushman who has survived the means taken to clear the country, and who is not in the service of the farmers, exists by sufferance only in a fugitive state . . ."[27]

The second point was that the Bushmen (and again, also for that matter the Hottentots), were still without land of their own to occupy and therefore in this respect the British had not brought relief. Quoting from the reliable work of George Thompson, Philip wrote:

"The Bushmen on this frontier", he [Thompson] observes, "whatever may have been their original condition, are now entirely destitute of cattle, or property of any description; and, now that the larger game has been almost entirely destroyed, or driven out of their country, by the guns of the boors and bastaards, they are reduced to the most wretched shifts to obtain a precarious subsistence, living chiefly on wild roots, locusts, and the larvae of insects."[28]

What was so alarming in Philip's judgment was that as extended as the present frontier of the Colony was, "it will not stop here":

"Within the last thirty years", he stated, "the frontier of the colony has been extending in every direction; and, as a proof that the colonists will not be satisfied to confine themselves within the bounds which have been fixed for them, the people of New Hantam had scarcely seated themselves in the Bushman country on the banks of the great Orange river, when they began to cross it to seek out new grazing grounds for their cattle, and to kill game (the only provision on which the natives had to depend) beyond it; and there on the other side of that river, and immediately beyond the eastern and northern limits of the colony, numerous and interesting nations must shortly share the melancholy fate of the hordes who occupied what was formerly known to us as the Bushman country, unless British humanity, and British justice, throw their protecting shield over them."[29]

27. Philip, *Researches,* ii, pp. 46–47.
28. *Ibid.,* p. 42.
29. *Ibid.,* p. 272.

The oppressed state of the Hottentots could be related to the supply and demand of labour, and Philip explained the reason for this. Before the abolition of the slave trade in 1807 when there had been a ready and cheap supply of labour, the missionaries had been permitted to continue their work unmolested even though they were generally held in contempt and ridiculed by the Boers as "Hottentot predikants". However, with the abolition of the slave trade and the ensuing scarcity of labour, even this unhappy state of affairs deteriorated. The Boers, who were "ready to seize upon every pretext for showing their enmity to the missionaries"[30] cast a "rapacious eye" at the Hottentots within the institutions and, with the assistance of the local authorities, "the final destruction of these institutions became the favourite object with an influential part of the community".[31] Prominent in this class of official, maintained Philip, had been Collins and the judges of the circuit courts since they had recommended that consideration be given to the closing of Bethelsdorp, or at least the curtailing of its activities to some extent. Many of their mission stations were indeed forced to close down, he stated, and those at Bethelsdorp and Theopolis very nearly suffered the same fate had not special measures been adopted to save them. Philip therefore charged that all white society at the Cape remained intent upon preserving the system which placed the Hottentots "subservient to the interests of the boors". Under these circumstances, then, the old system which had been pursued by the Dutch had been carried forward under the British "accompanied with all the authority and sanction of colonial law", as had been illustrated by their denying the Hottentots their human rights, while at the same time "the privileges of the missions within the colony were gradually curtailed, and the missions beyond its limits were not left undisturbed".[32]

---

30. Philip, *Researches,* i. p. 70.
31. *Ibid.,* pp. xviii–xix.
32. *Ibid.,* pp. xviii–xx.
As mentioned in an earlier chapter, the missionary institutions of the London Missionary Society had always been looked at askance by the official class in Cape Town. While Cradock had been obliged to institute the circuit courts to ascertain the charges of Read, Somerset clamped down on more than one London Missionary Society station beyond the colonial border. Whatever Somerset's feelings towards Philip might have been, the reason for this was simple enough: he feared that the extra-colonial missions might develop into strongholds for banditti who might have decided to raid the Colony.

Before entering into the collision between the Cape Government and John Philip it is worthwhile ascertaining what the Colonial Government officials themselves thought of the Afrikaners at this time as their opinions form the necessary background to understanding the Government's attitude towards Philip.

In 1822 Stockenström had remarked that experience had taught that "prudence, forbearance and kindness" were the best means to secure a peaceful frontier situation, a state which had also rendered the natives "very useful to us".[33] Whatever the past might have held – and he did not doubt that the practice of the commandos of taking women and children as prisoners had excited the Xhosas to revenge – "the present generation of colonists (with some exceptions indeed) show by their conduct of the Bushmen their conviction of this faith, and of the inhumanity of destroying them on every slight provocation".[34] In other words, irrespective of what the situation might have been on the frontier before 1795, the British Cape Government found the Afrikaners to be an acceptable group of people in 1822. The situation on the frontier was therefore most satisfactory. "The utmost cordiality" prevailed between the burghers and the military[35] and the colonists had "constituted an admirable description" of a fighting force – too much so, perhaps, as this gave rise to the Boer belief that they constituted the defence force of the Colony, a situation, some thought, which was unhealthy as a "trifling want of temper or conduct" could spark off an insurrection.[36] However, this fear did not materialise and in 1825 Somerset was able to report that even some of the burghers who had participated in the Slagter's Nek incident in 1815 had "subsequently evinced their loyalty and attachment to H.M. Government",[37] and in 1831 Cole described the Boers as "naturally a peaceable people".[38] Possibly the greatest commendation of all to the Afrikaner frontier colonists (or, perhaps it was no more than a denunciation of English frontier society), came from the philanthropically minded Bourke in 1827:

---

33. C.O. 48/84, Stockenström to Bird, 5 June 1822, f. 218: encl. to C.O. 48/84, Bourke to Hay, 29 Nov. 1826.
34. *Ibid.*
35. C.O. 48/39, Somerset to Bathurst, 22 May 1819, f. 12.
36. C.O. 48/40, Ellis to Goulburn, 19 Oct. 1819, f. 316.
37. C.O. 48/68, Somerset to Bathurst, 2 April 1825, f. 284.
38. C.O. 48/142, Cole to Goderich, 1 April 1831, f. 9.

"As far as I have discovered, there is but little difference of conduct between the old and the new colonists in matters where their interest is concerned, and I confess I think those of the Dutch may be as safely trusted on the frontier as those of the English race."[39]

In addition to this, it is a reflection of British opinion of the Afrikaners that the Secretary of State entertained no ideas of discrimination between the English and Afrikaners when it came to filling newly created government positions at the Cape as he declared that the "most respectable and most intelligent" of the colonists – "whether they be of Dutch origin or British born subjects" – would be successful,[40] yet at the same time the "very natural prejudices of many of the ancient Dutch Inhabitants" were to be borne in mind.[41] Although Bathurst had been informed of the "most profound ignorance" which existed among the "young Dutch and others educated here [at the Cape]" respecting all subjects of science,[42] and of the generally poor response to the educational facilities offered to the country Afrikaners,[43] as well as a certain slowness of the Boers in accepting new British innovations,[44] a change in the habits of the Afrikaners in the country districts was nonetheless discernible and in 1831 Francis had the following to say to Ellis about the Afrikaners:

"... I am happy to find that many of the Dutch inhabitants [at Uitenhage], approve of the plan of introducing [white British] labour, that is they begin to feel the want of it, as they now find a market for whatever they can produce, which induces them to use more and more exertion every day. Independent of which the young Cape Dutch, by associating with English, and the advantage of the National Schools, by which means they receive a certain degree of education, instilling principles and ideas into their minds, which their fathers have had little conception of. – I think we may justly look forward to more industry, more enterprise, a greater degree of intelligence, by which means there will be produced a better order of society (and speaking generally) a society better qualified to govern the affairs of the

---

39. C.O. 48/109, Bourke to Hay, 13 April 1827, f. 8.
40. G.H. 1/13, Goderich to Bourke, 14 June 1827.
41. *Ibid.*, 5 Aug. 1827.
42. C.O. 48/86, Atherton to Bathurst, 14 April 1826, f. 4.
43. C.O. 48/124, Bourke to Hushesson, 19 May 1828, f. 270.
44. C.O. 48/127, Welsford to Burton, 14 May 1828, f. 113.

Colony, when ever it shall legislate for itself, than can be found at present."[45]

The foregoing being representative of the trend in official Cape opinion for many years, it is clear that Philip would be expected to provide substantial proof to back his claims and accusations when they contradicted the findings and experience of the Cape authorities. Two arguments dominate the conflict between Philip and the Cape Government. The first, centring around the claims he made for additional land for the stations at Theopolis and Bethelsdorp and revealing Philip in the worst possible personal light in the eyes of the Government (for his veracity when put to the test was undoubtedly found wanting), need not be detailed here as it is of little relevance to the topic. The second, however, concerned allegations of atrocities perpetrated by the frontier farmers against the Griquas and certain other tribes outside the Colony[46] and more directly concerns this study as it involved the Afrikaners in particular.

Of the mission institution at Philipolis, Philip reported the following:

> "The [Afrikaner] farmers have for some years past been in the habit of crossing the Colonial Boundary and oppressing the Griquas in their own country. The Griquas have hitherto borne all this with admirable patience, waiting for the Colonial Government to put a stop to the causes of their grievances. If no stop be put to the rapacious conduct of the farmers, the Missionary [in charge of the station] states that he cannot be answerable for the consequences."[47]

Averting to the state of affairs at the L.M.S. Bushman Station, he added:

> "The Missionaries [at the station] suggest the vast importance of the farmers being prevented from migrating into the Bushman Country, where their Cattle depasture the lands required by the Bushmen, and where they either destroy the game, or drive it to such a distance that the Bushmen can no longer procure it.
>
> If the remnant of the Bushmen is not to be totally exterminated, as others of their countrymen have been in other parts

45. C.O. 48/145, Francis to Ellis, 22 Oct. 1831, f. 344.
46. C.O. 48/144, Philip to Bell, 17 Dec. 1830, ff. 69–80.
47. *Ibid.*, ff. 75–76.

of South Africa, it is of indispensable importance that the Colonial farmers be prevented from depasturing the lands of the people by driving their cattle beyond the boundaries of the Colony. That the evil complained of is one of great magnitude, is evident from the fact that such large numbers of farmers with their Cattle cross the Colonial Boundaries into the Bushman Country."[48]

Without wishing to enter into the pros and cons of Philip's allegations, it is necessary to briefly consider the reply made by Stockenström who, as Commissioner-General of the Eastern Province, completely disagreed with Philip's accusations that "the farmers have for some years past been in the habit of crossing the Colonial Boundary and oppressing the Griquas in their own country". According to Stockenström, such allegations were "destitute of foundation" on the grounds of there being "no such thing as a Griqua country anywhere near Philipolis unless Dr. Philip be disposed to justify the seizure by that Tribe of the Bushman Territory, about which he is so justly clamorous and indignant when committed by the Colonists . . . Exactly in the same way as the Boors gradually encroached on the Aborigines *within* the present Boundaries of the Colony (but with a great deal more cruelty because they were more irresponsible [under the Dutch Government]), the Griquas did *beyond* said limits . . . Let Mr. Moffat, who is employed by the L.M.S. at Latakoo, and has there done so much for the unfortunate Natives; let him say (he is now in Town) whether he does not know that within the last 15 months two opulent tribes of Bootchooanas . . . were without the slightest provocation attacked by these same Griquas, hundreds of them most inhumanely butchered and their cattle carried so clear off that starvation drove the Survivors to actual cannibalism. – Let the Missionaries and the Travellers (not Boors) say how many Tribes have been thus treated."[49]

What is especially interesting in Stockenström's reply is his preamble, when, speaking of the general feeling in England towards the

48. C.O. 48/144, Philip to Bell, 17 Dec. 1830, ff. 77–78.
49. C.O. 48/144, "Remarks of the Commissioner-General of the Eastern Province, Cape of Good Hope, on the return of Missions in South Africa belonging to the London Missionary Society, with accompanying documents forwarded to the Secretary to Government by the Rvd. Dr. Philip under cover of his letter of the 7th December, 1830", 31 Dec. 1830, ff. 100–101, 103–104.

Colony respecting the actual condition of the natives, he provides an excellent indication of both the mood of the British public and the tremendous influence philanthropists had over them. Not altogether unlike the situation which exists today, Stockenström wrote:

> "I am well aware that in making the following observations, I am placing myself in a very delicate position, in as much as experience has too well taught, that independent of the ignorant, prejudiced and deluded part of the community in England (whose opinion we might contemn,) even extensive circles among the truly worthy and respectable, whose approbation and support are in every respect desirable, will at once set down, as a narrow minded and oppressive enemy of the Aborigines and other coloured classes – and as hostile to every attempt at their amelioration, any man who shall presume in the least to differ with those from whom they have accustomed themselves to borrow their own notions as to the means by which that desideratum is to be attained, and to whose views they have made their own reasoning powers entirely subservient – yet with the perfect consciousness of the risk I incur, I consider the matter too momentous . . . to allow them to reach their high destination [the office of the Secretary of State] without submitting to His Excellency the Governor those elucidations in which I consider said documents defective – pointing out such parts as I think erroneous; and stating (with due deference) those opinions in which I find myself at variance with Dr. Philip."[50]

Such remarks were not entirely out of keeping when compared with those passed by Cole who said "Dr. Philip derives much of his importance from the enthusiasm of that party in England, whom he has taught to consider him, as the first, if not the only person, either here or at home, who has both the will and the courage to yield protection to the Hottentot population".[51]

Philanthropist power and sentiment had come of age and was to dominate British thinking until the early 1840's.

The *Commercial Advertiser* (whose editor, Fairbairn, was John Philip's son-in-law) had, from its earliest publications, closely associated itself with the missionary movement[52] by reason of the fact

---

50. C.O. 48/144, "Remarks of the Commissioner-General . . .", ff. 92–93.
51. *Ibid.*, Cole to Goderich, 10 May 1831, f. 17.
52. Such as, *Commercial Advertiser*, "Y", 10 March 1824; H. E. Rutherford, 17 March 1824; 24 March 1824.

that the elevation of the Hottentots, considered to be an integral part of the "new system" and so strongly advocated by this newspaper, would, it judged, be accelerated at the institutions.[53] Its attitude towards the natives losing possession of their lands is typical of the philanthropic school:

> "The Colonist has encroached upon the territory, or haunts, if you will, of the Bushman, without explaining to him, in a clear and satisfactory manner, his Right to do so. For more than a hundred years the Bushmen have been treated as an enemy to whom no quarter could be given. His cattle, for once he had cattle, were seized by way of reprisal for the losses, real or pretended, of his pursuers, and his children if caught, were distributed as slaves among his conquerors. Now, whether such proceedings were justified by the exigencies of the Service at the time, it is not the question at present; we only ask whether they were likely to generate any great degree of benevolence towards his new neighbours in the heart of the Bushmen? Being a mere savage, he thought that his being robbed by the Colonists was a natural reason for his robbing them in turn, when he could find a fit opportunity – and this turn of mind was enforced by the pangs of hunger, and it must be, by a love of vengeance, which even among ourselves will not be a stranger to the heart of a man who has been so abominably treated by those who ought to have known better. It is not intended to rake up the ashes of the Commandos of the last century, but it was necessary to refer to them to show that rapine and violence beget each other, and that the disturbed state of the frontier has had its origin in a false system of defence. If the Bushmen, like every other human being, has a love for property, he must be excused for resenting its loss. If he, like a beast, seeks only to satisfy the appetite of the moment, did you expect that he would lie down and die patiently when forcibly deprived of food?"[54]

In the same way as the "old system" pursued by the Dutch East India Company had adversely affected the development and character of the Afrikaner colonists and had required to be done away with, so the existing system respecting the relationship between the farmer

53. In the absence of land of their own, the missionary institutions were established to provide homes for the Hottentots where they were also educated in the ways of the Whiteman and taught the rudiments of Christianity. At most, the institutions provided a place to stay for some thousands of Hottentots, but never more than one-third of their total population.

54. *Commercial Advertiser,* 16 Aug. 1829.

and coloured servant – which had "long disgraced the Colony" and which the *Commercial Advertiser* had labelled "the unnatural state of society" – would need radical revision since it had been responsible for the decrepit state the Hottentots had sunk to, a condition which was all too clearly instanced by their ineffectiveness as a labour force.[55] The ultimate goal of the philanthropists (including the *Commercial Advertiser*) under the "new system" within the Colony was the general diffusion of education and knowledge amongst the Blackman so that they might be elevated to rank equally with themselves.[56] With this as its object, the *Commercial Advertiser* (until 1832 the Cape Colony's only newspaper) would naturally support any movement aimed at regularising the relationship between master and servant and generally improving the legal and social status of the Hottentots for, as it was remarked, the Hottentots had been the "original inhabitors and proprietors" of the country and while they had never been enslaved they had never had their personal liberty and property placed under the protection of the law.[57]

Without the restriction of a special vagrancy clause embodied in the Hottentot Ordinance of 1828, the Albany Settlers, who had never been allowed predial slaves, claimed that Hottentot labour, at best poor quality, would as a result of the ordinance become scarcer and even less efficient than before. During January 1829 "An Albany Farmer" wrote to the *Commercial Advertiser* to "point out an error" which he believed the newspaper and "all the inhabitants of towns who are unconnected with rural affairs" had made respecting the effects which the ordinance had had upon him as a farmer.[58] His letter "respecting the present condition of the Hottentots and the inadequacy of existing laws for maintenance of orderly conduct amongst them",[59] underlines the practical basis of the contention which arose between the east and west of the Colony on the issue of the treatment of the Hottentots. That the Hottentots had "gradually lost their possessions and independence" and had fallen under "the disabilities inconsistent with the most inherent rights of free people",[60] as the *Commercial Advertiser* had maintained, and that their con-

55. *Commercial Advertiser,* 19 Sept. 1829.
56. See for instance, *Commercial Advertiser,* 19 Sept. 1829.
57. *Commercial Advertiser,* 24 Dec. 1828. See also 27 Dec. 1828.
58. *Ibid.,* "An Albany Farmer", 21 Jan. 1829.
59. *Ibid.*
60. *Ibid.,* 27 Dec. 1828.

dition could be rectified by treating them as the free men they were when it would be seen that "this class of people is capable of fulfilling all the duties required [of them]"[61], (also claimed by Fairbairn), was of little consolation to the Albany farmer who had the following to say:

> "The circumstances to which I so confidently refer in support of my position are as follows: loss of stock, through the negligence of herdsmen — loss of time in performance of Agricultural operations, through the absence of servants without leave — and a greater indulgence than hereto-fore in their well known disposition to rest frequently from their labours — in other words to indulge in idleness."[62]

Maintaining that "it would be vain therefore for you or any other apologist of the Hottentots to maintain the sufficiency of the present laws for all just purposes", the farmer concluded by making his point:

> "You have really Mr. Editor, been contending with a phantom of your own creation: nobody wishes to impose compulsory service on the Hottentots or other free persons of colour; nothing is more desired than that some law be enacted to compel those persons to live honestly — that is, to satisfy the magistrate that they are engaged in some calling adequate to the maintenance of themselves and families, or that they have by former exertions acquired a competency, and are not under the necessity of levying contributions to the public, in their favourite and (in a land of industry) vicious propensities, which renders them either averse to engage in service at all — indifferent about the retention of a place in which they have been induced to engage, or careless about the performance of their duties during the period of their engagement."[63]

Such then was the basis of the issue which divided Englishmen from Englishmen within the Colony. The one group, resident in the eastern districts and who employed and relied upon Hottentot labour, claimed the necessity for a vagrancy law (other than that generally applicable to Europeans) because of the protection it afforded them as employers of labour and against Hottentot vagrants; and the other group, in Cape Town, who neither relied upon the Hottentots for

---

61. *Commercial Advertiser*, 24 Dec. 1828.
62. *Ibid.*, "An Albany Farmer", 21 Jan. 1829.
63. *Ibid.*

labour nor in fact came into contact with them to any extent, maintained that as free men the Hottentots should be treated as the white colonists were within colonial law. Typifying the breach between the eastern and western English colonists were the remarks passed by a correspondent to the *Commercial Advertiser* who, having visited the frontier, wrote the following:

> "I was induced, during my visit, to discover whether there were any solid grounds for the outcry against these people [the Hottentots]. My first question then was, what have been the effects produced by this so-much-talked-of ordinance? – Oh, it has given them leave to walk about without a pass; – there is no power allowed to the Field Cornets and Constables to lodge them in prison, and next morning to contract them, that they may gain a livelihood for themselves; they are now more idle than before, and getting insolent, and go about thieving at night, and lying in the bush by day, or go to those *nests of vice, the Schools!* I expected to have heard further – the want of labour, but that is satisfied in these districts as I shall presently show. My replies were short, and perhaps had no effect: – A pass, what! to walk abroad on the land of their forefathers! Contracts to bind them against their will. Idle, it is their own loss, and will soon work its own cure; what is termed insolent, may be only the consciousness of new possessing equal rights, and an unpolished way of asserting them which John Bull ought to be the last to complain of; – as to marauding, what are your Justices of the Peace about? they have the power to prevent trespassing, and ought to use it: as to the resorting to the schools, I have no means of judging, but perhaps may give you my opinion at a future time . . ."[64]

Complaints of a labour shortage in the eastern districts as a result of the ordinance was met in Cape Town with equal temerity. "The only remedy against [Hottentot] laziness is – the due and certain reward of industry",[65] judged the *Commercial Advertiser* – certainly little comfort to the eastern farmers who held that high wages in themselves were insufficient to solve their problem.[66] So the colonists were split on the question of a vagrancy clause, and on the one side were the Albany farmers (together with the Afrikaner colonists) who

---

64. *Commercial Advertiser,* from a correspondent on the frontier, 14 March 1829.
65. *Ibid.,* 7 Feb. 1829.
66. *Ibid.,* "An Albany Farmer", 11 March 1829.

claimed that losses, inflicted by the Hottentots, were sustained because of the system which missionary influence had caused to be introduced, and on the other, in Cape Town, led by the *Commercial Advertiser,* were those who maintained that the problems which the farmers in the interior said they experienced were imaginary simply because they believed that the problem did not exist. As a direct result of this opposition and the lack of representation of the interior farmers' interests, in December 1831 the *Graham's Town Journal* was established and in the years that followed this newspaper came to play a role as significant as that already played by the *Commercial Advertiser.*

CHAPTER SIX

No Holds Barred
1832–1836

By 1832 English opinion of the Afrikaners, both in Great Britain and the Cape Colony, had passed through a number of phases. In the beginning, when the British first occupied the Cape, only those immediately involved in the administrative affairs of the Colony were in a position to form any opinions and what they had to say of the Dutch colonists was intensely critical and condemnatory. It was during this period of temporary involvement that John Barrow, in his famous *Travels,* set about laying the foundations of future English opinion by describing the Afrikaners as a backward, indolent and cruel race of men – a trend which was reaffirmed and perpetuated by the small, yet influential wave of travellers and missionaries which reached the Cape shores in the early years of the nineteenth century. By 1810/1815, however, this general attitude towards the Dutch colonists, as held by the English within the Cape Colony, had come to be modified following government investigation into the difficulties on the frontier and the allegations brought by missionaries of the constant abuse sustained by the Hottentots at the hands of the Afrikaners. These investigations by British officials and circuit court judges, far from endorsing the accusations and complaints against the colonists, brought a better understanding of the problems involved and showed the Afrikaners in a more favourable and realistic light. In Great Britain, on the other hand, the impressions created by Barrow persisted, and as a result of the above-mentioned allegations made by missionaries, and because of their influence in Britain, a concept of Boer cruelty towards the coloured races took root in the minds of the British middle class.

From approximately 1815 to approximately 1828 the second phase unfolded when, as a result of the opinions expressed by the Colonial Government and the published works of travellers such as Burchell (1822) and Settlers such as Thompson (1827), plus the findings of the Commission of Enquiry in 1825, the Afrikaners gradually came to be viewed more generously in Great Britain and considered in a more balanced light, while in the Colony itself the earlier, more favourable opinions of the Afrikaner, continued to hold good.

In 1828, with the publication of Philip's *Researches* and the promulgation of the Hottentot Ordinance in the same year, the third phase of English opinion was entered upon. The attack launched by philanthropists against the master/servant relationship which existed at the Cape and the relationship between Xhosa and European on the frontier became the subject of much interest. It should, nevertheless, be pointed out that owing to the fact that until 1834 the man-in-the-street in Britain was primarily concerned with the abolition of slavery, the third phase did not get properly under way until after that had been accomplished, although certain parliamentarians had been made aware of the Cape missionary complaints long before. With the persistence of philanthropist agitation, however, and its influence continually gaining momentum, by the early to mid-1830's philanthropy had succeeded in completely dominating the British national attitude and government thinking on frontier affairs in the Cape Colony, with both English and Afrikaner colonists being regarded in the most unfavourable light in respect of their relationship with the Blackman. Meanwhile, at the Cape, the years immediately following the inception of the 50th Ordinance saw the relationship between the various parties within the Colony disintegrate into a state of conflict and confusion. During the period 1832–1836 feelings really ran high and hot controversy was the order of the day. As one contemporary commentator described the state of emotions at that time: "The elements of public feeling in the colony, or, as it may more properly be denominated, public animosity, are composed of three distinct exhibitions of hatred – First, the Dutch hate the English; next the Dutch and English hate the natives; and lastly, the natives hate the Dutch and English."[1] Unfortunately he did not mention what the *English* thought of the Dutch but other sources left no doubt about that.

1. John Fawcett, *An Account of Eighteen Months' Residence at the Cape of Good Hope in 1835–1836* p. 87.

The period after 1828, but particularly after 1834, was further characterised by a far greater interest being shown in the Colony by British parliamentarians,[2] by an upsurge of coverage given to the Cape press by British newspapers, and also by an increase in the number of publications dealing with Southern Africa.[3] And what was more important, the British people in general were directly interesting themselves in the affairs of the Colony – no doubt as a result of the redoubled effort on the part of philanthropists to draw the Cape Colony to their attention. The British reading public was changing – as *The Spectator* stated: "the causes which rendered an old traveller famous exist no longer"[4] (people were no longer primarily interested in flora and fauna), while *The Atlas* pointed specifically to what was wanted in Great Britain in the line of books on South Africa: ". . . a mixed history and commentary, a moral analysis of the people, of the means that have been taken to civilize them [the natives], of the progress of education diffusing itself gradually beyond the limits of European settlements, of the commercial intercourse and the domestic life of the interior, with suggestions, derived from experience, for the better conduct of our relations with the natives".[5] It is also interesting to read the opinion expressed by *The Atlas* in 1835 that, owing to the information already available on the Cape Colony, "it has, as it were, brought us [the British public] face to face with the land, which we know almost as well as if we were accustomed every day to gallop from one [field] cornet's station to another to arrive in time for the 12 o'clock dinner of the Dutch farmer".[6]

---

2. Such as: *Hansard,* 3rd Series, XXIV, 1 July 1834, cols. 1061–62; 3rd Series, XXVI, 19 Feb. 1835, cols. 725–729.
3. The more significant books published on South Africa during the period 1828–1836 are:
   Cowper Rose, *Four Years in Southern Africa;* Saxe Bannister, *Humane Policy;* William Wright, *Slavery at the Cape of Good Hope;* Stephen Kay, *Travels and Researches in Kaffraria;* Thomas Pringle, *African Sketches, and a Narrative of a Residence in South Africa;* J. W. D. Moodie, *Ten Years in South Africa;* Andrew Steadman, *Wanderings and Adventures in the Interior of Southern Africa;* Nathaniel Isaacs, *Travels and Adventures in Eastern Africa, Descriptive of the Zoolus, the Manners, Customs, etc. etc. with a Sketch of Natal;* Allen F. Gardiner, *Narrative of a Journey to the Zoolu Country, in South Africa;* John Fawcett, *An Account of Eighteen Months' Residence at the Cape of Good Hope in 1835–1836.*
4. *The Spectator,* 1 Aug. 1835.
5. *The Atlas,* 2 Aug. 1835, p. 487.
6. *Ibid.,* 26 April 1835, p. 262.

The two major publications on South Africa during the period under discussion were those of Thomas Pringle *(African Sketches)* and Lieut. J. W. D. Moodie *(Ten Years in South Africa),* both of whom were judged "respectable persons . . . both excellently qualified for describing human manners and natural scenery".[7] In fact, so highly thought of were these two works that the *Quarterly Review,* on referring to the publications of Kay and Steadman, remarked: ". . . quotations from their pages after Pringle and Moodie would hardly be endurable",[8] while *The Atlas,* on expressing disappointment in Steadman's work stated: "What we wanted was something like PRINGLE'S book."[9]

From the reviews in the press of books written on South Africa it is easy to guess what the British at home thought of the Afrikaners. Congratulating J. W. D. Moodie on the quality of his work, *Ten Years in South Africa, The Atlas* wrote: "Our author agrees with the majority of preceeding travellers in condemnation of the strange mixture of servility and coarseness that distinguishes the character of the Dutch population of the Cape."[10] On another occasion, when commenting upon Steadman's publication, this same journal briefly remarked on the state of isolation under which the frontier Boers lived and the effect which it had had upon their character, saying: "The state of the Boers on the borders presents a melancholy picture of moral degradation. It is satisfactory, however, to know that a prospect of improvement is dawning upon that desolate district."[11] Probably the best impression of how, and upon what basis the British public viewed both the Colony and the Afrikaners is gained from Pringle's *African Sketches,* as reviewed by *The Spectator.* Coming down squarely upon the main issue in the affairs of the Colony at that time, viz. the treatment and status of the coloured population, *The Spectator* quoted at length from Pringle's description of conditions within a colonial gaol which gave the impression that this was a reflection of the overall condition of the natives and of the treatment they received from the white colonists:

---

7. *Quarterly Review,* Dec. 1835, p. 74.
   It is well to remember that Philip's *Researches* cannot be considered as a major work simply because of the little public support it received in Britain.
8. *Quarterly Review,* Dec. 1835, p. 487.
9. *The Atlas,* 2 Aug. 1835, p. 487.
10. *Ibid.,* 26 April 1835, p. 262.
11. *Ibid.,* 2 Aug. 1835, p. 488.

> "The prisoners being desired to range themselves around the walls, exhibited a strange array of wild and swarthy visages, squalid with neglect and misery, and sickly with confinement. They were runaway slaves, standing with shackled limbs and lowering looks, sullenly awaiting their awarded punishment, and the arrival of their owners to drag them back to the house of bondage. There were Hottentots, clothed in costume half-native, half-European, – the sheep-skin caross of their forefathers, and the leathered trousers of the boor. Some of these were complainants at the drosdy against the fraud or oppression of the colonists to whom (agreeably to colonial *law*) they were bound in servitude; and they were immured (agreeably to colonial *practice*) in this vile tronk, until their masters found it convenient to answer their accusations, and probably to get them well flogged for daring to complain – such, at least, was then the usual result. Others were merely Hottentots out of service, who had been apprehended by the field-cornets, and sent here until some white man should apply to have them *given out* to him on contract."[12]

Even though Pringle had taken the precaution to state that some of the inmates of the prison mentioned were accused of the more "heinous crimes", his account nonetheless made its point and no doubt properly impressed the philanthropic public.

Following upon the attack launched by Philip on the Cape "system" (of Black/White relations), the *Quarterly Review,* and particularly *The Spectator,* drew attention to the two most important points dealt with in Pringle's narrative, both of which implicated the Afrikaners. First was the action of Somerset, and second was what was termed the Afrikaners' "constant collision of interests" with the natives.[13] Having found himself completely at loggerheads with the English settlers and hearing that their complaints had led to the appointment of a commission of enquiry into the administration of the Colony, Somerset "formed an underhand league with the frontier boors, the semi-savage *Dutch Africans;* winking at murder, permitting predatory excursions to harass the natives and plunder their property, finally, expelling a tribe from their possessions, and bestowing the lands (the Tory mode of rewarding people) upon his friends".[14] Elaborating further upon this so-called "system" at the

---

12. *The Spectator,* 17 May 1834, p. 468.
13. *Quarterly Review,* Feb. 1837, p. 2.
14. *The Spectator,* 17 May 1834, p. 469.

Cape under Somerset, *The Spectator* concluded its review with the following:

> "The narrative relating to the treatment of the Caffer tribes is one of painful interest, and cannot be read without feelings of disgust and indignation. By the stroke of a Governor's pen, they are deprived of large tracts of land, with their growing crops, and driven forth to destitution or starvation. For any real or fancied injury (such as the loss of cattle), it is in the power of the pettiest magistrate to send forth a *commando,* surprise and plunder the villages, burn the hovels, massacre the men and carry the women and children into captivity, frequently shooting them on the road out of wantonness, or impatience at their foot-sore pace. Their chieftans are grossly insulted, their envoys have been murdered, and the lives of the Caffer travellers are by no means safe; yet even all these things are *now* submitted to, for the tribes are too well aware of the British power to attempt reprisals; and unless some change of system should be enforced by the Government at home, the nation will gradually perish by murders, by massacres, and by want. The treatment of the aborigines by the colonists is one of the darkest and bloodiest stains upon the page of history; and scarcely any are equal in atrocity to the conduct of the Dutch boors, – ably seconded of late, according to Mr. PRINGLE, by some of the more degraded of the English settlers. If the volume contained nothing more than the account of this worse than slave-trade and the suggestions for its remedy it would be worthy of national perusal."[15]

15. *The Spectator,* 17 May 1834, p. 469.
Pringle entered into considerable detail about what he termed the "legalised butcheries" of the Bushmen. Quoting sources from Barrow to Philip, he also provided a personal example: "I well recollected the Field Commandant Van Wyk, generally considered one of the most respectable men in the Cradock district, halting at my cabin in 1821, as he returned with his commando of boors from an expedition against some hordes of Bushmen on the Bamboosberg, who had committed depredations at the Tarka. He and his men, as I was then told, had slain upwards of 80 souls, and had taken captive a considerable number of women and children – some of whom I afterwards saw at the residence of our neighbour Winzel Coetzer, in the service of one of his sons who had been on the expedition. It was an expedition ordered by the Government to repress the aggressions of the Bushmen; and this was the regular mode in which these affairs were managed. The kraal was surprised, the males consigned to indiscriminate slaughter, and such of the women and children as survived the massacre were carried off into captivity. Scores of such expeditions have taken place since, and the system continues to this very hour but little, I fear, if at all abated in its enormities. Nay, more atrocities still less excuseable, because altogether wanton and unprovoked, are even now perpetrated with impunity . . ." (pp. 371–372).

While Pringle's account of the Afrikaners' *mode* of life had contrasted sharply with the earlier descriptions provided by Barrow in that he spoke of the interior Boers as a most respectable race of men,[16] it was their "regard for the coloured races" which occupied his pen most notably. In an attempt to explain the Boer attitude towards the Blackman, he cited the Slagter's Nek incident. What had happened was that Bezuidenhout, the burgher concerned, had regarded the order of the magistrate to appear before him as "an interference between him (a free burgher), and *his Hottentot,* a presumptuous innovation upon his *rights,* and an intolerable usurpation of tyrannical authority".[17] During the earlier years of the Colony, continued Pringle, such thinking had been typical of the interior farmers when, as depicted by Barrow, "the Boors used to murder and mutilate the Hottentots at their discretion", but this had occurred when the Afrikaners had only *heard* of colonial legislation and when "rights of the natives" were held in contempt and when any challenge to their relationship with the native population (such as the Slagter's Nek incident had shown) would inevitably cause the Boers to react as "*insulted free burghers*".[18] Unfortunately, little had changed.

On all points, Pringle was in full agreement with Philip. The treatment of the natives remained deplorable and, within the system, oppression of the Hottentot population, stemming from labour requirements of the colonists and the mode of territorial expansion by the use of commandos, was still evident. However, there was hope in the future:

> "I am well disposed to concur in the opinion that the influence of religious instruction, combined with the high moral tone uniformly maintained by the *liberal* part of the press [the *Commercial Advertiser*] in regard to the coloured races, has done much, within the last few years, to humanise the sentiments of the more respectable portion of the Dutch-African colonists, yet we must not delude ourselves with the fallacious notion that the progress of light and knowledge *alone* will effect either a speedy or complete change in the state of things. Civilization and infor-

The commandos remained the main source of defence of the frontiers of the Colony until the 1850's. As in the old days, the problem remained of convincing the Government to undertake the costly garrisoning of the frontier, an area in which it had no direct interest.

16. Pringle, *African Sketches,* pp. 169–170.
17. *Ibid.,* p. 190.
18. *Ibid.,* p. 192.

mation must of necessity make but slow and feeble advances among a class of people so situated as the white backsettlers of the wild and thinly peopled regions on the Bushman frontier. Nor is it the knowledge simply of what is just and right that will induce men to act justly, or wisely, or humanely . . . I do not consider the Dutch-African colonists as worse than other people would be and have been in similar circumstances – not certainly worse than the British in Australia . . . Without strong *legal restraints,* such, alas! is human nature on the large scale, that merely humanity will always be too feeble for passion and selfishness."[19]

In 1835 Moodie, believed by the *Quarterly Review* to have been "excellently qualified for describing human manners and natural scenery",[20] published what must certainly be one of the most scathing attacks on the Afrikaners. Disregarding completely the shortcomings of Barrow, Moodie accepted his testimony respecting the Cape Dutch as one hundred percent accurate; in fact, he stated, "Barrow has described the Dutch manners so admirably, that I need not repeat them . . ."[21] His work is so crammed with condemnation that it is difficult to decide where to begin and what to omit:

> "Of all the people I have ever seen", he wrote, "the Cape-Dutch are the coarsest and least polished in their manners. The conversation of both sexes is marked by an almost total absence of common decency: the most disgusting oaths are used on all occasions by the men; and the women do not even feel ashamed to talk on the most indelicate subjects, hardly condescending to use any circumlocution. In this respect, indeed, they are even less refined than the Hottentots. Wherever they have had much intercourse with the English, however, a gradual improvement is observable. The females, though often handsome when very young, are from this coarseness of manners exceedingly distasteful to the English, and few even of the lower classes of our countrymen can bring themselves to marry into a Dutch family. The moment a Dutchwoman enters into the conjugal state, she takes her seat by a little table in the hall, from which she never stirs if she can help it; and they often laugh at the folly of the Englishwomen, in going about the house to attend to their domestic concerns, when they might have everything done by calling to their servants, without quitting their places. When the Dutch ladies marry, they become exceedingly torpid and phleg-

19. Pringle, *African Sketches,* pp. 370–371.
20. *Vide supra,* p. 124.
21. Moodie, *Ten Years in South Africa,* i, p. 66.

> matic in their manners and habits, dirty and slovenly in their dress; and, from their cold constitution and freedom of care, like the men, they generally at an early age grow to an unwieldy size."[22]

Moodie divided the inhabitants of Cape Town into six classes: first, the civil and military personnel and the clergy of the established churches; second, the professional classes, the merchants and those who lived by the letting out of their slaves; then there were the European and Cape Dutch artificers and labourers who composed a "very doubtful class" between the Whites and Blacks of the town, while the remaining three classes were made up of Malays, Hottentots and slaves. Despite their removal in distance from Holland, the Cape Dutch had retained something of both the good and the bad qualities of their European progenitors. "They have the same avaricious propensities and attention to small gains; the same persevering industry when they are sure of profit, but less energy in the pursuit of it; the same orderly, phlegmatic, and patient character".[23] As a group they were strongly attached to their own customs and unwilling to adopt the English language further than they required. Although they had some good points, such as their universal kindness and hospitality towards strangers, it was seldom that their philanthropy extended beyond their own race – a condition of mind which had found its origin in two things. First, their possession of slaves, which had made them "cruel and tyrannical to their dependents" and had caused them, as a group, to become callous to the suffering of others. (Moodie related how he had seen a man walking through the streets of Cape Town who, several years before, had "deliberately roasted a slave to death in an oven for presuming to smile at his master" and how, after some "trifling punishment for the deed, he was afterwards received into society "as if nothing of the kind had occurred".[24]) Second, in addition to their purely inward looking philosophy, was what Moodie described as the "rather extravagant notions which the Dutch colonists entertain of the privileges of Christians"[25] – in other words, the Afrikaner belief that the Blackman had been designated to an inferior position in the world.

---

22. Moodie, *Ten Years in South Africa,* i, pp. 169–170.
23. *Ibid.,* p. 33.
24. *Ibid.,* p. 34.
25. *Ibid.,* p. 158.

Family life also came under fire: "Love is almost an entire stranger to their breasts", he maintained, while marriage was considered as no more than "a matter of convenience, or a merely mercantile transaction".[26] Of course, this claim that the Cape Dutch were immoral, without love even for their own children was nothing new. It had been Barrow who had started the ball rolling in that direction by stating: "There is a great want of affection among near relatives . . . the members of the same family seldom meet together . . . there are scarcely two brothers in the Cape who will speak to each other", and speaking of the manner in which children were brought up, he considered that it did not "excite that harmony of sentiment and union of interests" which was to be found in English families.[27] The anonymous writer who had favoured the Colonial Office with his "Observations on the Cape of Good Hope" round about 1818 revealed more: "It is true that in general they not only marry, but both sexes marry *young,* and one should suppose this at least would be a check upon their future conduct, even if it did not originate in a virtuous principle, but the fact unfortunately is that the laxity of morals *before marriage* is not unfrequently *the cause of such unions.* The result therefore is not difficult to guess – *disgust* follows marriage and dissatisfaction follows disgust."[28] Taking the matter one step further, the author of the anonymous work *Notes on the Cape of Good Hope, made during an excursion in that Colony in the year 1820,*[29] made this accusation: "Conjugal fidelity is rarely to be met with here. The men have their slave girls, without any disagreeable feelings on the part of their wives; and these again have their cicisbeos with the good-will and permission of their husbands."[30] Reviewing this book in 1821, at a time when the British press was more kindly disposed towards the Afrikaners, the *Quarterly Review* had these comments to make:

> "It is no excuse to say that he only states what he heard; the gossip of a tap-room is not the most creditable authority, and, at any rate, should not be lightly trusted to the public ear . . . This is mere slander. If the Dutch ladies at the Cape excel in any one virtue it is that of 'conjugal fidelity'; and their habits are purely

26. Moodie, *Ten Years in South Africa,* i, p. 159.
27. Barrow, *Travels,* ii, pp. 103–104.
28. C.O. 48/38, anonymous, undated treatise, "Observations on the Cape of Good Hope", f. 313.
29. *Vide supra,* pp. 81–82.
30. Anon., *Notes on the Cape of Good Hope,* p. 27.

domestic. For the truth of this we appeal to the English families who have long been resident there. There were two, or three, we believe, who, shortly after the capture of the colony, made themselves ridiculous by the encouragement which they gave to certain naval and military officers of high rank, and their husbands equally so for suffering it; but we would ask, whether, if there should be found two or three vicious wives and mean-spirited husbands in an English town, the writer would consider himself warranted in asserting that conjugal fidelity was rarely to be met with in England! . . . Such stories, in fact, are told of all countries; and one or more of them may be found in every jest-book from Scoggins to Joe Miller."[31]

The change in attitude towards the Afrikaners between 1821 and 1835 is clearly illustrated by the fact that in a time when the Afrikaners were more realistically appraised, the *Quarterly Review* could not allow such exaggerated reporting to go unchecked, but under the influence of the prevailing philanthropic prejudices of the 1830's it accepted Moodie's findings and opinions without question.

More of what was represented as the personality of the Afrikaners was expressed by *The Atlas* in its review of Moodie's work:

" 'Slimmigheid', or cunning, is accounted among them the highest accomplishment, and the most undoubted proof of talent; and when they can obtain any petty advantage over a neighbour in a bargain, they do not scruple to boast of it in the most open manner, and rise in their own and their neighbour's estimation in proportion to their adroitness. No people can trick or lie with more apparent sincerity; their phlegmatic insensibility to shame and external simplicity of demeanour alike contribute to their success. Whenever they sell the most trifling article at the most exorbitant price, they try to persuade you that nothing but their personal friendship could induce them to part with it on such moderate terms. With all this cunning, there is a great want of talent and variety in the tricks they play upon strangers; so that if a person can bring himself to the ungenerous conclusion that they are still all rogues he need not be often deceived by them."[32]

Summing up his remarks on the Afrikaners, Moodie ("excellently qualified" to do so, it will be remembered) concluded:

---

31. *Quarterly Review,* July 1821, pp. 456–457.
32. *The Atlas,* 26 April 1835, p. 262.

"The Dutch at the Cape of Good Hope afford an instance of a people partially relapsed into barbarism from want of education, and from their intercourse wih a race of savages who they have subjected and demoralized; retaining most of the vices of Europeans, with the cruelty of the slave-holder and savage . . ."[33]

Before offering some commentary upon such slander — for slander it was — it is necessary to point out again that the significance of Pringle and Moodie lies in the fact that they were considered trustworthy and accurate recorders of the people and affairs of the Cape Colony. Pringle had impressed upon the British public that the old system which had disgraced the earlier Dutch administration with its commandos and suppression of the Hottentots and Bushmen had not, by 1834, relented, while Moodie had portrayed the Afrikaners as an immoral, cruel people who, in his own words, had "partially relapsed into barbarism". *This,* then, is what people in Britain were told of the Afrikaners on the eve of the Great Trek in 1836.

The descriptions of the Afrikaners outlined above cannot, under any circumstances, be considered as a correct or fair portrayal of their character, yet this is what people thought and for this reason it is necessary to show how this way of thinking came to be. At the bottom of the whole issue lies the fact that the period 1832 onwards (but particularly during and immediately after the highly emotional abolition of slavery in 1834) represented the golden age of philanthropy. It is not meant to be implied that philanthropists were unbalanced, yet with missionary zeal running high the spirit of the age was such that every aspect of colonial life came to be viewed in terms of morality. This meant that differences in national attitudes and customs were taken to have some special *moral* significance or implication and everything was seen in terms of being either right or wrong. Anything different which could not be understood or agreed upon was condemned outright. Under these circumstances the judgment of philanthropists was rendered unreliable, while the broad mass of the British public simply believed what they were told.

The prominent philanthropist, Fowel Buxton, in moving that a select committee inquire into the condition and treatment of the native inhabitants in and adjacent to British colonies,[34] backed his

33. Moodie, *Ten Years in South Africa,* i, p. 175.
34. *Report from the Select Committee on Aborigines (British Settlements),* 1836.

argument, when referring to the Cape Colony in Parliament, by echoing the words Barrow had uttered nearly *forty* years earlier when he said that in South Africa to shoot the natives was considered the most meritorious action a European could perform.[35] In its findings the committee, whose very appointment was further testimony to the pressure of philanthropic agitation, emphatically proclaimed that the treatment of the natives in South Africa was a blot on the good name of Britain, maintaining that "every law of humanity and justice has been forgotten and disregarded".[36]

Reaction to the 1835 Frontier War serves well to illustrate how Parliament regarded the Afrikaners and also indicates how completely the British attitude towards the Cape and its colonists had changed since the 1820's. The causes of the war were simple enough:

> "It was a lamentable fact that the state of this part of the colony [the Ceded Territory] could hardly be worse than it notoriously had been for some years past, owing in a great degree to the aggression of British subjects [the overwhelming majority] of whom had been Afrikaners upon the aboriginal inhabitants, and their endeavours to extend their territory in this quarter for selfish and interested purposes. The pretext for these enlargements of territory from year to year had been, the presumed necessity of increasing the security and safety of the colonists, by placing an intermediate territory between them and the Caffre tribes. The result was aggression on the part of the colonists often causeless and unprovoked, and, on the part of the aborigines, irruption and massacre . . . The prompt cession of the ceded territory was calculated to show, that, whatever had been the conduct of individuals, its subjects, the Government of Great Britain would be just when appealed to, and respect the rights of property, fully conscious that by so doing it might inspire a confidence as to its future conduct in the minds of the brave though barbarous people who had been encroached upon . . ."[37]

Sympathy for the Afrikaners in Parliament – not that it had ever been in much evidence – was a thing of the past. Demonstrating how

---

35. *Hansard,* 3rd Series, XXIV, 1 July 1834, col. 1062. For the original remarks of Barrow *vide supra,* p. 19.
36. *Report of the Parliamentary Select Committee on Aboriginal Tribes (British Settlements),* reprinted with comments by the Aboriginal Protection Society (1837), p. vi.
37. *Hansard,* 3rd Series, XLII, 10 July 1838, cols. 116–117.

great an influence the British attitude towards the natives had on determining what was thought of the Afrikaners, D'Urban's remarks in 1836 respecting the Frontier War tell their own story: "It is a source of deep regret," he wrote to Stockenström, that the Secretary of State "seems disposed to view these calamities as comparatively inconsiderable, and to think that the unfortunate frontier Colonists have been the injuring, and the enemy the injured party"[38] – sentiments echoed by Harry Smith who wrote of "our peaceable Farmers" as "*men* who duly paid their taxes, and therefore consider they have a right to be defended".[39] In fact, D'Urban's opinion of the Afrikaners – he saw them as a "brave, patient, industrious, orderly and religious people"[40] – was in direct opposition to what Englishmen in Britain were thinking of them.

Joined by certain British newspapers and pressure groups,[41] the L.M.S. set about weaving its web of influence around the Secretary of State for the Colonies, Lord Glenelg – or as Hockly put it: "the L.M.S. was busy doing its best to poison the mind of the recently appointed Secretary for the Colonies" and "unfortunately for the subsequent history of South Africa, suceeded in its endeavours".[42] In the Commons, Bagshaw sketched the background which had led to the "Caffre erruption" stating that the years preceeding the war had first been marked by the co-operation of the frontiersmen in following the policy of conciliation; *however*, a change had come about in the conduct of the colonists when "the boors became tired of the system of conciliation and adopted another", reverting to the old practice of commandos and the "spoor system" which resulted in renewed suffering for the natives.[43] "Was it to be wondered at", retorted Bagshaw, "that all forebearance was at last abandoned by the Caffres, and that they had taken the law into their own hands."[44]

---

38. C.O. 48/168, D'Urban to Stockenström, 1 Aug. 1836, f. 294. See also Muller, *Die Britse Owerheid en die Groot Trek*, pp. 47–48.
39. C.O. 48/168, Smith to D'Urban, 17 April 1836, f. 336: encl. to C.O. 48/168, D'Urban to Glenelg, 19 Sept. 1836.
40. G. C. Moore Smith (ed.), *The Autobiography of Lieut.-General Sir Harry Smith*, ii, pp. 224–226.
41. Such as *The British and Foreign Anti-Slavery Society, The Society for the Extinction of the Slave Trade and the Civilization of Africa, the African Civilization Society* and, of course, *The Aborigines Protection Society*.
42. Hockly, *The Story of the British Settlers of 1820 in South Africa*, p. 162.
43. *Hansard*, 3rd Series, XXVI, 19 Feb. 1835, col. 727.
44. *Ibid.*, col. 728.

This continuous battery of censure against the Cape resulted in Glenelg writing his famous despatch. Not only did it lay the entire onus for the past problems of the Colony upon the colonists, but D'Urban was recalled and his frontier policy reversed. Peace treaties were concluded with the natives and the annexed territory, the Province of Queen Adelaide, returned to them. The philanthropists had won the day.

As the previous chapter showed, the question of Hottentot vagrancy, resulting, it was claimed by those who were affected by it, from the application of the 50th Ordinance, divided the Colony between east and west and to counteract the pro-philanthropic voice of Fairbairn's *Commercial Advertiser* which had become increasingly unpopular in the eastern districts, the frontier gave birth to its own newspaper, the *Graham's Town Journal,* which was founded in the last month of 1831.

The period 1832–1836 was a time of great disharmony between the newspapers of the Cape. *De Zuid Afrikaan* (established as the Afrikaner reply to the Cape Town English press) and the *Commercial Advertiser* were engaged in a non-stop slinging match, while the *Graham's Town Journal* and the *Commercial Advertiser* were at continual loggerheads with each other. However, the importance of these years lies in the fact that it was during this period that the Cape press formulated its basic attitudes towards the Great Trek in 1836 and these attitudes were to continue into the 1840's.

While various arguments in favour of a vagrancy law were brought up by the *Graham's Town Journal* between 1832 and 1833,[45] what mainly attracted the attention of the newspaper's editor, Godlonton, and that of the English inhabitants of the eastern districts were the libellous charges brought against the Colony by certain travellers and missionaries, and in particular Philip in his *Researches,* for, amongst other things, it was asserted that had it not been for the publication of Philip's work, there was "little doubt ere this we should have had a Legislative Assembly, or some legal and constitutional check on the amount of our taxation, and the manner of its expenditure".[46] Referring to philanthropists such as Philip as "that ambitious and over-bearing faction", one correspondent to the *Graham's Town Journal* maintained that the contents of Philip's *Researches* "must

45. Such as 27 Jan. 1832; 1 Nov. 1832; 11 Sept. 1833.
46. *GHT Journal,* "A.B.", 24 Feb. 1832.

call up a blush on the cheek of every sincere missionary";[47] another spoke of it as a "specimen of malicious falsehood" brought against the character of the Colony in general,[48] while the correspondent "A.B." called Philip's integrity into question when he refuted the accusation that the colonists had aided and abetted the plunder of the Bechuanas, "then virtually making slaves of them".[49]

Naturally, there was more to the rejection of Philip's *Researches* than just the condemnation of his statements on the grounds of their being false – it opened the entire question of frontier policy towards the Xhosas, and the treatment they received at the hand of the colonists, both English and Afrikaner. In short, the remarks of the *Graham's Town Journal* represented the reaction of those living contiguous to the frontier to philanthropic influence in these matters – or simply the reaction against what was often referred to as the "mistaken philanthropy" of missionaries.

> ". . . when the ruling powers at home," wrote Godlonton in his *Journal,* "are apathetic and incredulous, and when we find that this is induced by the unfounded representations or the extravagant proposals of visionary speculators, it is high time that those who are well informed on the subject, and at the same time immediately interested, should make common cause, and endeavour to arouse the public attention to a question of so vital consequence to their future prosperity."[50]

Understandably, then, the *Graham's Town Journal* would be critical of the traveller body in general which, it claimed, had supported the missionary movement and had determined both British opinion of and policy towards the Cape frontier.[51] In 1835 Godlonton wrote:

47. *GHT Journal,* "An Observer", 27 Jan. 1832. See also "An Observer", 13 July 1832. On 14 Feb. 1832 the *GHT Journal* referred to the remarks of the missionary, Boyce, who had refuted allegations brought by Saxe Bannister in his *Humane Policy,* adding: "One [Boyce] has had the benefit of sound *practical* knowledge, and sees facts as they really are – the other [Bannister] was an amiable enthusiast who saw everything through a false medium, and whose plans are the mere dreams of a distempered but warm imagination."
48. *GHT Journal,* "X.Y.", 10 Feb. 1832.
49. *Ibid.,* "A.B.", 24 Feb. 1832.
50. *Ibid.,* 24 Jan. 1833.
51. See for instance: *GHT Journal,* 20 Dec. 1832; W. Chalmers, 20 Dec. 1832; 3 Jan. 1833; William Southey, 10 Jan. 1833; 24 Jan. 1833; 4 Sept. 1834; "A.B.", 11 Dec. 1834; 9 Jan. 1835; 16 Jan. 1835; 30 Jan. 1835; 16 July 1835; 3 Sept. 1835; 18 Feb. 1836.

"This part of the British dominions has long been a favourite and fertile field for the operations of political umpires — Utopian dreamers — and of mistaken philanthropists; and it is worthy of note that the united labour of these has tended to produce that state of affairs under which we are now so severely suffering. Who can peruse, with any attention, the writings of PHILIP, SAXE BANNISTER, BRUCE, KAY and last but not least of MR. PRINGLE, without a full conviction of the erroneous impression which has been made upon the British Public, by their several lucubrations. Our actual characters and condition — our wants — our prospects — our capabilities — our dispositions — our difficulties, have all been placed before the eye of the public under a false medium; and the consequences resulting from all of this is, the annihilation of our dearest hopes, and the disruption of all those ties which bind us to a particular soil — that stimulate us to industrious exertion, — and that inspire confidence in the Government of the country."[52]

A publication which particularly attracted the attention of the *Graham's Town Journal* was that of Thomas Pringle's *African Sketches:*

"At the time when MR. BRUCE was favouring the world with his lucubrations, it was predicted that from the wide deviations from truth which they contained . . . that those letters were written solely for effect, and in order to be quoted by certain parties in England as if they were gospel.

This opinion is now fully corroborated by the appearance of MR. PRINGLE'S book on South Africa, for its one-sided statements and adroit deceptiveness, equals or exceeds all its forerunners, — Pringle quotes Bruce, Philip, Wright, Bannister, Fairbairn, Kay etc. and they quote him; thus each quoting the other as sacred texts of their sinister assertions."[53]

It will be remembered that this publication was deemed "worthy of national perusal" by *The Spectator* and, together with that of Moodie, was regarded in Britain with almost scriptural reverence.[54] It will also be remembered that *The Spectator* had given prominence to Pringle's accounts respecting the abuses recently perpetrated by both English and Afrikaner colonists under the commando system. In its struggle to represent the colonists of the Eastern Province in what

52. *GHT Journal,* 30 Jan. 1835.
53. *Ibid.,* "A.B.", 11 Dec. 1834.
54. *The Spectator,* 17 May 1834, p. 469; *vide supra,* p. 124.

was thought to be their true colours, the reaction of the *Graham's Town Journal* to Pringle's work and the review it obtained in Britain is straight-forward:

> "Whether the account of MR. THOMAS PRINGLE is worthy of national perusal or not, is a question which is not very important to discuss; it, however, may be of some moment to warn those who do peruse it that the above remarks [of *The Spectator*] are a flagitious libel both on the Colonial authorities and on that class of inhabitants alluded to, and that it, therefore, should be perused with considerable reservations."[55]

Before proceeding any further it is necessary to briefly portray the feelings generated by the *Commercial Advertiser* towards *De Zuid Afrikaan* representing, as it did, the Afrikaner population of the Western Province. Here, where there was a large-scale dependence upon slave labour, the abolition of slavery caused great agitation in the press and together with the old issue of the Colony obtaining a legislative assembly, the scene was set for a heated confrontation between the followers of the *Commercial Advertiser* and *De Zuid Afrikaan*.

As has already been indicated, this period in the Cape Town press was marked by one continuous slinging match between the two newspapers who "watched and denounced each other" without mercy.[56] The *Commercial Advertiser* still stated that its aim was to see the Colony with its own legislative assembly,[57] although after 1832 it dropped its protective attitude towards what it had earlier thought of as the 'misrepresentation' the Afrikaners had suffered at the hand of travellers. Times were changing. Because of the conservative views held by *De Zuid Afrikaan* respecting the abolition of slavery and the conditions set by 105 Koeberg farmers before they would accept the freeing of their slaves[58] (viewed by the *Commercial Advertiser* as

---

55. *GHT Journal,* 4 Sept. 1834. See also 9 Oct. 1834; 11 Dec. 1834; 16 Jan. 1835.
56. *C.H.B.E.,* viii, p. 263.
57. Such as *Commercial Advertiser,* 1 Jan. 1834; 4 Jan. 1834.
58. See *De Zuid Afrikaan,* 13 May 1832; *Commercial Advertiser,* 16 May 1832; 30 May 1832. See also *Commercial Advertiser,* 24 Oct. 1832, regarding the petition of 216 farmers of the Beaufort district to the Governor, in which they had stated: "we do not intend to obey certain enactments and many others contained in the new Slave Order formed by the King in Council".

showing defiance to "Law, Loyalty and Common Sense"[59] and thought to be "containing the sentiments formerly held in the West Indian Colonies"[60]) the *Commercial Advertiser* and its various correspondents placed unreservedly the full blame on the Afrikaners for having "destroyed any prospect we had of an Assembly".[61]

The *Commercial Advertiser* maintained that *De Zuid Afrikaan* – "that Seditious little Faction"[62] – was out to mislead the colonists, and asked:

> "Is it that they propose to separate this Colony from the British Empire? or to place the European population in an attitude of hostility against the people of colour? or would they be satisfied if a spirit of Jealousy and mutual Hatred could be kept alive between the English and Dutch?"[63]

In fact, *De Zuid Afrikaan* was nick-named *"Firebrands"* for having prompted the farmers mentioned above to adopt their rebellious attitude towards the authority of government over the issue of the abolition of slavery.[64] Because the farmers of the country districts – "especially those of Koeberg and Stellenbosch" – had declared their intention of not reading the *Commercial Advertiser,* Fairbairn stated: "Are men *ripe* for Free Institutions who refuse or attempt to suppress the Liberty of Free Discussion, who publicly declare that they will not hear *both sides* of a question?"[65] And so intense was the feeling against the proprietors of *De Zuid Afrikaan* that in 1832 a correspondent expressed the following view:

> "Into what good society are they admitted? What gentleman in the Colony would not think it necessary to make an apology, if, by accident, he were seen conversing with any one of them? . . ."[66]

On 8 October 1834 a very significant meeting was held in Cape Town in order that a further petition for a legislative assembly for the

---

59. *Commercial Advertiser,* 30 May 1832.
60. *Ibid.,* 16 May 1832.
61. *Ibid.,* "R. near Q. in the Corner", 4 Jan. 1832.
62. *Ibid.,* 21 Jan. 1832. See also 19 Jan. 1833
63. *Ibid.,* 21 Jan. 1832.
64. *Ibid.,* 30 May 1832. See also 27 Jan. 1832; 30 June 1832.
65. *Ibid.,* "An Abolutionist", 29 Sept. 1832. See also 11 Oct. 1834 and 18 Oct. 1834.
66. *Ibid.,* "R. near Q. in the Corner", 4 Jan. 1832.

Colony might be drawn up by the colonists. What transpired on this occasion is of supreme importance as it shows, admittedly under somewhat trying circumstances, what the *Commercial Advertiser* thought of those who opposed it through the columns of *De Zuid Afrikaan*. Two important things took place that evening. First, a Mr. Buckton opposed the resolution that the Colony was ready for such an institution. The *Commercial Advertiser* reported:

> "... but he [Buckton] feared that the present adult Dutch population were not sufficiently acquainted with the principles of Legislation to render so great a trust safe for themselves or for the other classes of the Inhabitants. From unfortunate circumstances their Education has been necessarily very defective – that they themselves could not deny this – that they already felt their inability to frame wise and salutary laws for a whole community – and ought not to be offended at his publicly stating what they all confessed and deplored in private. The rising generation, he had no doubt, would furnish a class of better educated men, who would thus be better able to serve their country and protect the rights and the reputation of this Colony."[67]

However, his motion that a legislative assembly be withheld from the Colony on these grounds was rejected outright. Referring to the second part of the proceedings of the evening, the *Commercial Advertiser* reported:

> "But a more serious argument against this important Resolution, was furnished most unhappily by the Dutch part of the Meeting, which also composed an overwhelming majority. It was moved by one of their number, that seven persons should be appointed as a Committee, to draw up a petition on the basis of the Resolution that had been agreed to, and out of the 7 only *two* were Englishmen – the chairman, who could not decently be omitted, and Mr. Prince, who had moved and supported the Resolution, to pass over whom would also have been rather too gross an outrage on decorum. *Five-sevenths* were thus Dutch, and not one of whom had signed the Requisition. The Requisition, it should be remarked, had been signed by 37 Englishmen . . . in this instance, the exclusion of the English was so manifestly the result of a bad spirit towards them as a body, that they thought it incumbent upon them to notice it, and it was accordingly moved and seconded, that a certain number of the Requisitioners, all

67. *Commercial Advertiser,* 11 Oct. 1834.

of whom were English, should be added to the Committee. This was violently opposed by the leaders of the Dutch, and rejected on a division, by an immense majority. The majority consisted entirely of Dutchmen, and the minority, with a few exceptions of English."[68]

In a subsequent edition the *Commercial Advertiser* based its entire evaluation of the Afrikaners on the outcome of the proceedings at the meeting of the 8th:

"The fact is, John Bull seldom opens his mouth when he thinks a wink or a nod will be enough. Besides, on this occasion he was not called upon to acquire a character. Nobody questions *his* "ripeness" to enjoy the rights and liberties of his forefathers. His Cousin *Dikkop* was in a different predicament. John Bull had a character to *lose; Dikkop* had a character to *make;* John, therefore, contented himself with charging his Cousin to the muzzle with English *ammunition,* and let him to *go off after his own fashion.*

Of the *two* English speakers, it is but fair to add, that MR. BUCKTON had his motion handed to him only about half a minute before he rose to begin the Play; and MR. PRINCE'S conscience was too tough to admit of his speaking of his Cousin's *"ripeness"* otherwise than in the *future tense.* All these things were against John Bull reaping much glory on the 8th of October. Do we, then, surrender forever our hopes of Political Liberty in South Africa? On the contrary, we think a most important step towards it has been secured. John Bull has been awakened from his dream of confidence in the Afrikaner; and all danger of *Dutch Domination* is at an end. If this is not LIBERTY – it is SECURITY, and John knows full well that these two are brethren.

For, who composed the enemy's host on this occasion? – The Watermeyers, the Polemanns, the Thalwitzers, the Ludwigs, or such like, of German blood, and brain, and nerve? No! They were *absent* to a man. And in their stead we saw the Brans, the Smutses, and De Wets, and Cloetes, and Hofmeyers, and other eminent growers of cabbages, shareholders and committee men, and subscribers to, and advertisers in, the *"Zuid Afrikaan"* Newspaper!"[69]

The result of the whole episode was that it had "united the English Inhabitants as one man to resist all further insolence on the part of

---

68. *Commercial Advertiser,* 11 Oct. 1834.
69. *Ibid.,* 18 Oct. 1834.

the Africander".[70] The split between the *Commercial Advertiser*, which represented part of the English population of Cape Town and environs, and *De Zuid Afrikaan*, which represented the Afrikaners in the western province and even further afield, was complete.

Of more importance to this study, however, than the argument the *Commercial Advertiser* had with the Afrikaners of the western districts was its collision with the *Graham's Town Journal* and its English contributors, of whom it wrote that they should "give up their childish disputes, and, instead of wasting their time writing mischievous nonsense for slanderous journals, prosecute their real object as Farmers, namely, – the growing of wool, flax, and the rearing of bullocks"![71] After 1832 the old question of Hottentot vagrancy still cropped up,[72] though it did not interest the *Commercial Advertiser* so much since it considered that the matter had been fully discussed in 1828. Of the Draft Vagrancy Law, submitted to the British Government in 1834, the *Commercial Advertiser* said it "seems to be almost universally dreaded and condemned".[73] The main issue, however, was the frontier relations with the Xhosas and this, in turn, opened the entire question of the reliability of the travellers' accounts which, of course, had particular bearing upon what was thought of the colonists in general, and the Afrikaners in particular.

Writing in 1834, the *Commercial Advertiser* stated that it was a "reproach" to the Colonial and Home Governments that since the turn of the century there had not been the "slightest perceptible improvement" in the system of intercourse with the Xhosa.[74] What made matters more difficult was that the mutual arrangements "supposed to exist" between the Colonial Government and the native tribes were not made publicly known. The only information they had were "the reports of ignorant or interested Tourists, Traders or Field Cornets – or of anonymous writers in Party Newspapers [naturally the *Graham's Town Journal* and *De Zuid Afrikaan*[75]] who may be

70. *Commercial Advertiser*, 18 Oct. 1834.
71. *Ibid.*, 12 Jan. 1833.
72. Such as *Commercial Advertiser*, 17 May 1834, 24 May 1834, 14 June 1834, 28 June 1834.
73. *Commercial Advertiser*, 28 June 1834.
74. *Ibid.*, 22 Feb. 1834.
75. It is interesting to note that Fawcett, the author of *An Account of Eighteen Months' Residence at the Cape of Good Hope, 1835–1836*, p. 22, referred to *De Zuid Afrikaan* and its "sister print" the *Graham's Town Journal* as being "the disgrace and the cross of the colony".

both ignorant and interested . . . these are, with a few exceptions, so vague, stupid, narrow, or contradictory, that a writer, whose only object is to arrive at the real truth, is often forced to give up the case in despair".[76] The state of affairs on the frontier and the policy pursued towards the natives suited nobody. The colonists claimed that the Government afforded them neither protection nor redress, while the Xhosas had represented the whole system as being "founded on false principles".[77] "To recommend Justice, Humanity, and Generosity to the stronger party [Great Britain]", wrote the *Commercial Advertiser,* "may gain a man credit for good feelings, but it is to be feared that these principles have been too often lost sight of by the Colonial Government and its servants on the frontier" – unfortunately, the "old system of Commandos and Patrols seem to be indolently acquiesced in, as if nothing better could be devised".[78] Of course, the wisdom of the commandos themselves was open to question and the *Commercial Advertiser* reported that military men with whom it had spoken and "whose honour and sincerity were above all suspicion" said that the commandos could be regarded as either "a just and necessary act of self-defence characterised by humanity and forebearance" or "a causeless and savage butchery" of the natives.[79] "Whatever the frontier system may have been", judged Fairbairn, "it has notoriously failed" since "the punishments inflicted on those [Xhosa] people by the Commandos were absurd in principle, and necessarily sowed the seeds for future aggression . . ."[80]

Before proceeding further it is necessary to clarify the term "colonist" as applicable to the frontier. It will be remembered that Pringle in his *African Sketches* and *The Spectator* in its review of that book had brought allegations against the "colonists" – the colonists being "the Dutch boors" and "some of the more degraded English settlers". Therefore, when the *Commercial Advertiser* (closely aligned with Pringle) spoke of the "colonists" it meant the Afrikaners and *some* of the English living in the interior districts. It would seem that the *Graham's Town Journal* understood the term "frontier colonists" to refer mainly to the Afrikaners, simply because more of them resided on the actual frontier than the English.

76. *Commercial Advertiser,* 28 April 1832.
77. *Ibid.,* 22 Feb. 1834.
78. *Ibid.*
79. *Ibid.,* 28 April 1832.
80. *Ibid.*

To return to the opinion expressed by the *Commercial Advertiser* above regarding the commando system, it continued by pointing out that *all* the travellers of the Cape since the time of Le Vaillant and Sparrman, who had preceded Barrow, right up to the present time when Pringle had published his work – not to mention the Commission of Enquiry in 1825 – had held the same reservations about the wisdom of the system. "And all these gentlemen", wrote the *Commercial Advertiser,* "agree condemning the System as impolitic, inefficient, injurious to the Colonists and to the Natives . . ."[81] Furthermore, "to suppose that all these writers have been mistaken . . . have fallen into the same error, or been misled by the same prejudices, is to deny the value of all human testimony".[82] The *Commercial Advertiser* made it clear where the actual responsibility for the system lay:

> "The source of the evil is to be found in the present state of the Law – in the weakness of the Government – in the laxity of the Frontier Authorities – and in the bloodthirsty disposition of certain individuals . . . ["the Dutch boors" and "some of the more degraded English settlers"] whom Government has not thought fit either to restrain or to punish . . ."[83]

With the foregoing as background, then, what the *Commercial Advertiser* thought of the "colonists" in the interior – or more specifically of the Afrikaners – it revealed in 1834:

> "Now we know that the Colonists are not savages or barbarians; and even those who have arraigned us at the bar of PUBLIC JUSTICE, particularly MR. THOMAS PRINGLE, speak of them – as *private individuals* – in terms of respect and affection. Indeed, MR. PRINGLE'S picture of the Frontier Farmers afford some of the most pleasing examples of rustic virtue and rural happiness that are to be found in history or romance. But the evidences of our *National* criminality are distinct, specific, and overwhelming."[84]

In other words, while the Afrikaners might have been acceptable as *"private individuals"*, when it came to frontier relations, they were responsible for the *"National* criminality".

81. *Commercial Advertiser,* 14 June 1834. See also 27 Aug. 1834.
82. *Ibid.,* 14 June 1834.
83. *Ibid.,* 27 Aug. 1834.
84. *Ibid.*

The *Graham's Town Journal* viewed matters differently. While accepting that the commando system was the basis of the frontier relationship with the Xhosas and, as such, was "full of defects" – "not least of which is that it engenders desultory habits in our Frontier Farmers"[85] – the *Graham's Town Journal* was of the opinion that "it is, however, extremely difficult to point out a mode by which the Frontier could be defended against the irruptions of the tribes beyond us without such a system".[86] It will be remembered that the *Graham's Town Journal* had refused to accept the testimony of travellers and such people as Pringle in regard to the practical aspects of frontier politics. With this in mind, then, this is how the *Graham's Town Journal* presented its opinion of the Afrikaners – the "Frontier Farmers":

> "We are not of those who would depict the Colonists as a set of heartless, unprincipled, and unfeeling beings, who would wantonly inflict the most barbarous cruelties on an inoffensive people, and who would plunder them of their property and slaughter the unresisting inhabitants to glut a ferocious appetite for blood and rapine. Neither do we hold the notion that our Farmers of the present day benefit by their approximation to Caffer territories in the way which has been stated; on the contrary, we believe that they soldom complain without reasonable cause for it, and that they are kept in a constant state of excitement, and their herds within a very moderate compass by the continual inroads of this people, and the adroitness with which they execute their enterprise. It is too much the practice for strangers visiting the Frontier to give undue credit to all the unreasonable stories they hear of the predatory expeditions of the Farmers against the Caffers. But it has become fashionable for tourists to post from hence to Cape Town, there to display their vituperative talent at the expense of those from whom, perhaps, they have met with the greatest attention, and the kindest hospitality on their journey . . ."[87]

The attitudes adopted by the colonial press towards the frontier system and their opinions of the Afrikaners were only strengthened by the outbreak of the 1834/35 Frontier War which witnessed the frontier districts being overrun by some 12 000 Xhosa warriors. Their

85. *GHT Journal,* 13 Dec. 1832.
86. *Ibid.* See also 13 March 1834, 2 June 1836.
87. *Ibid.,* 13 Dec. 1832.

reactions are almost predictable. On the one hand, the *Commercial Advertiser* held the following point of view:

> "The '*aggressors*', as all the witnesses agree, have been robbed of their land and harrassed by an ill-digested border policy, which is indiscriminately destructive of life and property. Yet it is coolly talked of taking revenge upon a people who can bear such oppressions no longer, and who at last exercise their right to what Lord Bacon correctly calls 'Wild Justice' . . .",[88]

while the *Graham's Town Journal*, on the other hand, protested vehemently against what it termed "slander" and "misrepresentation" of the colonial character.[89]

In the ensuing months such cries were to become the hallmarks of these newspapers and in the light of later events were to provide the basis for the storm of reaction within the Cape Colony which followed upon the turning point in South African history – the Great Trek.

---

88. *Commercial Advertiser*, 23 Jan. 1836.
89. *Vide infra*, Chapt. VIII.

CHAPTER SEVEN

To Natal
1836–1844

> "The history of this colony, whether under Batavian or British rule, proves that, notwithstanding every attempt which, even under the more rigid laws of the Dutch Government, was made, from time to time, to stem the further advance of the Colonists, they still continued to press forward, and the Government was obliged to overtake these Pioneers, and bring them again under the authority of the law. The consequence of this policy has been seen in the massacre of the Native Tribes, the course of the Emigrants having always been traced in blood, much of which might have been saved, had the hand of Government directed and controlled an Emigration, which it was impossible to prevent."[1]

In 1797 John Barrow had spoken of a frontier society which would, under certain circumstances, react in such a way as to remove "the shackles imposed upon it by the parent state" – the "shackles", in effect, being any form of interference which might encroach upon the traditional way of life pursued by the interior colonists.[2] In 1800, Dundas, on outlining what he thought to be the most solicitous policy to be adopted towards these same Graaff-Reinet burghers, maintained that owing to their "rude and uncultivated state" and because of their "wild notions of independence" any attempt to "introduce civilization" and a strict administration of justice would be slow and, indeed, if not proceeded upon with caution and management would create a spirit of resistance – "or a disposition to migrate still further from the seat of Government".[3] In 1819 the *Quarterly*

---

1. C.O. 48/220, Napier to Stanley, 25 July 1842, ff. 187–188.
2. *Vide supra,* p. 15.
3. *Vide supra,* p. 52.

Review, on referring to the imminent advent of the British Settlers to the Colony, considered that the frontier Boers, "hemmed in on every side, and his old habits broken in upon . . . would betake themselves beyond the Snowy Mountains".[4]

Whether the causes of the Great Trek can be wholly attributed to the factors expressed in the above opinions is debatable; however, the remarks of Napier[5] and Glenelg in 1838 show clearly what was at the heart of philanthropic thinking regarding the Afrikaners when considered in the light of what Stanley, the new Secretary of State, said represented "one of the most singular passages in modern history"[6] and which the Cape Governor could not "perceive any way or means of preventing"[7]:

> "Such are the desires of the Boers to reside on lands more fertile than their own," said the Secretary of State, "and to inhabit a country in which they hope to escape taxation – the drought which has rendered their lands within the Colony unproductive – the scattered state of the population which makes it difficult for any man to remain behind who has been deserted by a very few of his neighbours – the discontent at the abolition of Slavery, and the amount of compensation awarded – and a dislike to the policy of H.M. Government towards the Kaffre Tribes. These sources of discontent (all I think originating in popular misconceptions) can be arrested by no other [means] than the slow process of education and advancing knowledge."[8]

In other words, the situation which had given rise to the Great Trek had been the Boers' doing and the situation thus created could only be remedied by the Boers becoming civilised, educated, etc. – much the same judgment as critics of the Afrikaners had been repeating since Barrow had first adopted this line of thinking.

Of course, trekking was nothing new to the Cape Colony where it had come to be accepted as a way of life for a certain section of the population. The graziers, or trek boers had long been living the life of semi-nomadic pastoralists and had for some years been crossing the frontier to pastures new – as Philip had so frequently complained. Therefore, to have predicted that such a migration would take place

---

4. *Vide supra,* pp. 73–74.
5. C.O. 48/191, Napier to Glenelg, 18 May 1838, ff. 65–73.
6. *Hansard,* 3rd Series, LXII, 7 April 1842, col. 1168.
7. C.O. 48/191, Napier to Glenelg, 19 March 1838, f. 41.
8. C.O. 48/191, Glenelg to Napier, 15 Sept. 1838, ff. 77–78.

did not require as much imaginative insight or foresight as might be expected, since it may safely be argued that sooner or later the Cape Colony would have burst its seams – as proved the case in the great western migration of the U.S.A. – owing to the fundamental need for more land. However, why the Great Trek assumes such prominence in the history of South Africa and what renders the above opinions significant and, furthermore, what distinguishes it from being simply an expansionist movement by a large section of the Cape Afrikaner population, is that it represented the political, ideological and social rejection of all that was British and brought about the birth of the Afrikaner *nation*. Whatever divergencies of opinion may exist on the causes of the Great Trek, it may be said that the Great Trek was a reactionary movement – a bloodless revolution against what might be termed 'changing times', manifesting itself in the form of political assertion.

In the South Africa which rose upon the old Cape Colony after 1836, the Afrikaners assumed a new importance and what divided English opinion of the Afrikaners (those who left the Colony, that is) was whether the Great Trek represented a legitimate expression of legitimate frontier grievances, as was maintained by the *Graham's Town Journal*, or whether its origin was to be found elsewhere, as suggested by the above opinions and expounded in the *Commercial Advertiser*.

Official feeling regarding its causes was merely the reflection of those earlier liberalist attitudes held towards the Afrikaners when they had been judged in terms of those events (such as the 1835 Frontier War) which had led to the actual Trek. It certainly did not seem to present a crisis to British parliamentarians and other than the explicit pronouncement of Glenelg in 1838 (quoted above) not a great deal exists on official *opinion* of the Voortrekkers.[9] Nonetheless, from the preceeding chapter it must be obvious that official opinion on the Great Trek would permit little scope for sympathy towards the fate or fortunes of the Afrikaner emigrants – good or otherwise – as they rambled on their way to Natal over the wide plains of the interior.

9. It is again necessary to emphasise that this study is not concerned with British *policy,* as such, towards South Africa. Such information can be gleaned from any general work on South Africa or more particularly from the specialist works of C. F. J. Muller *(Die Britse Owerheid en die Groot Trek),* F. A. van Jaarsveld *(Die Tydgenootlike Beoordeling van die Groot Trek, 1836–1842)* and, to a lesser extent, from Walker's *The Great Trek.*

What most concerned the British Government about the course of action embarked upon by the Trekkers, apart from humanitarian considerations, was that the inevitable warfare which must result in the interior would jeopardise the safety of the Cape Colony's own eastern frontier. Soon condemnation was directed against the Afrikaners for having created a situation which had led to the "inhuman warfare by which Southern Africa has recently been desolated"[10] and which had caused the "destruction of human life";[11] while Stockenström, on referring to the reported "extermination of whole tribes of blacks by H.M. Subjects",[12] had considered it absolutely necessary that "some serious and effective steps be taken by the British Government to control the said Emigration to prevent all blacks in the interior being reduced to the same state in which the Hottentots were lately".[13] Impressions of the Afrikaners under these circumstances were hardly favourable and it did not help matters at all for the British Government to have its attention drawn to the "Brazilia" episode or the election of Maritz and Retief as Voortrekker leaders, or hear of the Afrikaners beyond the colonial boundaries talking of "the third month of our Independence" for, as it was stated, "it gives the whole proceeding a more serious aspect".[14] Neither, indeed, did reports of child stealing[15] and of slaves being illegally carried out of the Colony by the Emigrants[16] help annul official reservations respecting the nature and causes of the Great Trek. On the contrary, they only added weight to the already unsympathetic feeling held towards the Afrikaner frontiersmen, now turned Voortrekkers.

Much of the official attitude towards these people is revealed in the manner by which the murder of Retief was received. While Napier showed some inclination towards sympathy on hearing of the

---

10. G.H. 1/26, Glenelg to Napier, 30 June 1839, f. 760.
11. G.H. 1/26, Glenelg to Napier, 13 Jan. 1839, f. 46.
12. C.O. 48/203, Stockenström to Glenelg, 12 Jan. 1839, f. 16.
13. C.O. 48/191, Stockenström to Napier, 12 March 1838, f. 59.
14. C.O. 48/173, Gardiner to Bell, 9 Sept. 1837, f. 74: encl. to C.O. 48/173, D'Urban to Glenelg, 28 Oct. 1837. See also, C.O. 48/219, Napier to Stanley, 13 June 1842, ff. 339–343.
15. See, C.O. 48/194, Stockenström to D'Urban, 29 July 1837, f. 113; C.O. 48/195, Stockenström to D'Urban, 23 Nov. 1837, ff. 127–128; C.O. 48/195, Stockenström to D'Urban, 11 Oct. 137, ff. 20–21.
16. See, G.H. 1/25, Glenelg to Napier, 24 April 1838, ff. 1–9; G.H. 1/26, Glenelg to Napier, 12 Jan. 1839, ff. 40–41.

massacre,[17] the Secretary of State adopted a somewhat cooler attitude:

> "Much as I lament the disastrous fate of these misguided men, I cannot feel surprise at this result of their proceedings. It was not to be expected that the Natives of the Countries adjacent to the Colony would suffer themselves to be overrun by these invaders; and still less was it to be expected that those who had quitted their home and in some instances entered on a career of plunder and aggression, could receive at a distance from the Frontier that protection which they had voluntarily renounced."[18]

Throughout, it is clear that the British Government could not credit the actions of the Voortrekkers to a well-balanced society and every so often reference was made by both the Secretary of State and the Cape Governor to the Afrikaners as 'these misguided men' who had embarked on a most "mischievous' course of action.

The despatch of troops under Capt. Smith in 1842 to occupy Port Natal so as "to afford the native tribes of Africa the protection of British arms against the aggression of H.M. Subjects"[19] opened the entire question of the annexation of Natal to the British dominions.

There were two main reasons behind the reluctance of Britain to annex Natal to its dominions in the December of 1842, both of which exerted tremendous influence upon English thinking regarding the Afrikaners and ultimately led to the Afrikaners being granted their long sought after political independence during the 1850's. First was economy, which had so powerfully influenced British policies immediately after the Napoleonic Wars and which was still very much a pressing factor in British politics during the 1830's and 1840's. In practice this meant that unless a colony or prospective colony could pay its way within the framework of empire, it would come under sharp attack.[20] In addition to this was the fact that the Report of the Aborigines Committee in 1837 had pointed to the dangers and probable financial involvement likely to arise from further imperial expansion,[21] while the troublesome events in Canada that same year

17. C.O. 48/191, Napier to Glenelg, 17 March 1838, ff. 39–40.
18. C.O. 48/191, Glenelg to Napier, 8 June 1838, f. 46.
19. C.O. 48/214, Napier to Russel, 6 Dec. 1841, f. 200.
20. *C.H.B.E.*, ii, p. 809.
21. *Ibid.*, pp. 330–331, 354.

tended to confirm the view shared by both Whigs and Tories that the second empire, like the first, was destined to dissolve.[22] The second factor, closely bound to the first but perhaps having greater significance, was that with the abolition of slavery in 1834 philanthropists lost much of their political momentum, which meant that by 1836/37 they had passed the height of their political influence. However, this is not meant to imply that philanthropy in British politics was dead – it was not. Statesmen continued to be moved by humanitarian motives, yet subsequent events (such as those in Natal and in the interior of South Africa), although hotly deliberated upon by the Aborigines Protection Society, failed to rekindle the fervent political and public enthusiasm which emancipation had generated. At home, agitation for the abolition of the Corn Laws, plus an increased interest in the free trade movement pushed philanthropy into the background and as far as colonial policy was concerned it was economics which held precedence.

What Napier hoped to achieve was to bring "these misguided Emigrants to a just sense of the folly of persevering in the line of conduct so inconsistent with justice, and so detrimental to their own ultimate welfare".[23] He doubted whether the Boers would resist Smith – in fact, there was not the *"least risk of collision"* – owing to the reports he had received which spoke of the large and increasing party among the Voortrekkers in Natal who were weary of the "anarchy and confusion of their present Government".[24] Referring to the Afrikaner population there, Napier wrote:

> "If these people are to be empowered [in the event of Natal becoming a separate colony under the British Crown] to make and execute Laws, it appears to me that they should shew themselves capable of appreciating the principles of justice and humanity. I by no means wish to depreciate their merits, for there are many among them who, under proper restraint, would become again as they were heretofore, useful and respectable members of society; but I know enough of the South African born farmer to be convinced that the proceedings of the Emigrants would be directed by a few men who possess perhaps more activity and intelligence than their neighbours, and are more willing to devote their time to public business of their com-

22. *C.H.B.E.*, ii, pp. 336–338.
23. *Ibid.*, f. 201.
24. C.O. 48/214, Napier to Russel, 6 Dec. 1841, f. 201.

munity, but who are animated by no feelings of good will either to H.M. Government, or to the native tribes; and who fear that the occupation of Natal is a prelude to the [*decimation*] of their importance."[25]

Stanley's reply in 1842 to Napier's suggestions concerning the establishment of a new British colony at Natal shows something of British policy towards the Afrikaners and also, of course, what was thought of them:

> "With this view it is necessary that you should open a Direct Communication with the Emigrants, and distinctly inform them that Her Majesty's Government are fully impressed with the magnitude of the mischiefs which have arisen, and which are likely to result, from the Emigration of the Dutch Colonists to the neighbourhood of Port Natal, and from their Settlement there. They contemplate with deep regret the calamities to which these misguided people have exposed themselves, nor can they regard, without lively indignation, the slaughter and oppressions, to which, in the prosecution of their enterprise, they have subjected the Native Tribes, [and they] regard, as altogether inadmissible, and even as extravagant, the pretention which they make to be regarded as an independent State or Community . . ."[26]

The defeat of Smith at the hands of the Boers further heightened the indignance felt towards the Voortrekkers at Natal. Commenting on the episode, Napier wrote: "That the Boers would have been so misguided as to subject the troops to such annoyances as would make it necessary to have recourse to arms I never seriously apprehended – that they would write manifestos and either submit with great unwillingness or retire from the neighbourhood of Natal, I never doubted", and on referring specifically to the complicity of Smellenkamp, whose actions as supercargo of the Dutch brig "Brazilia" had led the Voortrekkers to assume that Holland was prepared to back their political aspirations, he continued: "The Boers are ignorant and credulous, and give ear to every story, no matter how absurd, provided it is told to them by those in whom they confide . . ."[27]

Again Napier elaborated on his opinion of the Afrikaners at Port Natal:

25. C.O. 48/214, Napier to Russel, 6 Dec. 1841, f. 202.
26. G.H. 1/29, Stanley to Napier, 10 April 1842.
27. C.O. 48/219, Napier to Stanley, 13 June 1842, ff. 340–341.

> "I cannot too often repeat that no one acquainted with the previous character of the Dutch South African Colonists, and whose opinions, founded on that knowledge, were entitled to due consideration, ever imagined that their madness and folly would have led them into open rebellion . . . The duplicity and determined spirit of hostility towards Great Britain which mark the character and conduct of those who have acquired a least [*say*] in their council, and the pertinacity with which they [*cling*] to the idea that the Dutch Government will espouse their cause, will show Your Lordship how impossible it is to reason with men whose ignorance would only excite compassion were it not for the scenes of bloodshed consequent to their rebellion. The Emigrants are now probably engaged in all their horrors of a savage and murderous strife with the Natives, as calamitous to contemplate as it is impossible to check."[28]

While it has been stated that philanthropic agitation since 1828 concerning the Cape Colony was great, it would be a mistake to imagine that the Great Trek received front page coverage in the British press or that it was considered as a setback to British national interests. Reaction in Great Britain was hardly noticeable and press reaction was slight. Of course, in the Cape Colony it was an event of colonial or 'national' importance since the Great Trek represented the culmination of the great split, or the 'parting of the ways', which had been brewing since 1828 when Philip's *Researches* had sparked off the controversy over the 50th Ordinance and, indeed, which had been in the air since Barrow had published his *Travels* at the turn of the century. So great, in fact, was the friction between the various parties during the period just before the Great Trek that in 1838 the *Graham's Town Journal* reflected that the Afrikaner emigration had operated as a *"safety valve"* to the whole of the eastern province.[29]

In the early days of the Trek the *Commercial Advertiser* expressed regret that so large a number of the frontier colonists had abandoned the Colony, regarding the exodus as a "serious loss", although it doubted whether "a change of scene [would] improve the prospects of the Emigrants".[30] Its chief fear was that with the evacuation of

---

28. C.O. 48/220, Napier to Stanley, 13 July 1842, f. 148. See also, C.O. 48/220, A. J. Cloete to Napier, 6 July 1842, ff. 280–284; C.O. 48/220, Napier to Stanley, 25 July 1842, ff. 186–190.
29. *GHT Journal,* 22 March 1838.
30. *Commercial Advertiser,* 4 May 1836.

the frontier districts the whole area would be thrown back into the state it had been in twenty or thirty years before[31] – an argument which, although undoubtedly true, had been put forward as an attempt to stay the flow of colonists abandoning the frontier districts. In fact, when it became apparent that an even greater number of the colonists were likely to follow suit, the newspaper advocated the prevention, or at least the checking of the Trek.[32] It could not be denied, admitted the *Commercial Advertiser,* that there were faults in the colonial administration – "but they are not such as can be evaded by pushing farther into the interior of Africa".[33]

Since its inception the *Commercial Advertiser* had advocated the development of the Colony's interior, with special emphasis on the advancement or development of the Afrikaner colonists residing there. Comparisons had been drawn between the English and Afrikaner farmers wherein it was argued that because of their African environment the older colonists did not show the same spirit of experiment and enterprise which the English so prided themselves in. It was felt that much of the Afrikaners' apathy towards improvement was due largely to what Cradock had earlier referred to as the fact that they were largely graziers and therefore not closely bound to the soil. *Herein,* considered the *Commercial Advertiser,* lay the root of the Great Trek:

> "Most of the Emigrants are Cattle Farmers, and a cattle farmer in this colony is bound to the soil by very slender ties. He lives alone. The few wants of his family are supplied from his herds and flocks, and from a few acres of virgin ground slightly scratched by a plough of his own manufacture, once a year. Even the luxury of bread is by no means universal amongst them. To such men any country, where grass and water can be found for their cattle, is as good and as valuable as the farms on which they have been born. They abandon nothing of value. They carry with them all that they love – their wagons, the family pot, their cattle, and their wives and children . . ."[34]

Closely aligned to this absence of ties was the grazier's love of independence, a requisite fundamental to his concept of life:

---

31. *Commercial Advertiser,* 4 May 1836.
32. *Ibid.,* 10 Sept. 1836.
33. *Ibid.,* 4 May 1836.
34. *Ibid.,* 27 Aug. 1836.

"For though a social animal, he acknowledges other instincts besides the love of intercourse with his kind. He loves land as such, and cattle as such, without reference to the produce or the money they can furnish. He loves ease, and he likes to have his own way in everything, which he calls being independent."[35]

Reports that the farmers of Swellendam, far removed from the frontier, had also joined the Trek provided the *Commercial Advertiser* with its evidence that the cause of the Great Trek was "something else than Caffre depredations; or even the delay of compensation for the losses of the late war".[36]

Migrations were nothing new to the world as men had universally spread themselves until they met some insurmountable natural or artificial barrier such as the sea, an uninhabitable desert, or some nation too strong to be moved. While the love of adventure might have played its role, the main cause for such movements was land:

". . . a preference in favour of *land* that costs nothing, over *land* which must be purchased and paid for, subject, moreover, to the burdens which are necessary for the support of a regular government . . . minor causes operate at different periods, in producing particular movements. But to obtain land for nothing, and to escape taxation, are the motives of Emigration. These motives have carried the colonists of South Africa from Table Bay to the Fish and Orange Rivers. The same motives are now carrying them over those rivers towards Port Natal, and Dela Goa Bay, and onwards the same motives will carry them until they meet some impassable desert, – the Mediterranean, – *or some African nation too strong to be moved to a safer distance, and which holds land as private property.*"[37]

Or, as the *Commercial Advertiser* more humorously put it:

"The cause of this tendency to break the ties that bind men to their native soil, in Ireland, is said to be redundant population – that is, *a greater number of mouths than there is meat for.* In this country, the causes of Emigration is in substance nearly, the same – namely, *a greater number of legs than there is land for!*"[38]

---

35. *Commercial Advertiser,* 5 Aug. 1837.
36. *Ibid.,* 27 Aug. 1836.
37. *Ibid.,* 3 Sept. 1836.
38. *Ibid.,* 5 Aug. 1837.

As the months passed the *Commercial Advertiser* showed less alarm at the vacation of the frontier districts since it claimed that "the country thus abandoned will be speedily thus occupied by Sheep-farmers and Agriculturalists with capital, skill and enterprise, who will do justice to the soil, climate, and position of South Africa".[39] In other words the Colony would survive!

In the same way as the Great Trek could not be stopped inasmuch as the Afrikaners were simply "following the instincts of the Human Race",[40] so also the progress of the Colony would continue. In fact, the step the Emigrants had taken fell perfectly into the mould or pattern which all developing countries followed in the path to maturity. A further quotation from the *Commercial Advertiser* illustrates as never before exactly the standpoint it assumed in passing opinion on the Afrikaner Emigrants:

> "In the Boundless Interior the Frontier Boer sees, or fancies he sees scope for the gratification and indulgence of all these propensities; and looking with pity on the busy hive of condensed humanity in cities, or even in villages; and regarding with disdain the grand, but to him the unintelligible results of combined industry, the beauty of which he cannot know because they are intellectually discerned, he tosses up his head like the wild horse, utters a neigh of exultation, and plunges into the wilderness.
>
> These are the cattle farmers, who may be called the aerial class of our community, who, like the wind, always wander where they will.
>
> Into the space thus evacuated, flows the second class who rear sheep and occasionally cultivate the soil. These are more gregarious and less mobile. They frequent markets; entertain less aversion to Churches, Courts of Justice, or Schools, and though not immovably rooted, they manifest a constant tendency to take root.
>
> Into their neighbourhood, but without displacing them, creeps the cultivator of the soil, followed gradually by the mechanic, and the artisan. And now civilization properly begins. Things more precious than mere land, or mere cattle, or ease, or uncontrolled self-will, begin to make their appearance, and to exert an influence more powerful than the repelling instincts of rude nature. Mutual assistance, or the division of labour; the exchange in *small quantities* of all things necessary or ornamental; security for the person without arms; and for property during

39. *Commercial Advertiser,* 27 Aug. 1836.
40. *Ibid.,* 3 Sept. 1836.

> sleep and absence; discourse, books, refined manners — and riches beyond the imagination of him who boasts that he is master of all he can see from his saddle. These things draw Mankind into what may be called the *solid state,* from which single particles, or individuals, can only be detected by a considerable force.
>
> In this colony these states of society are all co-existing, nor are they without the mutual advantages, though we would wish that the proportion were somewhat different. By the abundant supply of food, the Cattle Boer has greatly promoted the rate of increase in all the other classes of the people; but he excludes the present amount both of labour and capital in the colony, from their due share of surface. His time is come, therefore, and he feels it, when he must either advance geographically, or fall partially to the ranks of *social* labour. Accordingly, we see some of his class becoming more solid, that is, acquiring sheep, and putting their oxen to the plough; whilst others proceed as their fathers have done, towards the north and the rising sun."[41]

For these reasons the *Commercial Advertiser* refused to accept that the Great Trek could be attributed simply to the emancipation of the Hottentots, the abolition of slavery and the late frontier war and generally those factors held by the Afrikaners to account for their action.[42] Its total and outright rejection and ridicule of the reasons for the Trek as submitted by Retief in his "Manifesto", round off perfectly what the *Commercial Advertiser* thought of the Afrikaners in their endeavour to rid themselves of the British Government.[43] Indeed, "it is on such imaginery and fallacious grounds that the . . . Farmers have been induced to withdraw from under a settled Christian Government, to seek a '*quiet life*' among the gentle kings of central Africa!"[44]

The frontier press, on the other hand, held somewhat different ideas respecting the causes of the Great Trek and as Harington says, as soon as the evidence presented before the Aborigines Committee reached Grahamstown, Godlonton "took up the cudgels on behalf of the colonists".[45] As far as the *Graham's Town Journal* was concerned, for so large a body of people to disassociate themselves "with

---

41. *Commercial Advertiser,* 5 Aug. 1837.
42. *Ibid.*
43. *Ibid.,* 11 Feb. 1837.
44. *Ibid.*
45. A. L. Harington, *The Graham's Town Journal and the Great Trek,* p. 32.

one accord"[46] from the "many endearing associations connected with the land of one's birth", there needed to be "the most weighty reasons".[47] Despite the agitation against the colonial character by philanthropists – the *"pretended* champions of liberty"[48] and "adepts" in making the "worse appear the better cause and whose sophistry appears to have had, of late, more weight with those who control our affairs than the substantial demands of reason and justice"[49] – the causes of the Great Trek to those who resided on the frontier were evident enough and it was not "a matter of surprise or of ingenious speculation".[50]

The first cause was the enactment of the 50th Ordinance, "so ostentatiously lauded as the Hottentot Magna Carta". It was not that "any liberal minded man" objected to the act itself, explained the *Graham's Town Journal,* since obviously it was founded on benevolence and justice; "but whilst we cheerfully make this admission, we contend it was due to the mass of the [Hottentot] people that proper checks should have been provided for the reaction which it required but very little political sagacity to discover would be the inevitable consequence".[51] What, however, was the most trying part was that "losses daily sustained by vagrants who were spread over the country, subsisting on the flocks and herds of the plundered farmers – were met by the most unfair and unfeeling taunts; their [the farmers] real condition was shamefully misrepresented; and they were held up to the scorn and abhorrence of the world, as the oppressors of the poor and the defenceless . . ."[52]

Then there was the question of the abolition of slavery. It was pointed out that in no country was the mandate more favourably received and more promptly obeyed than in the Cape Colony but what was so incredible, maintained the *Graham's Town Journal,* was the "crying injustice" of compelling the inhabitants of the Colony to apply in London for the compensation due to them, which meant

---

46. *GHT Journal,* 13 July 1837. See also, 15 Feb. 1838.
47. *Ibid.,* 11 Aug. 1836.
48. *Ibid.,* 13 April 1837.
49. *Ibid.,* 11 Aug. 1836.
50. *Ibid.*
51. *Ibid.*
52. *Ibid.*

that they received only one-third of the appraised value of their slaves.[53]

The third cause which had led to the Great Trek was the actual state of the frontier districts – a direct result of the native depredations which had stemmed from the "refusal of any adequate military protection and the prohibition of the government against the people defending themselves".[54] To substantiate this statement the *Graham's Town Journal* published a firsthand account illustrating the condition of the colonists under the existing government policy:

> "I called at a house on the road to my farm, where I saw a farmer, named Niemand, and another named Coester. The former has a wife and seven children, and the latter a wife and four children; they have nothing left them; but are wholly dependent upon the kindness of friends; and I assert, as a fact, that the whole of the clothing that all of them had, on their bodies, were not worth more than 30/-; they had nothing to purchase more with; their children were crying for milk and victuals; but they had nothing to give them. The one possessed two oxen, one cow, and 70 sheep and goats, and the other had no cattle at all. They were both well off before the Caffre Invasion, and now they have not a house left, or oxen to move their wagons. Many on the same neighbourhood are in similar circumstances. Let anyone, we repeat, read such statements as this", asserted Godlonton, "and then say whether it is just or decent, that whilst a people are suffering such intolerable privations, it should be bruited abroad, that their grievances are visionary; and that they are in flourishing circumstances; and that abandonment of home and country arises from disaffection to lawful authority, or is the consequence of those endeavours which have been made to awaken the public mind to a true estimate of their character and condition?"[55]

For these reasons the Afrikaners had "abandoned the land in search of a more peaceful home"[56] – a state of affairs which cannot "fail to excite the deepest sympathy, and the greatest possible commiseration",[57] commented the *Graham's Town Journal.*

With such opposite points of view on the causes of the Great Trek the colonial newspapers could be expected to take up very different

53. *GHT Journal,* 11 Aug. 1836.
54. *Ibid.*
55. *Ibid.* (paragraph in italics).
56. *Ibid.,* 30 May 1839.
57. *Ibid.,* 13 July 1837.

stands on the proper course of action to be followed by the Government.

According to the *Commercial Advertiser* it was in the best interests of the Colony that the depopulation of the frontier districts should be halted. The course open to the Government was therefore plain: The "physical and moral" improvements of the Colony should be such that "no man shall be able to leave it for the wild regions of the interior"; secondly, immigration from Britain to the Colony should be encouraged so as to make up for the already depopulated areas, the effect of which would be excellent as a greater demand for land would increase its value.[58] However, apart from the depopulation of the Colony, a more sobering consequence of the Great Trek was the actual presence of the Emigrants in the interior as this, it was considered, would plunge the sub-continent into a state of turmoil. The *Commercial Advertiser* maintained that a collision with the native tribes was inevitable[59] since even the annual excursions of certain of the frontier farmers over the past eight or nine years across the colonial boundary had caused "much inconvenience" to the Government, the frontier inhabitants and the native tribes on whose land these colonists had encroached.[60] A mass emigration such as the Colony was then witnessing could only "throw the whole country into a combustion".[61] It was therefore necessary for the Government to adopt such measures "for the protection of both the Colony and the Natives, whose existence is thus compromised".[62]

As far as the *Graham's Town Journal* was concerned the "self-expatriation" of the Afrikaner colonists called for the "deepest consideration".[63] "With what sedulous care", it judged, "should it [the Government] proceed to discover the *cause* of such an unheard of procedure, – and with what wisdom should it endeavour to heal the wounds which have been inflicted".[64] In view of the fact that it was in the interest of the Colony that the emigration of those persons

58. *Commercial Advertiser,* 3 Sept. 1836.
59. *Ibid.,* 4 May 1836; 3 Dec. 1836.
60. *Ibid.,* 10 Sept. 1836.
61. *Ibid.,* 3 Sept. 1836.
62. *Ibid.,* 30 Nov. 1836.
63. *GHT Journal,* 11 Aug. 1836.
64. *Ibid.,* 13 July 1837.

considered "our most valuable hands"[65] be halted, the *Graham's Town Journal* warned:

> "We again repeat that the circumstances of the frontier farmers require the most attentive and humane consideration on the part of the government; hitherto they have been treated without the slightest regard to their personal feelings or their prejudices; and we do not now hesitate to declare – and we sincerely trust that the caution may not pass unheeded – that if those who exercise control over their affairs do not adopt such just, efficient and conciliatory measures as the people have a right to expect, the eastern frontier districts of this colony will be extensively abandoned."[66]

Both the *Commercial Advertiser* and the *Graham's Town Journal* were of the opinion that the presence of the Emigrant Farmers in the interior would inevitably lead to hostilities with the natives. To the *Commercial Advertiser* this would result from the justifiable reaction of the natives to the Trekkers' intrusion on their lands; to a correspondent of the *Graham's Town Journal* there was another reason for the expected hostilities:

> ". . . The natives, seeing plenty of fine cattle and horses, and an abundance of fat sheep, will immediately begin to steal secretly, or plunder and murder openly, according to their force and strength."[67]

Furthermore, "depend on it", stressed this writer, "the Dutch farmers will not injure the natives, unless the natives *first* injure them".[68]

---

65. *GHT Journal,* 7 Feb. 1839.
66. *Ibid.,* 11 Aug. 1836.
67. *Ibid.,* "A Frontier Farmer", 13 April 1837.
68. *Ibid.*

CHAPTER EIGHT

To Natal and Beyond
1836–1844

> "Our government may not be aware of the fact, but it is nevertheless true, that the Kaffirs are much better affected towards the Dutch Boers than to the British government. They are conscious that the former are not wont to trifle with them; that they are pertinacious in the maintenance of their ground; prompt in punishing injury, and persevering in seeking redress for actual wrong. They understand all this perfectly, but they cannot comprehend the motives which actuate the Colonial authorities; *their* proceedings are altogether inexplicable . . ."[1]

The overall attitudes of the colonial press (the *Commercial Advertiser,* the *Graham's Town Journal,* in 1840 the *Cape Town Mail,* and the *Cape Frontier Times* in 1841) towards the Afrikaners who had gone on the Great Trek can best be revealed by elaborating upon the major aspects of that event section by section. Into the first section comes the reaction of the press to the Government's handling of the Great Trek as a whole, to Natal being opened to the Whiteman and to the reported fortunes and experiences of the Voortrekkers. Into the second section falls their reaction to the Afrikaner's attempts to establish a republic and to the alleged abuses perpetrated against the natives by them. The final section deals with the reaction to Capt. Smith's defeat by the Boers at Port Natal.

I. *Press reaction to Government handling of the Great Trek, the opening of Natal and the fortunes of the Voortrekkers there*

From the outset the *Graham's Town Journal* was critical of the Government for not "adopting that line of policy which would have

---

1. *GHT Journal,* 21 Aug. 1845.

restored confidence",[2] which might have resulted in halting the exodus and might even have gone so far as to cause the Trekkers to return; instead, it stated, the Government had done "nothing". "We have looked on with criminal apathy, and while death stalked through the land, we have been indulging ourselves in copious libations of moonshines."[3] As a result the emigration "has taken exactly that course which has tended most effectually to cause exasperation, and which has led so many valuable hands to plunge, with the recklessness of despair, into the tractless wilderness, and to place themselves beyond the pale of civilization".[4] What the Government had done was cause the Boers to "cherish eternal enmity towards the British name and Government".[5] In fact, the *Graham's Town Journal* seriously wondered whether the measures adopted by the Government towards the frontier had not been *intentionally* ineffective, and that the dispersion of the Emigrants into the interior had not been actually *hoped* for by the British Government.[6] By early 1838, however, and throughout 1839 the *Graham's Town Journal* was convinced that the tide of the emigration could not be stemmed nor would the Emigrants ever be persuaded to return[7] despite the fact that they would be received back into the Colony with the "most cordial welcome" by both Dutch and English.[8] With the murder of Retief and his party – a "most painful subject"[9] – the course of the Voortrekkers had been irreversibly set:

> ". . . we at present have strong reasons to doubt whether it will have this tendency [to make the Emigrants return], and are much more inclined to believe, that this wanton and savage butchery will rather tend to consolidate their [the Emigrants'] power, to unite their jarring interests, and ultimately that it will lead to the entire subversion of a power [the Zulu nation]".[10]

What best illustrates the practical attitude of the *Graham's Town Journal* towards frontier matters is the view it held on the ultimate

2. *GHT Journal,* 9 Aug. 1838.
3. *Ibid.,* 14 Feb. 1839.
4. *Ibid.,* 9 Aug. 1838.
5. *Ibid.,* 14 Feb. 1839.
6. *Ibid.,* 9 Aug. 1838.
7. *Ibid.,* 14 Feb. 1839; 22 March 1838.
8. *Ibid.,* 22 March 1838.
9. *Ibid.*
10. *Ibid.*

outcome of the Great Trek. Firstly, with the British establishing a firm hold on Natal, trade with the interior would be better facilitated, the development of which would compensate for the already declining resources of Kaffraria;[11] and secondly, such control on Natal would help reduce the pressure on the Colony's eastern frontier or, as Godlonton expressed it in more detail:

> "Deeply as we regret the emigration of the farmers, both as respects the immediate consequences of the step to the colony and to themselves; yet we are not among those who look to the *result* with every gloomy foreboding. We, on the contrary, are rather disposed to regard it as affording the strongest hope of future safety. This colony, whatever may be thought at a distance, is fast verging towards a momentous crisis. Should the process which is now going on continue, the country must be completely overrun — and that at no distant period — by a black population. Every day this force is felt to be stronger, and the resistance opposed thereto weaker; it is pressing steadily and surely upon us from the eastward, and if there be anything that can cause a re-action, it will be the firm establishment of a colony of whites in the Natal country. Of this fact every intelligent person must be convinced, by a single glance of a map of South Africa, as well as of the great importance of Natal to this colony, both politically and commercially. The voice of humanity calls itself loudly upon the British Government to take up this measure with a zeal correspondent to its importance."[12]

Of course, the attitude of the *Commercial Advertiser* was completely the opposite to that of its counterpart in Grahamstown. The idea of "attempting to settle in independent masses among the native tribes"[13] was referred to as plain "mischief"[14] since it was argued that nothing could be gained from such an excursion, while it exposed the Colony to obvious dangers. The early collision of the Trekkers with Mzilikatzi had shown the natives that the Whiteman was not invincible and "nothing", declared the *Commercial Advertiser,* "can be imagined more dangerous to our frontier than exhibitions, on our part, of injurious dispositions and apparent weakness".[15] The greatest danger lay in creating the impression in the minds of the natives that "we

11. Harington, *The Graham's Town Journal and the Great Trek,* p. 3.
12. *GHT Journal,* 14 Feb. 1839.
13. *Commercial Advertiser,* 2 June 1838.
14. *Ibid.,* 4 Feb. 1837.
15. *Ibid.* See also, 2 June 1838.

intend to advance, and that we consider our right to African Soil unlimited" as, in the opinion of the *Commercial Advertiser,* this would result in a general retaliation against the Whiteman which, naturally, would also embrace the Colony.[16] "Should not the Government at all hazards", it therefore advocated, "consult for the safety of the colony by interposing its *power* between those madmen who propose to provoke a hostility which they cannot, and we may not be able to resist, and the tribes who may not *yet* ascribe the invasion of their country to the cupidity of the British, or the success against the Boers, to the weakness of our arms?"[17]

Besides pointing out the illegality of the action,[18] the election of Retief as Governor of the Emigrant Farmers led the *Commercial Advertiser* to advocate strong action on the part of the Government. Retief was to be summoned and all further intercourse with the Trekkers was to be prohibited.[19] The massacre of Retief and his party —"the calamity which has befallen the Emigrant Boers"—was greeted with little surprise. Retief and his men had acted imprudently[20] — armed bodies of foreigners found within the limits of the Colony, even though they were natives of Africa, were *"considered enemies, and treated as such",* so why therefore should Retief have been treated otherwise?[21] The newspaper's reaction to the massacre also demonstrates its underlying attitude to the Great Trek as a whole: "Bloodshed and devastation must mark its progress, and it can end no otherwise than in the ruin and dispersion of the unhappy people who have so wantonly renounced the support and protection of their lawful government",[22] while its views on the important question of persuading the Trekkers to return to the Colony consolidate that attitude:

> "However we may feel for the sufferings of these unfortunate people, it is perfectly clear that assistance, in any shape, can be afforded them only on condition of their returning to the colony.

---

16. *Commercial Advertiser,* 2 June 1838.
17. *Ibid.,* 2 June 1838.
18. The *Commercial Advertiser* repeatedly put forward arguments against the legality of the actions of the Voortrekkers in Natal, especially when the "*original* [English] *settlers*" at the port of Natal greeted Retief as "Governor of the Emigrant Farmers". (16 Dec. 1837.) See also, Harington, *The Graham's Town Journal and the Great Trek,* p. 123.
19. *Commercial Advertiser,* 4 Nov. 1837.
20. *Ibid.,* 7 March 1838.
21. *Ibid.,* 25 April 1838.
22. *Ibid.,* 7 March 1838.

Relief on any other terms would but protract their sufferings, and keep alive the flame which their irruption into the interior has kindled. Should they return in obedience to the Government's invitation, they will be received with kindness and liberality."[23]

II. *Press reaction to Afrikaner attempts at independence and reports of abuse of the natives*

In dealing with the reaction of the *Graham's Town Journal* and the *Commercial Advertiser* to the actions of the Afrikaners in Natal, specifically with regard to their desire to establish an independent Afrikaner state, it is necessary, by way of introduction, to show those areas in which these two newspapers, together with the *Cape Town Mail* and the pro-philanthropic *Cape Frontier Times*,[24] were in agreement and disagreement.

It has already been shown how, in 1839, the *Graham's Town Journal* foresaw ultimate good resulting from the Great Trek and throughout the Great Trek period this newspaper, together with the *Cape Town Mail*, advanced further such pragmatic arguments favouring the expansion of the Colony. "The Trusteeship of South Africa", wrote the *Graham's Town Journal* in 1841, "has been given to the British Crown, not for the mere selfish purpose of aggrandisement, but for incalculable benefits to Africa itself, by the conversion of the heathen from barbarism to civilization",[25] while a year later it spoke of the "great duty"[26] which had befallen the British people to become the "conservators of peace in South Africa".[27]

The *Cape Town Mail* was of the opinion that the emigration of the frontier colonists could not be halted[28] and shared the views of the *Graham's Town Journal* as to the expansion and the ultimate future of South Africa. Indeed, it "looked forward to the peopling of Southern Africa, – and of Central Africa, – with British subjects".[29] On the question of the inevitable collision of interests of the White and Black man, particularly with regard to the possession of land, the *Cape Town Mail* was of the opinion that positive British involve-

---

23. *Commercial Advertiser*, 17 Nov. 1838.
24. Its predecessor, *The Colonial Times*, lasted for only eighteen editions during the early months of 1840.
25. *GHT Journal*, 22 July 1841.
26. *Ibid.*, 24 Feb. 1842.
27. *Ibid.*, 23 June 1842.
28. See *Cape Town Mail*, 13 March 1841; 10 Sept. 1842; 29 Oct. 1842.
29. *Cape Town Mail*, 10 Sept. 1842.

ment in the affairs of South Africa was even more imperative since it was argued that it was the responsibility of Great Britain "to preserve, or compensate, whatever of just right belongs to the Native, while the high and beneficient designs of Providence for the peopling of this fair world may no longer be thus blindly thwarted"[30] – Natal was to be the "instrument" placed by Providence in the hands of Great Britain for "effecting, in part, this high and beneficial purpose".[31] It goes without saying that the *Commercial Advertiser* disagreed vehemently with its counterparts, declaring that expansion beyond the colonial limit would be detrimental to the interests of the Blackman and in fact throughout this period the *Commercial Advertiser* could only foresee "evils arising from the swarming of British subjects towards the Interior".[32]

On one point, however, the colonial press did take a united stand – they all whole-heartedly repudiated any attempt by the Natal Afrikeners to establish an independent state. While the *Graham's Town Journal* could understand what had brought the Emigrants to hoist the Dutch flag at Port Natal when Capt. Jervis' force abandoned the port in 1840, it utterly ridiculed any idea of foreign intervention in the settlement.[33] "The sooner, therefore, this chimerical idea is removed from the minds of the emigrants the better", wrote the *Graham's Town Journal*[34] – a feeling fully endorsed by the *Cape Town Mail.*[35] And in 1842 the Smellenkamp episode evoked the following reaction – a reaction which was representative of all colonial feeling at the time:

> "Let the Natal emigrants well understand, that neither Holland nor any other state dare interfere . . . Natal is British territory, and British supremacy *must and will be* maintained over all that dwell there."[36]

---

30. *Cape Town Mail,* 29 Oct. 1842.
31. *Ibid.,* 10 Sept. 1842.
32. *Commercial Advertiser,* 5 June 1839.
33. *GHT Journal,* 16 Jan. 1840.
34. *Ibid.*
35. *Cape Town Mail,* 30 July 1842; 14 Jan. 1843.
36. *GHT Journal,* 29 Sept. 1842.
    Harington in his dissertation, *The Graham's Town Journal and the Great Trek,* sums up the attitude of this newspaper to the political aspirations of the Voortrekkers in Natal perfectly. Quoting a leading article in the *Graham's Town Journal,* dated 20 Feb. 1834, respecting "the ultimate determination of many of the Farmers to pass the Colonial Boundary, and

The Cape Town Mail was not far behind in its view: "No credence . . . is to be attached to any rumours professing to disclose the final determination of Her Majesty's Government on these subjects"[37] (that the British Government might consider granting the Boers their independence); while the *Frontier Times* maintained that any such claims to independence made by the Boers "can scarcely be treated with seriousness".[38] To the *Commercial Advertiser* the granting of political independence to the Emigrant Farmers was ludicrous and it mainly interested itself with suggesting ways and means of stopping the exodus by prohibiting contact with the emigrants.[39]

Whether Great Britain should or should not annex was another important question which featured prominently in the colonial press. At first, the *Commercial Advertiser* had been against British involvement in Natal other than through the adoption of those measures which would curtail or prevent the emigration of British subjects into that territory, but once the Great Trek became an established fact the *Commercial Advertiser* begrudgingly advocated such a course of action on the grounds that if Natal was to be invaded by British subjects it had better be done under the control of the British Government.[40] The threatened interests of the natives in Natal at the hands

---

there to form themselves into a distinct and independent people", Harington writes that this was "a scheme which it dismissed with contempt as a 'hare-brained undertaking', drawing scornful attention to the absurdity of expecting 'to produce from the very elements of discord and confusion, order and good government'. Though the idea possessed one merit, in that it might rid the Colony of 'factious persons', its execution would have to be prevented, for the sake of the natives whom they would try to dominate, and for the sake of the colony, which would suffer when the dispossessed natives were driven towards the frontier and when trade with the interior was upset" (p. 48).

37. *Cape Town Mail,* 14 Jan. 1843. See also, 30 July 1842.
38. *Frontier Times,* 3 June 1840.
The attitude of the *Frontier Times* towards the causes of the Great Trek is interesting. Like the *Commercial Advertiser,* this newspaper became increasingly more interested in involving itself with immigration and the financial development of the Colony. As long as the emigrant colonists did not disrupt the peace of the Colony nor adversely effect its development, then it was content. On the subject of the Great Trek it merely presented its readers with what it considered to be all the possible factors which might have led the Afrikaners to deserting the Colony without involving itself in a feud similar to that engaged in by the *Commercial Advertiser* and the *Graham's Town Journal* and without stating what it personally believed to be the main causes.
39. *Commercial Advertiser,* 5 June 1839, 19 June 1839, 26 June 1839.
40. *Ibid.,* 28 Nov. 1840; 15 May 1841; 17 Dec. 1842.

of the Emigrants was generally accepted by the colonial press as grounds for British annexation. The *Graham's Town Journal,* for instance, considered that the collision between the Emigrants in Natal and the native chief, Faku, provided just that proof required to demonstrate the need for British intervention in Natal;[41] furthermore, it maintained that the Boers themselves by that time had tired of the "restless wandering which had been their lot"[42] – they were tired of "wandering from place to place"[43] – and it pointed out that there were at Natal "many influential persons who are most favourable to British interests, and who, as lovers of good order, are most anxious to see the establishment, on reasonable conditions, of British rule amongst them"[44] – a view sustained by the *Commercial Advertiser.*[45] As far as the *Frontier Times* was concerned "the position of the Boers themselves, and a benevolent regard to the lives and well-being of the native tribes, alike demand . . . that Natal should be occupied by the British".[46] Warfare in the interior was inevitable, and there had been sufficient bloodshed already to prove this, therefore:

> "The permanent occupation of the Natal territory, with the restoration of the emigrants to British dominion, under circumstances conciliating their attachment to its sway, would effectually hinder these demonstrations [the bloodshed], and in doing so, not only save thousands of lives, and the infliction of inappreciable suffering, but promote the internal peace of the various native tribes, and their steady advances in civilized life."[47]

III. *Press reaction to the defeat of Capt. Smith*

Undoubtedly, the most important single occurrence of the period to highlight the various opinions held by the colonial newspapers towards the Natal Afrikaners in their efforts to create an independent state, was the defeat of Smith at the hands of the Boers in 1842. This, together with those factors already elaborated upon and the endeavours of the Emigrants beyond the Drakensberg to establish inde-

41. *GHT Journal,* 21 Jan. 1840.
42. *Ibid.*
43. *Ibid.,* 16 Jan. 1840.
44. *Ibid.,* 14 Oct. 1841.
45. *Commercial Advertiser,* 15 May 1841.
46. *Frontier Times,* 3 June 1840.
47. *Ibid.,* 12 Aug. 1840.

pendence, and their relationship with the Griquas and Basutos, provides the foundation upon which actual opinion of the Afrikaner emigrants can be gauged.

Before elaborating further it is perhaps advisable to first pause and reflect upon the basic differences which separated the two main parties in the Colony. The colonial split of 1832 was still very much evident in 1836 and 1844 with the *Commercial Advertiser* on the one side and the *Graham's Town Journal* on the other, and the two newcomers (the liberal *Cape Frontier Times* and the conservative *Cape Town Mail*) ranged between them. The division in the colonial press on the issues surrounding the Great Trek was merely an extension of the old question of the expanding and conflicting interests of the natives and Europeans, the ensuing contact between the two groups and, of course, the outcome of this contact. The *Graham's Town Journal,* speaking on behalf of those in the eastern districts whom it represented during the 1830's,[48] held the view that the colonists were not responsible for the aggressions of the past as they had acted only in retaliation, claiming that the frontier situation stemmed from the Government who, for reasons of its own, had not fully accepted or honoured its responsibility to keep peace on the frontier. Others, such as the *Commercial Advertiser,* the Secretary of State (Glenelg), the Aborigines Protection Society and the early liberal group of travellers, thought differently and reacted against what was termed the "old system".[49] It will be remembered that in its first years the *Commercial Advertiser* had strongly condemned the relationship between the Whites and Blacks under the Dutch administration which had been "exposed and condemned", it stated in 1836, by the wise and humane action of the British Government; otherwise, had the system continued, it would have become a *"National sin"*.[50]

Perhaps herein lie the roots of the great paradox in South African history. The contact between the Whites and Blacks on a or any frontier has inevitably resulted in the Blackman becoming subjected to the will of the Whiteman – how this came about or whether it is a good or bad state of affairs is not the purpose of this discussion, the

48. It should be noted that the *Cape Frontier Times* was established in 1840 because, as its editor stated on 6 May 1840, the *Graham's Town Journal* could no longer claim to represent all the colonists on the frontier.
49. See *Commercial Advertiser,* 24 Sept. 1836.
50. *Commercial Advertiser,* 24 Sept. 1836.

point is that in such contact the outcome has been universally the same. The obvious and apparently only means of preventing this state of affairs in South Africa was to prevent the initial contact taking place – long advocated by philanthropic bodies such as the Aborigines Protection Society – and the obvious and apparently only way to achieve this was for the government of the day to prevent such contact through a militarised frontier system. Without such preventative measures the inevitable had to occur. The two pastoralist societies, both on the move and seeking room to expand and live, collided; the weaker became subject to the stronger and the victor possessed the disputed lands, the result being that the Blackman became economically dependent upon the Whiteman.

The underlying attitude of the *Graham's Town Journal* towards the Great Trek was a reaction to what it repeatedly termed 'misrepresentation' – a misrepresentation of the colonial character by travellers and missionaries dating back to the days of Barrow[51] and relating specifically to the question of land and the treatment of the aborigines. "Trace the history of this frontier", maintained Godlonton, "and it will be found to be a record of plunderings on the one side, and of feeble public retaliatory measures on the other. The Whites have been charged with a series of encroachments on the aboriginal inhabitants; but certainly there is not a shadow of proof that any encroachment has even been made on the *Kafir* tribes. These, it is proved beyond doubt, have always been pressing forward towards the westward".[52] The Hottentots, it was readily conceded, represented an altogether different case . . . "but as the latter [Hottentots] are now amalgamated with the former [the Whites]", it argued, "as their interests are inseparably blended, – as they enjoy equal laws, have the benefits of the same institutions, live under the protection of the same Government, profess to have the same faith . . . they are made ample amends in those great moral advantages of which they are now the recipients".[53]

The division between Englishmen on what they thought of the interior Afrikaners may be gauged by how they attributed blame for the situation on the frontier. Either the responsibility rested upon the Government for not maintaining peace on the frontier, or upon

51. See *GHT Journal,* 16 Feb. 1837; 15 Feb. 1838.
52. *GHT Journal,* 19 Jan. 1837.
53. *Ibid.*

the frontier colonists who, like the natives beyond the frontier, were seeing to their own interests. The *Graham's Town Journal* maintained that their legitimate interests and rights as citizens of the Empire had been denied as they had been exposed to the incursions of the Xhosas without government protection, yet at the same time they had been prohibited from taking the law into their own hands (as the Afrikaners had done during the Dutch administration), whilst the Xhosas were free to do so as they pleased. As far as the frontiersmen then were concerned the full onus for the frontier problems rested squarely upon the Government. From the other side, the argument was put forward that the state of the frontier was the result of the 'old system' being continued by the colonists who were not prepared to change their way of life (that of land-hungry, semi-nomadic pastoralists) and whose 'state of civilisation' rendered them uncouth, semi-barbaric and in dire need of enlightenment. The native tribes were held to be the injured party and because of the contact which the system on the frontier allowed, the Blackman gradually came to find himself in a subjected position, for this reason the frontier colonists were thought of in the blackest of terms.

As already mentioned, the *Graham's Town Journal's* reply to the accusations brought against the frontier society was "misrepresentation". It sympathised with the Voortrekkers simply because it understood more perfectly what had driven them to leave the Colony; in fact, the *Graham's Town Journal* has been judged to be the Voortrekkers' "official organ".[54] It is also important to remember that because of the accusations brought against the frontier society (especially over the issue of the 5th Frontier War),[55] the English colonists found themselves to be in much the same boat as the Afrikaners. With this in mind, then, the *Graham's Town Journal's* pronouncements on the Great Trek must be regarded as its reaction against the slander levelled at frontier society.

It is important that this be understood and it is also necessary to appreciate that while, as Harington says, a "cordial" relationship existed between the English and Afrikaners within the frontier

---

54. F. A. van Jaarsveld, *Die Tydgenootlike Beoordeling van die Groot Trek, 1836–1842,* p. 5. See also the work of Harington, *The Graham's Town Journal and the Great Trek,* pp. 68–70.
55. Harington in *The Graham's Town Journal and the Great Trek,* p. 42, points out that as a result of the 1835 Frontier War, "Godlonton became less liberal" towards the border tribes.

districts,[56] this amity or harmony should not be over-emphasised as the two groups never really amalgamated. The chief difference between them was clearly pointed to in 1839 when in retrospect the *Graham's Town Journal* explained that while the Afrikaners had felt themselves at liberty to foresake the Colony, the English, because of their closer association with Britain and Empire, had been obliged to accept the "oppressor's wrongs" and console themselves with the fact that while British justice might be "tardy . . . persevere and it will be sure".[57] What the *Graham's Town Journal* therefore set out to show was that the Great Trek was a reaction against the same kind of liberal thinking which had given rise to the misrepresentations of frontier character in the first place, to which both the Afrikaners and English had been subject.

The split which existed in the public mind is well illustrated in the remarks passed upon the Government's conciliatory policy adopted towards the Trekkers in Natal under which Capt. Jervis was despatched to "treat" with them in 1840. The *Commercial Advertiser* was adamant that because the Boers had revolted they should be treated as rebels and nothing else,[58] whereas the *Graham's Town Journal* took quite the opposite view. The Afrikaners were far from being rebels – rather, they were people who had acted in the only way possible under the circumstances and perhaps, it was argued, the British Government had even learned a lesson from the episode. However, the defeat of Smith in 1842 at the hands of the Boers was met with condemnation throughout the colonial press, although the state of affairs surrounding the incident lent itself to more than one interpretation.

The *Graham's Town Journal,* for one, had long been critical of the Government for its handling of colonial affairs, and Natal was simply further evidence of this.[59] "Coercive and violent measures", it had stated in 1840, "may be most injurious, while a conciliatory tone and moderate requirements, may be eminently successful".[60] It was sincerely hoped that some kind of *"agent"* be appointed to negotiate

---

56. Harington, *The Graham's Town Journal and the Great Trek,* p. 126.
57. *GHT Journal,* 30 May 1839.
58. *Commercial Advertiser,* 19 June 1839; 26 June 1839.
59. *GHT Journal,* 4 July 1839. See also, 19 Jan. 1843.
60. See, for instance, *GHT Journal,* 14 Oct. 1841. 16 Dec. 1841; 27 Oct. 1842; 10 Nov. 1842; 12 Jan. 1843.

with the Emigrant Boers.[61] The despatch of troops, therefore, under Capt. Smith was viewed with considerable reserve as it was maintained that what they required was not a military government but the establishment of a civil administration: "If Port Natal is to be made a military station, and nothing more, then the troops had better remain where they are, as every farthing expended in their removal [to Natal] will be a sheer waste of time and of public money."[62] The defeat of Smith, considered the *Graham's Town Journal,* "too fully justifies the opinions entertained at the outset of the folly and imprudence of the whole proceedings relative to that country [Natal]".[63] What was responsible for the "blunder" of Smith in Natal was the "temporising policy" of the Cape executive which had allowed the Natal Boers to imagine that they would ultimately be considered independent by Great Britain; then there was the utter "audacity" of despatching a military force incapable of doing the job of work it had been sent to do – and that its commander should have been a man with no experience whatever with the people with whom he was to deal, and that the detachment had been despatched to Natal by way of the three to four month land route was simply beyond their comprehension. *If* military might had really been necessary then a *"suitable"* force should have been sent, or nothing.[64]

In spite of this state of affairs, the *Graham's Town Journal* pointed out that "we would guard the expatriate colonists from falling into the error of supposing that the blame resting upon the local government is to be carried to the account of sympathy for them".[65] It was the duty of every British subject to "give his best support" to those measures which would rectify the situation in Natal. The *Graham's Town Journal* sympathised with the Natal Afrikaners for their "lamentable mistake" and pointed out that as British subjects they had placed themselves in the situation of rebels and as such were exposed to an "ignominious punishment":

> "They have now by their own rashness *compelled* the British Government to vindicate its authority and avenge the blood

---

61. *GHT Journal,* 14 Oct. 1841.
62. *Ibid.,* 16 Dec. 1841.
63. *Ibid.,* 9 June 1842.
64. *Ibid.,* 9 June 1842; 28 July 1842.
65. *Ibid.,* 9 June 1842.

which has been spilled, and they may depend that it will do both, amply and speedily."[66]

The attitude of the *Commercial Advertiser* was different. It will be remembered that from the start it had viewed the emigrant Afrikaners as rebels,[67] and by the end of 1839 had adopted the view that the main characteristic of or motive behind the Great Trek had been the desire on the part of the Afrikaners to establish an independent state.[68] So intense was this feeling to renounce their allegiance to Great Britain, maintained the *Commercial Advertiser,* that the Emigrants had threatened *"death and massacre to all strangers landing as Emigrants at the Port of Natal without their previous consent"* and that this had been especially directed at British subjects.[69] The despatch of Smith in 1842 to occupy Port Natal – though the *Commercial Advertiser* strongly suspected that "the place is good for nothing" – had been undertaken to "prevent the formation of a community of British subjects, calling themselves independent, and affecting to be irresponsible to their Sovereign for their conduct, particularly towards the natives, with whom they have had several destructive contests".[70] The news of Smith's defeat only served to reinforce the belief that "the Boers had not yet laid aside their enterprise of founding an independent state, or at least an African Commonwealth, in some kind of connection with the Kingdom of Holland".[71] The outcome of the episode was plain to the eye: "British supremacy must be re-established; – this Revolt must be suppressed", though it was allowed that it would take a somewhat larger force than that which had been at the disposal of Capt. Smith.[72]

Before considering the reaction of the *Frontier Times* to the defeat of Smith, a brief investigation into its general attitude towards the Great Trek is called for. To begin with, it had adopted a moderate attitude towards the causes, providing its readers with what it considered were all the possible reasons for it, yet not committing itself to a personal opinion.[73] Generally, its feeling towards the Trek had

---

66. *GHT Journal,* 9 June 1842.
67. Such as *Commercial Advertiser,* 19 June 1839; 26 June 1839.
68. *Commercial Advertiser,* 4 Dec. 1839.
69. *Ibid.,* 14 Dec. 1839.
70. *Ibid.,* 11 June 1842.
71. *Ibid.,* 15 June 1842.
72. *Ibid.* See also, 18 June 1842; 25 June 1842; 2 July 1842.
73. *Frontier Times,* 3 June 1840.

been that the movement (which it considered inevitable) should have been embarked upon under the control of the British Government and for that reason it "claims the prompt attention of those in power".[74] It also fell in with the stand adopted by all the colonial newspapers which totally disallowed the Boers being granted independence at Natal. With the despatch of Smith to Port Natal, the *Frontier Times* provided the following prophetic criticism of the Government's handling of the situation:

> "Should the spirit of insubordination unhappily so far prevail as to produce actual resistance it cannot be sufficiently deplored that the force sent is so feeble."[75]

The reaction to Smith's defeat is therefore no surprise:

> ". . . the force sent is ridiculously inadequate to the occasion; and instead of inspiring those who spurn at British dominion with terror, and by its simple demonstration compelling them to submission, is every way calculated to incite them to acts of aggression with confidence of success. The government must have had singular confidence in the paper pellets by which the detachment was preceded, to suppose that its strength was sufficient for the service on which it was sent."[76]

As for its feelings towards the Afrikaners in their new position as conquerors, the *Frontier Times* was straight-forward:

> "The sword having been drawn, and the British force having suffered defeat, nothing remains but that the Boers should be reduced to subjection, and justice and humanity alike demand that this should be effected with the least possible delay, and with the smallest effusion of blood."[77]

While the defeat of Smith had given rise to a certain amount of anti-Afrikaner feeling among the English colonists resulting, as one correspondent to the *Cape Town Mail* wrote, in "widening the breach between the English and the old Colonists",[78] this same newspaper

---

74. *Frontier Times,* 3 June 1840.
75. *Ibid.,* 17 March 1842.
76. *Ibid.,* 24 March 1842. See also, 9 June 1842; 16 June 1842; 23 June 1842.
77. *Ibid.,* 23 June 1842.
78. *Cape Town Mail,* "Justus", 17 Sept. 1842.

could, in the same month, report that the intense antagonism felt on the part of the English towards the Afrikaners had calmed considerably since the first news of the incident. Nonetheless, the *Graham's Town Journal* in January 1843 considered it necessary to refer to "the estrangement of feeling" which was still apparent in the relationship between the English and Afrikaners and criticised the English in the Colony for the long-standing prejudices harboured against the Afrikaners.[79]

* * *

What added to the anti-Afrikaner feeling in the Colony were the reports received of the actions of the Emigrant Farmers residing beyond the Drakensberg. Towards the end of 1840 the *Frontier Times* carried reports of abuses inflicted upon the natives, particularly the Bushmen, by those Boers who had migrated beyond the Orange River.[80] One report spoke of inhuman actions "worthy of those good old times", natives were being shot with "reckless cruelty", while children were being taken into the service of the farmers and were being transacted "from hand to hand". "This is slavery", cried the *Frontier Times,* "call it by what mitigated terms we may."[81] Taking up this report, the *Commercial Advertiser*[82] stated that it had been precisely this state of affairs that it had earlier warned against: "The time we chose for pointing out the evils that would necessarily flow from this Emigration was — when it was first projected and announced as a separation from British rule".[83] In other words: "we told you so". Filled with righteous indignation that such things could "*really*" be perpetrated on the "very verge" of a British colony, the *Frontier Times,* on referring to the Boers who had "trampled upon the sacred rights of humanity and justice", wrote:

> "Let the faintest indications of reviving this abomination, almost at our hearth, awaken the honest indignation, and the firm negative, of Britons, and the sons of Britons, who, claiming freedom for themselves, would give it to the world!"[84]

---

79. *GHT Journal,* 19 Jan. 1843.
80. *Frontier Times,* 11 Nov. 1840.
81. *Ibid.*
82. Also reported in *GHT Journal,* 19 Nov. 1840.
83. *Commercial Advertiser,* 28 Nov. 1840.
84. *Frontier Times,* 11 Nov. 1840.

What added insult to injury – bearing in mind that it had been Great Britain "in the plenitude of her mercy" who had liberated slaves throughout the Empire and paid compensation to the tune of £20 million – was that the Boers in the interior of South Africa now "dared to insult her humanity and justice, by seizing upon the children of the natives around them, and selling them into slavery amongst themselves".[85] "This", stated the *Frontier Times,* "must excite the aversion and reprobation of every British heart."[86]

While this intensity of feeling was not the mood of the press in general – and certainly not that of the *Graham's Town Journal* and *Cape Town Mail* – the actions of the Afrikaners as a whole in the interior provided strong arguments for extending British control and went a long way to creating the impression in the colonial mind that the Boers beyond the colonial boundary would always require British supervision.

What, then, did the colonial newspapers really think of the Afrikaner Voortrekkers?

In 1838 the *Graham's Town Journal* said that the Afrikaner image was so poor that "the very name of 'Dutch Boer' is the equivalent to a term of reproach".[87]

> "The people in England", it explained, "have heard so much of the oppressive character of the Boers – and, as the result of this, the inhabitants of the Colony, both British and Dutch, have both seen and *felt* the evil effects of that false philanthropy which gives audacity and frequency to crime by unduly interfering in matters but partially known; – thus, by exciting sympathy towards those actually injured, not only has positive injustice been done, but a state of things has arisen, the issue of which is seen in the present disturbed state of this country."[88]

Whatever the motives behind such thinking might have been, the result of philanthropic "meddling" had nonetheless been disastrous.[89] The culprit was the Whig Government (in power since 1830) whose "political tinkering" had been characteristic of its colonial policy: "We have had various changes of official men, – we have had

85. *Frontier Times,* 3 Nov. 1842.
86. *Ibid.,* 19 Jan. 1843.
87. *GHT Journal,* 15 Feb. 1838.
88. *Ibid.,* 5 Jan. 1843.
89. *Ibid.*

numerous alterations but no improvements, while we have seen that best bulwark of a country – its own native yeomanry – either being driven from the frontier by insult or rendered comparatively powerless . . ."[90] As far as the *Graham's Town Journal* was concerned, the Emigrants had taken the only course open to them,[91] and what was so remarkable was that the Afrikaners in Natal had, after their initial difficulties, arrived at an amicable arrangement with the natives.[92]

The faulty policy of the Government towards colonial matters and the incorrect impression held in the British mind of the colonies could be attributed to two factors. In the first place, the actual condition of the natives in South Africa was unknown in Britain;[93] and secondly, a false impression had been gained of the interior graziers of the Colony following the "hasty accounts" of travellers – not least of whom had been John Barrow.[94] "A bad and degrading opinion has been formed . . . but nothing can be more senseless and unjust. They have been termed indolent, avaricious and cruel . . ."[95] "We, however, declare, in the teeth of such calumniations", it later wrote, "that taking the frontier inhabitants as a body, they are not surpassed by any people in the world (we include in this category the inhabitants of the United Kingdom) for hospitality, for benevolence, for good order, and for everything that constitutes a really valuable member of society".[96] The Afrikaners were nothing like the disreputable group of people they were represented to be, maintained the *Graham's Town Journal*. There had been a "libel" on the character of the Afrikaner colonists to term them "a factious, a discontented, or a turbulent people" whereas, in fact, they were quite the reverse of this.[97] In any event, enquired Godlonton, how would the English themselves have reacted had they been in the position of the Boers? "Where is a native of the British Isles", it was asked, "who would not feel thus [as the Afrikaners], or who does not cherish, as amongst his most ardent feelings, a sacred attachment to the land of his birth, to

90. *GHT Journal,* 16 June 1842.
91. *Ibid.,* 4 July 1839.
92. *Ibid.,* 5 Jan. 1843.
93. *Ibid.,* 5 Jan. 1848.
94. *Ibid.,* 21 Nov. 1839.
95. *Ibid.*
96. *Ibid.,* 15 Feb. 1838.
97. *Ibid.,* 19 Jan. 1843.

the [national prejudices and] home of his forefathers?"[98] The Boers in Natal were not as a body averse to British supremacy nor, indeed, as hostile to the natives as others had made them out to be. Besides, the British were hardly the people to level accusations of cruelty against the Afrikaners for had they not themselves exterminated "whole races of natives" at Van Diemens Land and elsewhere?[99]

The settlement of Natal arrived at by Henry Cloete and the despatch of troops under Col. Hare beyond the colonial boundary to quell the Afrikaners in the interior, bring out more of the moderate attitude exercised by the *Graham's Town Journal* towards the Afrikaners, particularly when moved to criticise the Emigrants.

"If the intention", wrote Godlonton of the Lieut. Governor's decision to send troops across the Orange River "be purely belligerent, then, we think, the decision is much to be regretted."[1]

> "Let it be carefully remembered", the *Graham's Town Journal* wrote as Col. Hare was marching with a strong detachment to meet the interior Afrikaners, "that the interior of Southern Africa presents but small temptation to military ambition. There are few laurels to be won there. It is emphatically a *poor* country – a wilderness – and does not hold out the remotest prospect of ever refunding . . . the expenses of a war. Although, therefore, it is the true policy of Great Britain to maintain her supremacy over that territory – it is not her desire nor her interest to do this by the *sword*. *It will not pay* to do so . . . we wish to see this accomplished in such a manner as shall be consonant with reason and justice."[2]

On the other hand, the indecision of the Natal Afrikaners to re-accept their allegiance to the British Government as offered by Commissioner Cloete "cannot do otherwise than cause deep regret as well as excite warm indignation in every one who can appreciate unexampled generosity".[3] More of this attitude towards the Afrikaners is clearly shown in this newspaper's reaction to the conduct of the Boers in the interior. The *Graham's Town Journal* could hardly credit the reports received that the Boers residing on the Orange River and

98. *GHT Journal,* 19 Jan. 1843.
99. *Ibid.,* 16 March 1843, under the heading "The Character of the Cape-Dutch Emigrants, at Natal".
1. *Ibid.,* 12 Jan. 1843.
2. *Ibid.*
3. *Ibid.,* 13 July 1843.

beyond were parcelling out lands irrespective of native claims and that an immediate attack was said to be planned upon the native tribes living on the Caledon River.[4] While it conceded that it could understand how "ignorant men" could be tempted to try "their luck" in defying the British Government, it cautioned them against going too far and rebelling.[5] Reports received a week later, which included accounts of the Boers abusing missionaries in the Bechuana country, induced the *Graham's Town Journal* to adopt a somewhat stiffer tone:

> "The Boers, it would seem, who have taken possession of that [Orange River] territory, are determined not to be a whit behind their fellow compatriots at Natal – and hence have proceeded to parcel out and appropriate the lands among themselves, to declare their independence and to hurl defiance at the British government."[6]

British prestige was at stake and clearly things had got out of hand and it was therefore necessary "to crush this spirit of rebellion".[7] In view of this, the action taken by Judge Menzies beyond the colonial boundary was welcomed inasmuch as it was a step in the right direction, and while he might have departed from custom, it was at least a positive step.[8] "We agree that he acted entirely from patriotic motives, and from an anxious desire to anticipate and thus prevent a threatened evil."[9]

The annexation of Natal was a "wise and human measure";[10] however, the matter was not to rest there:

> ". . . it is not sufficient", stated the *Graham's Town Journal,* "to proclaim Natal British territory and under the operation of British Law – but the *whole* of South Africa must come within the same circle and be subject to the same interdicts. There must be no imaginary boundaries beyond which the emigrants may step, and there defy with impunity the British power – the whole must be appended to the British dominions – the British Crown

---

4. *GHT Journal,* 20 Oct. 1842.
5. *Ibid.*
6. *Ibid.,* 27 Oct. 1842; 1 Dec. 1842.
7. *Ibid.,* 27 Oct. 1842.
8. *Ibid.*
9. *Ibid.,* 10 Nov. 1842.
10. *Ibid.,* 14 Dec. 1843.

must be declared as the conservator of the peace in this section of Africa; and the emigrants must be convinced it is not in their power, by falling a little further back, to get beyond the limits of British jurisdiction. Humanity alike to the Emigrants and to the natives demands that this measure should be adopted."[11]

Owing to the fact that the Cape Town based *Commercial Advertiser* did not share the same relationship with the frontier Afrikaners as the *Graham's Town Journal*, and as it recognised no grounds for defending them, it is clear that it would not have quite so much to say about them for, to its way of thinking, all that needed to be said of the frontier society had already been written down by the travellers. It will, in fact, be recalled how in 1834, on discussing the demerits of the frontier "system", the *Commercial Advertiser* had accepted as fact the statements the travellers had made respecting the 'system', asserting that to ignore their findings was "to deny the value of all human testimony".[12] As far as the *Commercial Advertiser* was concerned there had been *no* misrepresentation of the Afrikaner colonists on the frontier — had it not warned that the Great Trek, unless stopped, would lead to the further abuse of the natives, which abuse now filled the columns of the colonial press?

Unfortunately, because of a greater interest shown by this newspaper in matters such as immigration, the *Commercial Advertiser* was not all that interested in the fate or fortunes of the Voortrekkers and therefore did not take the trouble to describe them as did the *Graham's Town Journal*. What this newspaper then thought of the Afrikaners must be gleaned from its reaction to events in which the Afrikaners were involved.

As can be expected, the *Commercial Advertiser* viewed the actions of the Afrikaners in the interior with exceeding disquiet. Their determination under Mocke to cast off their allegiance to the British Government, together with reports received of further ill-treatment of the natives,[13] confirmed its worst fears and could but lead to one course of action — British intervention.[14] Its attitude towards the step taken by Judge Menzies is interesting, for it felt that in view of the fact that the Government would not follow up his action, the natives

11. *GHT Journal,* 7 Sept. 1843. See also, 22 Feb. 1844; 25 April 1844.
12. *Commercial Advertiser,* 14 June 1834.
13. *Ibid.,* 10 Dec. 1842; 17 Dec. 1842.
14. *Ibid.,* 26 Nov. 1842.

could easily misconstrue the situation and assume that the Boers and the British Government were working hand in hand towards their overthrow.[15] The attitude of the *Commercial Advertiser* to the despatch of troops under Col. Hare is almost predictable. It was convinced that the troops, then on their way to Colesberg, would not permit the Boers to get off scot-free.[16] Indeed, they were convinced that Col. Hare would *"do his duty"* and, what is more, "from the whole of his conduct, and from the tone of his language, we also infer that he knows what that duty is . . . *'strangle'* rebellion"![17]

The feeling of the *Commercial Advertiser* towards the Afrikaners cannot be better nor more clearly illustrated than by quoting at length what must be, in terms of this topic, by far its most significant editorial. Appearing in the edition of 10 May 1843, it reads:

> "The motives of . . . [Natal's] founders, even granting that they rose from mistakes or ignorance, were substantially the same as those which carried the Pilgrim Fathers to Boston, namely, a desire to escape from the restraining power of a Government acting on principles which they did not understand, or did not approve of; and a wish to live under some form of Rule more agreeable to their peculiar notions of Liberty.
>
> The Pilgrim Fathers were not enlightened men. They did not leave an intolerant government because they hated Intolerance. They abandoned their native land because they were in a minority on a question as to what opinions should be maintained, and what opinions [were] restrained or punished by government, not on a question as to whether Toleration or Liberty of Conscience, were among the rights which mankind retain in all conditions or stages of society. They agreed with their antagonists in the doctrine, that the heretic should be smitten with the sword. They only differed with them as to what was heresy . . .
>
> In the same manner the Frontier Boers, who lately left the Colony for Natal, felt that they were restrained in the treatment of their households, by certain new laws and ordinances relative to the natives, and that their poverty in, as well as their power over their Slaves, were dealt with in a way they could not but disapprove of. Some, it is said many, of them also really believed that their *Religion* was about to be meddled with by the British Government, not to mention some assertions still more wild and monstrous, with which designing men contrived to alarm the minds of these simple people.

15. *Commercial Advertiser,* 26 Nov. 1842.
16. *Ibid.,* 7 Jan. 1843.
17. *Ibid.,* 28 Jan. 1843.

Thus the characters of the two migrations coincide to a greater extent than would at first sight be thought probable. Both fled from Restraint in matters where they thought they should have their hands free; and both sought what they called Liberty, but which they understood to be Independence or rather Power.

In a rude state the human mind does not generalize like modern Philosophers. It delights in *privileges* or *special* distinctions. For instance, the good people of England two hundred and fifty years ago, would not say *'Every man'* has a right to be judged by his peers or equals, or only to be taxed by his representatives; they would say *'We'* or *'Every Englishman'*. It was the same with regard to higher things. They did not say *'Every man* has a right to worship God according to his own conscience.' They confined this right entirely to the People of God, to those whose consciences were enlightened, in short, to themselves. They said, *'We* have this right, and will die for it.' But they also said 'Those who worship in a different manner should be restrained even to bonds, imprisonment, or in extreme cases, to the shedding of blood.'

It is thus, by the illustrations of contemporaneous events, that the pride of ancient history is brought down to its proper human level. The Boer's conduct is condemned because the whole of his case is seen, and chiefly, the bad parts of it. The Pilgrim Father is extolled because the bad parts of his case disappear in the distance of time and place, and a falsely-favourable meaning is given to his words.

The truth which results from a severe analysis in both cases is, – that the Pilgrim Father and the Boer were moved to abandon their country for various reasons, some good some bad, but chiefly because (to use a vulgar phrase from the land of the Pilgrims,) they were restrained in the *Liberty of walloping their own niggers*."[18]

As already shown, the reaction of the *Frontier Times* to the reported aggressive tactics of the Afrikaners in the interior was one of outrage and indignation. The lawless state of the interior, the abuse of the natives, and the defiance of the Boers, together with the fact that the Boers had cast off their allegiance to the British Government, drew the retort that the "spark of sedition" should be extinguished, and the "rebellion put down for ever".[19] It was along these lines that the *Frontier Times* set forth its feelings. Unfortunately, like the *Commercial Advertiser,* during this period, this newspaper did not find it

---

18. *Commercial Advertiser,* 10 May 1843.
19. *Frontier Times,* 1 Dec. 1842.

necessary to set down its opinions on the Afrikaners in so many words, and because of this, detailed descriptions of the Afrikaners do not appear. The *Frontier Times* said little regarding the despatch of troops under Col. Hare, but what it did say was perfectly to the point:

> "Treason, instead of limiting itself to the Natal territory, has spread like wildfire from thence to Colesberg, and compels the assumption of a military attitude which only the urgency of the case could justify. But the case *is* urgent and requires all the wisdom and energy which the strongest minds can put forth, to avert consequences from which the mind shrinks with dismay."[20]

From the foregoing study of the Cape press it can be concluded that, disregarding party views, the colonial English in *general* were apprehensive about the character of the Afrikaners as manifested by the Great Trek. The conduct of the Afrikaners towards the Blackman (especially in the interior) had brought the Cape English to the conclusion that British control of Southern Africa was imperative – without such control bloodshed and bondage would be the fate of the Blackman. The Great Trek had also established in the minds of the English that a certain section of the Emigrants would be satisfied with nothing less than independence. But underlying all English opinion of the Emigrants was the view that the Great Trek was the result of ignorance – a strange mentality which had preferred the hazards of the unknown to the benefits of an established colony.

The initial reaction of the *Commercial Advertiser,* it will be remembered, was that it doubted whether "a change of scenery will improve the prospects of the Emigrants" and while there were undoubtedly faults within the colonial administration, they were hardly to be solved or "evaded by pushing farther into the interior of Africa".[21] The *Graham's Town Journal,* on referring to the identical hardships which the English and Afrikaners had had to face on the frontier, enquired why it had been that the English had not joined "this extravagant enterprise". Answering its own question it maintained that the reason for this was the "better acquaintance" of the English "with passing events":[22]

---

20. *Frontier Times,* 8 Dec. 1842.
21. *Commercial Advertiser,* 4 May 1836. *Vide supra,* p. 155.
22. *GHT Journal,* 23 Aug. 1838.

". . . can anyone for the moment suppose that if education had been more general", wrote Godlonton, "the emigration mania would have spread to the fearful extent it has done? By no means. Had the people been better informed, instead of flying from the country, they would have sought redress of their grievances by all those means which they are armed by the constitution of that empire to which they belong; nor would they have ceased the use of them till they had fully obtained it.

What has kept the British [English] residents in this province from joining this extravagant enterprise? It is their better acquaintance with passing events. The light which has been reflected, through various mediums, by an independent PRESS in their midst, diffusing intelligence amongst all classes, has indicated clearly their true position in the social system, as well as the proper remedy for the existing grievances. Like a chart to the tempest-tossed mariner, which warns him of the rocks and shoals and currents, education, and the ready means of information, have enabled the British [English] inhabitants to avoid these errors into which others less favourably circumstanced have fallen, and have led them to pursue that course which is befitting the character of those who are members of the British Empire, and who, as such, possess the rights and privileges, which cannot be set at naught and trampled on with impunity."[23]

As far as the *Frontier Times* was concerned, the general lack of education among the frontier Boers – "the profound and rayless ignorance which broods over them", or "the gloom of intellectual night in which a large portion of this class of our fellow colonists is involved" – was largely responsible for the events which had led to the situation in Natal.[24] Herein, no doubt, lies the reason why all sections of the colonial press ridiculed the Afrikaners' mentality for imagining, for instance, that Great Britain would *ever* permit them to establish an independent Afrikaner state. Of course, this is not meant to imply that the English thought of the Afrikaners as outright fools – it was just something in their make-up and something which distinguished them from the English. It would seem, however, that "ignorance" was equated by the English to whether a person was prepared to submit himself to British rule or not. Hence the *Graham's Town Journal's* description of the majority of the Afrikaners who left

23. *GHT Journal,* 23 Aug. 1838.
24. *Frontier Times,* 20 Oct. 1842.

Natal and migrated beyond the Orange River as "ignorant men"[25] – a view endorsed by Henry Cloete, H.M. Commissioner to Natal, who spoke of the *bulk* of the Natal Emigrants as being a most "respectable" group of men, but referred to the fringe of die-hards who chose rather to live in the wilds of Africa than under British rule, as a group which would be no loss at all to the infant Natal.[26]

When considering the reaction of the British press to the Great Trek, it is necessary to realise that although the press had shown greater interest in South Africa during 1835/36 than in the past – as the reception received by Moodie's and Pringle's works attest – there still remained a section of the press which did not regard the affairs of the Cape Colony as justifying coverage and therefore many of the most prominent newspapers of the day such as *The Observer* and *Manchester Guardian* did not mention the Great Trek even in passing.

Of course, as Britain launched into the 1840's philanthropists were still attempting to influence the Secretary of State and humanitarianism still had its place in British politics, but the British press was beginning to show a swing away from philanthropy in colonial matters. Although *The Atlas* adopted an attitude of condemnation towards the Boers because of the "butcheries committed on the Zoolas",[27] and looked forward to the time when the British flag would be hoisted at Port Natal when, amongst other advantages, it would afford "equally to the White man and the Black, the blessing of British freedom and the security of British law",[28] such feelings were not typical. Rather, the consensus of opinion was that the entire episode of the Great Trek was a pitiful example of bad government – both home and colonial.[29] The remarks of *The Spectator* were straightforward:

> "It would appear . . . that these men disliked and despised the English, and their rule. They complained of the abolition of slavery, which deprived them of the work of their labourers, and exposed them to their depredations; they alleged they were

25. *GHT Journal,* 20 Oct. 1842.
26. S.G.O. II/I, Cloete to Montagu, July 1843, ff. 32–33.
27. *The Atlas,* 26 June 1841.
28. *Ibid.,* 2 July 1842.
29. *The Spectator,* 2 March 1839; 17 Sept. 1842; 24 Sept. 1842; 29 Oct. 1842. *The Times,* 18 Jan. 1839; 25 Aug. 1842; 12 Sept. 1842. *The Colonial Gazette,* 19 Jan. 1839; 4 May 1839; 18 Sept. 1839.

left without protection against the Caffre incursions, and were crippled in defending themselves; they were also troubled by some other grievances; and to make short of it, nearly two thousand fighting men with their families and properties emigrated from the colony . . . whose fate, whether they have been foolish or not, is another example of the misgovernment of the Colonial Office."[30]

The Times, too, left no doubt as to where its sympathies lay and particularly condemned the steps taken by the Colonial Government to prohibit the shipment of all supplies to the distressed emigrants of Port Natal as "unnecessarily harsh" since although the proclamation was primarily aimed at cutting the supplies of gunpowder "to prevent them from carrying on war against the Zollas, by whom they had been so ferociously assailed", it also deprived the Emigrants of such essentials as food, clothing and agricultural utensils.[31] Referring to the causes of the Great Trek, the *Colonial Gazette* sharply criticised the Aborogines Protection Society for attempting to make the British public believe that the "extraordinary emigration" had originated in a disaffection to the British Government stemming from the emancipation of slaves.[32] Besides describing the frontier colonists as "industrious and peaceable white inhabitants"[33] and reporting that the Rev. Lindley had spoken of the Boers in Natal in terms of "piety, industry and good feeling – of forebearance towards the Zoolas",[34] the *Colonial Gazette* referred to the opinions expressed by Capt. Stockenström who, although known in the past to have shown up his countrymen in an unfavourable light, had "been constrained to admit that the Dutch inhabitants of this colony are not by any means a factious people; that they are easily governed – and hence the fair inference is, that they possess the germ of those principles which only require a congenial soil, and a fostering hand to shoot up to vigorous maturity and to produce a rich and abundant harvest".[35]

"Strange then", judged its editor, "that the Government should still cherish their erroneous notions – should still cling to their darling [philanthropic] prejudices; and that, notwithstanding all

30. *The Spectator,* 2 March 1839.
31. *The Times,* 18 Jan. 1839.
32. *Colonial Gazette,* 19 Jan. 1839.
33. *Ibid.,* 15 Dec. 1838.
34. *Ibid.,* 18 Dec. 1839.
35. *Ibid.,* 19 Jan. 1839.

that has been said, and all the light which has been thrown upon the subject, the Under Secretary for the Colonies should put forth before the British Parliament the hackneyed sentiment, that the unsettled state of this district was 'owing, in a great degree, to the aggressions of British subjects upon the Aboriginal inhabitants, and their endeavours to extend their territory in this quarter, for selfish and interested purposes'. Why, there never was made a more unjust misrepresentation than this . . ."[36]

Smith's defeat at the hands of the Afrikaners at Natal – "the little war in which Great Britain has become engaged without knowing it"[37] – drew sharp reaction from the press. The pro-philanthropic *Atlas* cried that "the words *'defeat of British troops'* sound harshly to our ears" and called for positive corrective action,[38] whereas *The Times* sought an explanation of the "unfortunate affair, which is now becoming really serious", in the factors which had caused the Boers to emigrate in the first place.[39] "The origin of the affair", it reported, "was the departure of several of the emigrants . . . in consequence of the imperfect protection offered by the Colonial Government against the incursions of the Kafirs",[40] and the fact that such a small force had been despatched to Port Natal and then by way of the tedious overland route, showed that "altogether, the greatest blame appears to attach to the temporising and irresolute policy adopted by the late Cape Government".[41] All-in-all, criticism was directed against those in the seat of government for having been lax when the Afrikaner emigration had first commenced and also for the "fast-and-loose" policy pursued which had permitted the Boers to set up a government of their own.[42]

Two letters to *The Times* during 1842 expressed the growing exasperation felt by at least one section of the public towards the Government's handling of the situation in Natal. The first correspondent wrote: "Lord Glenelg wrote an admirable paper upon the occasion. Sir Benjamin [D'Urban] was disgraced and 7,000 men, the best of the colony, in despair, departed into the wilderness in

---

36. *Colonial Gazette,* 19 Jan. 1839.
37. *The Spectator,* 27 Aug. 1842.
38. *The Atlas,* 27 Aug. 1842.
39. *The Times,* 25 Aug. 1842.
40. *Ibid.*
41. *Ibid.* See also, *The Spectator,* 17 Sept. 1842.
42. *The Spectator,* 17 Sept. 1842.

disgust";[43] while the other said: "The beneficial results arising to the colony from his Excellency the Governor's recent measures will be a debt of not less than £100,000 incurred by the two military expeditions, a feeling of mistrust and ill-will between the English and Dutch settlers deeply injurious to their political and social interests, and not improbably another Caffre war!"[44]

After 1836/37, the influence of the philanthropists began its downward course thus making possible the rise of a more moderate picture of the Afrikaners such as had been expressed by the colonial authorities during 1815–1828, immediately prior to the commencement of the philanthropic agitation against the colonial character when the writings of Moodie in particular had found their mark. Early indications of the 'new era' in public opinion can be found in the works of Donald Moodie[45] and William Boyce[46] published in the late 1830's. Actually, during the period 1828–1836, certain of the philanthropists, and even the *Commercial Advertiser*,[47] on writing about the conditions within the Colony, had indicated that the Afrikaners, when viewed as *individuals* and not in a political sense, were really quite fine fellows. Pringle had been of the opinion that the Boers had shown them, the Settlers, a kindness which could hardly have been expected, as did Phillips, Rose, Thompson and others, while in 1830 Bannister, a staunch philanthropist, had gone to lengths to show that Barrow's original general judgment had been ill-founded and that, indeed, the findings of the Commissioners of Enquiry had "not [been] unfavourable to the general colonial character".[48] In 1836, Fawcett, also a philanthropist — "a friend of Dr. Philip" — had spoken of the Afri-

43. *The Times*, "C", 12 Sept. 1842.
44. *Ibid.*, "Sentinel", 29 Sept. 1842.
45. *The Record; or a series of official papers relative to the Condition and Treatment of the Native Tribes of South Africa.* Moodie was commissioned by the Cape Government to compile a record of the dealings the colonists had had with the aborigines since their first contact to counter the defamation brought against the colonial character by the Aborigines Committee.
46. *Notes on South Africa Affairs from 1834 to 1838.* Boyce, a Wesleyan missionary, refuted that the responsibility for the 1835 Frontier War rested on the colonists.
47. *Vide supra*, p. 144.
48. Bannister, *Humane Policy*, p. 187.

kaners as "these kind simple folks".[49] What, then, accounts for the hostility during the years 1828–1834/36 was that the Afrikaners had been judged on their 'politics' by philanthropists and a liberal biased British public. In future the Afrikaners would be evaluated less critically, with the viewpoints of the *Graham's Town Journal* becoming more widespread.

---

49. Fawcett, *An Account of Eighteen Months' Residence at the Cape of Good Hope, 1835–1836,* p. 20.

CHAPTER NINE

Winds of Change
1844–1854

> "What are the Caffres to us, or we to the Caffres? What have the peaceful inhabitants of the British Isles to do with the barbarous nomads of the inland districts of the great African promontory? What end of religion, of morality, of commerce, or of ambition is served by this remote and ignominious conflict? How is our national power consolidated, or commerce protected, or our welfare in any shape promoted, by a war costing us . . . nearly a million and a half a year, and denuding these shores at a time when the menacing state of the continent barely affords us security from day to day of 15 fine regiments, the *elite* and the flower of our troops?"[1]

The reluctant annexation of Natal in 1843, the treaties with the Griquas and Moshesh, and the military demonstrations beyond the frontier, all of which were to culminate in the annexation of the territory between the Orange and Vaal Rivers in February 1848, were but successive attempts to cope with new developments, and it would not be until 1852/54 that the British Government would emerge for the first time with an unambiguous attitude towards South African affairs – an attitude which showed the complete acceptance of the Great Trek and its result.[2]

---

1. *The Times,* 22 Jan. 1852. The war referred to was the lengthy Eighth Frontier War, 1850–1853.
2. *C.H.B.E.,* viii, p. 400. In considering the period of transition in British opinion regarding the Afrikaners which shifted from being motivated by philanthropic considerations to political withdrawal from the interior of South Africa, it should be borne in mind that until 1842 official concern had been directed towards Natal, while Transorangia was left to take care of itself; after the annexation of Natal in 1843 the situation was reversed and British interest was turned to the interior. Because of this and the fact

Under these circumstances, those factors which in the past had provided the basis whereupon Englishmen had formed their opinion of the Afrikaners[3] would, during the years 1844–1854, come to be considered from a rather different viewpoint. First was the question of the political aspirations of the Afrikaners. With the prospect of further costly involvement in the shaky Orange River Sovereignty (not to mention the situation beyond the Vaal) Britain reaffirmed its policy of withdrawal from the interior regions of South Africa, thus promising greater freedom to the political aspirations of the extra-Cape and Natal Afrikaners and by 1854 events had so unfolded as to witness the creation of two Afrikaner republics – the Transvaal Republic (1852) and the Orange Free State (1854). In keeping with the mood of the day and as a result of the heavy expenditure incurred during the 8th Frontier War in British Kaffraria, public feeling in Britain demanded that the Cape Colony be responsible and pay for its own internal affairs[4] and so the Cape Colony was granted its long sought after representative government in 1854.

The second factor was the Afrikaners' relationship with the Blackman. With the gradual but certain demise of the philanthropic sentiment in British policy-making (as the above remarks of *The Times* in 1852 certainly attest), Great Britain came to regard the Blackman in an entirely new light. By 1854 general public opinion and official policy towards the natives of South Africa had changed to such a marked extent that the Afrikaner attitude and dealings with the natives were no longer real points of contention – certainly Englishmen were not prepared to allow philanthropic considerations to dictate official policy.

The British attitude to the third factor, that of the relationship between the English and Afrikaners within the Colony, also found itself changing, particularly as a result of the Anti-Convict Agitation which commenced during the second half of the 1840's when colonists,

---

that by 1848/49 the majority of the Natal Voortrekkers were fast abandoning Natal for the interior regions, Natal drifts into insignificance until the second half of the century as far as English opinion of the Afrikaners is concerned.

3. *Vide supra*, p. 3.
4. *C.H.B.E.*, viii, p. 4; See also, *Hansard*, 3rd Series, XCIX, 29 May 1848, cols. 249–250; 3rd Series, CXIV, 6 March 1851, col. 1093; 3rd Series, XCIV, 10 March 1851, cols. 1167–1173; 3rd Series, CXVIII, 15 July 1851, cols. 694–778; 3rd Series, XCIX, 5, 6, 13, 19 Feb. 1852, cols. 174, 187, 476, 746. *Vide infra* for the remarks passed by the British press.

both English and Afrikaners, were drawn together in a common cause to fight against the deportation of convicts to South Africa. Such was their oneness over this issue that people within the Colony even spoke of "colonial unity".[5] This improved state of affairs went far to remove the barriers which had separated the two groups in the past and definitely had bearing upon how the colonial English regarded the Afrikaners in their daily contact with them.

Owing to the fact that the British attitude towards the political aspirations of the Afrikaners is so closely bound to what the English thought of the Afrikaners' relationship with the Blackman, these two aspects may be discussed together. The rise of the more real and pragmatic considerations and the accompanying change in British heart towards the interior Afrikaners was a gradual process starting round about 1844. While the appointment of Maitland as Governor (1844–1847) was some indication that the British Government was veering away from its former philanthropy, still official policy, was as willy-nilly as ever and in essence hardly differed from that of the past. In fact it was only with the appointment of Sir Harry Smith in late 1847 as Governor and High Commissioner that strong elements of the future trends in British thinking towards South Africa really came to the fore. Stanley, the Secretary of State (1841–1845), had declared that British policy regarding the Great Trek was to encourage the Trekkers to return to the Colony, otherwise communications with them would be severed, and if the Trekkers attacked the tribes, the tribes would be protected and their assailants treated as rebels[6] – or, as the Colonial Office plainly worded it: "What is really important is not to prevent these Emigrants from leaving the colony . . . but enabling the natives to resist them."[7] Maitland's attitude was typical of the old school. His aim was to frame such measures in the "existing entanglement" between the Griquas, the Basutos and the Boers "as will tend permanently to secure the Native tribes against aggression from the Emigrant Farmers"[8] and while he was aware that scarcely a tribe in all Transorangia occupied its "own hereditary soil", the "peculiar character" of the Emigrant Farmers only complicated the issue further:

5. A. F. Hattersley, *Convict Crisis and the Growth of Unity,* pp. 80–92.
6. Walker, *A History of South Africa,* pp. 224–225.
7. C.O. 48/276, Pottinger to Grey, 2 Nov. 1847, comment by Merwaite, f. 272.
8. C.O. 48/255, Maitland to Stanley, 13 May 1845, f. 6. See also, C.O. 48/255, Maitland to Stanley, 1 Aug. 1845, f. 266.

"... their independent and migratory habits, their impatience at restraint, their disaffection towards the British Government from which they were so removed, their readiness to plunge deeper into the interior to escape the least pressure of an external power upon them, and their contempt of the natives, their indifference to native rights and native life, rendered them difficult to be blended satisfactorily into any scheme for restraining their tendency to commit outrage, and for maintaining the native population in enjoyment of its just rights."[9]

A strong consideration in the outlook adopted by Britain at that time was that the emigrant Afrikaners were taking possession of lands to which they had "not a shadow of a claim".[10] However, while such sentiments were to crop up throughout the remainder of the century when British officials discussed the Afrikaners,[11] the attitude of Sir Harry Smith[12] respecting the natives is more indicative of the line of thinking which came to hold sway in the minds of the British during the 1850's.

"I freely and candidly admit," he wrote to Grey in 1851, "that my opinions as to the Civilisation and conversion to Christianity of the Natives Tribes has undergone a complete change. The treacherous conduct of the Kaffirs staggered me as to the correctness of my previous views. Still more so the Revolt of the Hottentot Race after the treatment they had received from this Government, under which they possessed every Right and Privilege of the most favoured Citizen, and owing to whose care they were provided with Seminaries, Schoolmasters and Ministers. The fact that these men quote the Holy Scriptures as the authority under which they aim at the destruction of their former protectors, proves that curly headed man of colour is not to be abruptly reclaimed from his savage nature and propensities. Such a change in his character can only be affected after many

9. C.O. 48/255, Maitland to Stanley, 1 Aug. 1845, ff. 266–267.
10. C.O. 48/276, Pottinger to Grey, 2 Nov. 1847, comment by Merwaite, f. 272. See also, C.O. 48/255, Maitland to Stanley, 13 May 1845, ff. 4–6.
11. Such as, C.O. 48/307, Smith to Grey, 18 Sept. 1850, comment by Grey, f. 295.
12. A vigorous man, Smith had within a few months of his assuming office in South Africa annexed the Ceded Territory and British Kaffraria on the eastern frontier and bullied the natives into accepting the Queen's authority over them. He then turned his attention to Transorangia where he found the usual friction between the Emigrants and Griquas, the ripples of which were also affecting the Basuto borderlands. He bullied Adam Kok into abandoning his jurisdiction over the Griquas outside his inalienable reserve and attemped to do the same with Moshesh.

years and successive generations. He must in the meantime be held in complete subjection by the irresistible power of the sword, while his children are brought gradually to understand the duties of social life and to entertain a love for their neighbour be he black or white . . ."[13]

With such an attitude (dovetailing ideally into what both colonial Englishmen and Afrikaners were thinking) it is not at all remarkable that Harry Smith was well liked by the colonists as a whole. Almost immediately upon his arrival at the end of 1847 he set about showing the Emigrants the confidence which he placed in their "possession of personal attachment".[14] He was in some respects a paternal figure and he spoke of the Boers as "his children".[15] To him the Emigrants represented a "deluded" body of men[16] and the state of affairs in the interior represented to Smith by many of the Voortrekkers only further convinced him of the necessity to annex the territory which was to become the Orange River Sovereignty:[17]

"Look around you, Sir," he was told, "we are under no authority, no Government; you see the Barbarian provided with Ministers and Teachers of the Gospel, Schools . . . while we, in consequence of our own voluntary expatriation, cannot even marry or bury the dead, and must eventually fall back to savage life — we cannot return to the colony — our property there is sold, and our means here are nearly exhausted by the expenses which attended our emigration — our hopes rest entirely upon your measures."[18]

Be this as it may, all was not plain sailing in his dealings with the interior Afrikaners and Smith spoke of the body of men "who style themselves most unworthily Patriots" and who, "ruined in circumstances and blackened in heart, have endeavoured to excite . . . a restless and unhappy People".[19] With conditions being as unsettled as they were in the interior, if Smith was at all to unite the Emigrants under the British flag it was above all necessary to establish British

13. C.O. 48/319, Smith to Grey, 7 Nov. 1851, ff. 86–87.
14. C.O. 48/283, Smith to Grey, 3 Jan. 1848, f. 151.
15. G.C. Moore Smith (ed.), *The Autobiography of Lieut.-General Sir Harry Smith*, ii, p. 236.
16. C.O. 48/283, Smith to Grey, 3 Jan. 1848, ff. 153–155.
17. *C.H.B.E.*, viii, p. 345.
18. C.O. 48/283, Smith to Grey, 3 Jan. 1848, f. 155.
19. C.O. 48/284, Smith to Grey, 30 March 1848, ff. 488–489.

ascendancy over such opponents as Pretorius (referred to by Smith as "a shrewd fellow"[20] and an "arch agitator" who was bent on furthering "mutual distrust" in the "already divided society"[21]) which, in fact, he accomplished when he confronted the Boers under Pretorius in August 1848 at Boomplaats. The Boers were defeated and British supremacy was extended to the Vaal.

One year later, after the creation of the Sovereignty, Smith had the following to say about the situation in the territory between the Orange and Vaal:

> "It must not be expected that perfect cordiality can at once be established among men who have for so many years led so unsettled a life as these Emigrant Farmers — men moreover of strong prejudices — most credulous in all respects, especially where the Government is concerned — jealous to a degree of what they regard their rights — constantly at variance with one another — and evincing the want of mutual confidence, which I hope will be speedily removed by the measures in progress, aided by the Ministers of the Gospel and the Churches now actually in course of erection. Distrust will, I feel convinced, soon give place to that feeling of Religion, Piety, and Morality, which the social compact demands. The character of the Dutch Farmer is peculiar; he is kind and hospitable, affectionate and grateful for kindness when really convinced of its sincerity; inclined to be very religious, and entertaining the highest respect for the Ministers of his Church . . ."[22]

Progress and improvement became more marked as time went by and later in the same year Smith was able to report:

> "The Dutch Farmers are settling down most amicably; and readily pay their Quit Rents, when the Surveyors Certificates of their Farms are delivered to them. Churches and Schools are established, or in process of erection, at the seats of the different magistracies. There is already a Clergyman at the DR Church at Bloemfontein; and I daily expect two Ministers from Holland, whose passages I have paid, for the express purpose of proceeding to this territory. The Council has assembled for the first time at Bloemfontein — its proceedings were very satisfactory — and the unofficial members evinced much gratification.

20. C.O. 48/287, Smith to Grey, 10 Aug. 1848, f. 5.
21. C.O. 48/286, Smith to Grey, 26 July 1848, ff. 49–50.
22. C.O. 48/295, Smith to Grey, 26 March 1849, ff. 118–119.
23. C.O. 48/298, Smith to Grey, 21 Aug. 1849, ff. 54–55.

So rapid has been this increase of Bloemfontein, that it was proposed that a municipality should be granted to it."[23]

In August 1849 Smith was able to say that even beyond the Vaal the Boers were "perfectly quiet" and many of those who had fled across the Vaal as a result of the Boomplaats episode were returning to the Sovereignty.[24] Yet, "this man Pretorius" remained a problem: "[he] is a most determined agitator; and notwithstanding the hold which we now possess over the Sovereignty by means of a strong, well garrisoned, and well provisioned fortress, serving to check the evil disposed, and to form a rallying point for the loyal, White as well as Native, this unsettled and Proscribed rebel will lose no opportunity to excite the discontented and stir up dissention".[25]

In 1851 Grey had indicated that the main reason for the Sovereignty having been annexed in 1848 was that Smith had maintained that only annexation would prevent "disorder and bloodshed"; [26] nonetheless the subsequent clashes between the Emigrants and natives showed that despite British involvement the peace and security of the interior had not been secured and, in fact, as Walker has put it, the "British Government had had enough of it".[27]

The arrival of the commissioners Hogge and Owen to investigate the state of the Sovereignty during late 1851 was a clear indication that Great Britain was seeking to extricate herself from the turbulent state of affairs in the interior of South Africa and it could therefore be anticipated that a change in the British attitude towards the interior Afrikaners was imminent. First of all, the earlier hard-line attitude adopted by Harry Smith towards the "proscribed rebel", Pretorius, and his followers – followed through in his victory over the Boers at Boomplaats – would need to be reassessed since the success of Hogge and Owen's mission was largely dependent upon the neutrality of the trans-Vaal Afrikaners.[28] What particularly acted to modify official opinion in this direction, was the pressure brought to bear upon the Secretary of State by a certain individual, J. S.

---

24. C.O. 48/298, Smith to Grey, 21 Aug. 1849, ff. 57–58.
25. C.O. 48/305, Smith to Grey, 15 March 1850, f. 4.
26. G.H. 1/44, Grey to Smith, 15 Sept. 1851.
27. Walker, *A History of South Africa,* p. 265.
28. C. J. Uys, *In the Era of Shepstone,* p. 32.

Christopher, of Natal.[29] What Christopher did was to impress upon the Colonial Office the extent to which the English were indebted to Pretorius for their peace and safety. "Dare you move against the English", Pretorius is purported to have warned both Panda and Moshesh, "and I will sweep you from the face of the earth."[30] Christopher continued:

> "Pretorius may thus be said to have saved us and yet he remains a proscribed man . . . Did you, Sir, know the Dutchman, know his vigor, his endurance, his prowess and his aim . . . you would I am convinced, feel the importance of having the Dutch people thoroughly satisfied; no people are more sensible to kindness."[31]

The impact Christopher's despatch had upon the Colonial Office is evidenced by the fact that Earl Desart, the Parliamentary Under Secretary, was sufficiently impressed to add this footnote to the letter:

> "I am satisfied that by a judicious policy of conciliation towards the Boers, our difficulties at the Cape would, comparatively speaking, disappear. If we could obtain the co-operation of Pretorius and his followers – and I see no reason whatever to doubt the faith of Pretorius – men trained and accustomed to bush warfare, the Caffir would no longer appear such a formidable enemy. No time should be lost in taking steps to repair the errors that have made these men our enemies instead of friends and valuable allies."[32]

Such was the new approach to the Afrikaners of the interior and it is therefore little wonder that the earlier tension between north and south subsided[33] and that Smith and Cathcart were able to report that the incalcitrant Boers under Pretorius were at last showing a

---

29. Of Christopher's impact upon the Secretary of State, Uys, in *In the Era of Shepstone,* p. 32, has the following to say: "And it would not be wide of the truth to assert that Christopher was largely responsible for both the ratification of the Sand River Convention and for the subsequent abandonment of the Orange River Sovereignty."
30. Uys, *In the Era of Shepstone,* p. 32.
31. As quoted by Uys, *In the Era of Shepstone,* pp. 32–33.
32. C.O. 48/335, J. S. Christopher to Pakington, 8 Feb. 1852. Also quoted by Uys, *In the Era of Shepstone,* p. 33.
33. F. A. van Jaarsveld, *Die Eenheidstrewe van die Republikeinse Afrikaners, Deel I, Pioniershartstogte (1836–1864),* pp. 118–119.

desire to co-operate with Britain.[34] The fruits of this new turn of events was that in 1852 Britain accorded the Afrikaner Emigrants beyond the Vaal the "freedom to manage their own affairs without let or hindrance and promised to abstain from encroachment on their territory north of the river provided they did not encroach upon what lay to the south of it".[35]

In support of the changing tide of British official opinion of the republican-minded Afrikaners was the warm reception Pretorius received in Port Natal after the Sand River Convention had been signed when he was lauded as a hero. Preller recreates the feeling the English in Natal had for him:

> "Die mense, – en baie van hulle het deur Pretorius se hande gegaan tydens Smith se beleg, – was een en al geesdrif en blydskap, om gastvryheid te kan bewys aan die man van Dingaansdag, Kongela, Boomplaats en Zand rivier, – die man wat geweier had om die Zulus op hulle los te laat. Hulle het hom as held vereer. Na afloop van die ontvangs het die menigte hom 'n hartelike ‚hoera' toegeroep, wat, volgens die lokale blad, ‚die hart van die ou veteraan blykbaar verwarm het,' want hy het daar die wens uitgespreek, dat baie ander van sy landgenote getuie kon gewees het van hierdie hartelike vriendskap, – en, dat die handel tussen Natal en Transvaal mag bloei en groei!"[36]

In 1853, however, the retention of the Sovereignty was still open to question and in November of that year Sir George Clerk arrived in South Africa to investigate the affairs of the Sovereignty. Without wishing to enter upon the pros and cons of the abandonment of the Sovereignty, Clerk's report on the O.R.S. casts light on the current thinking of official British opinion towards the Afrikaners – an opinion which made abandonment possible:

> "Few Dutch Settlers or Boers reside in this part of the Territory [Bloemfontein]. I have had interviews however with some; and with two or three who deplore the withdrawal of the British Government. These are men, who during the times of disturbances, or of actual collision between the British troops and the Boers, have sided with the former, or during peace have

34. C.O. 48/323, Smith to Grey, 14 Jan. 1852, ff. 247–248; C.O. 48/324, Smith to Grey, 16 Feb. 1852, ff. 215–216; C.O. 48/326, Cathcart to Grey, 20 April 1852, ff. 140–141.
35. Quoted by Walker, *A History of South Africa,* p. 261.
36. G. Preller, *Andries Pretorius,* p. 469.

occasionally lent their time and zealous services to the British Authorities in a way to assist their administrative measures. But Your Grace is, no doubt aware that, in reviewing the former policy of the British Government, one cannot escape from the painful conviction, with reference to the interests and feelings of the Dutch Inhabitants of the Cape Colony, that the measures which, with few exceptions, it pursued towards them, and the neglect or disdain with which it habitually regarded them, have engendered a spirit which leaves them, with few exceptions, by no means desirous of remaining anywhere under British Dominion; and least so in this quarter, to which and beyond it, as a last resort, migrated many years ago with wives and children, that portion of the Dutch community who felt their position within the Colony was so unsatisfactory and insecure as to be insufferable. It may be anticipated therefore, that a large majority of the Dutch settlers here, who are to the British as 8 to one, if left to the exercise of their own judgements, will rejoice in the prospect of being allowed to govern themselves. There may, no doubt, be some among them of a reckless character, and others who will seize any such occasion as the present to manifest openly their malevolence. But these I imagine are few, and when a State chooses to occupy Territory too remote in position, and too poor in revenue, to admit of that occupation, with its attendant vast and complicated responsibilities, being followed up with such measures as are calculated to render control efficient and authority respected throughout its limits, no surprise can be felt that it should now and then be resorted to by some who may seek to screen their past misconduct, and to escape from restraint upon their evil propensities."[37]

What is significant is that while the Cape Colonists' appeals for the introduction of a *legislative assembly* had been turned down during the late 1820's and 1830's because the British feared how the Afrikaner majority would "treat" the dependent Hottentots – or, as one British parliamentarian had worded it, a legislative assembly could not be granted to the Cape until the colonists revealed "a disposition of the strong to protect the weak"[38] – during the early 1850's the British Government was prepared to grant two Afrikaner republics their *independence* without, as it were, batting an eyelid. Actually, the fact that the Cape Colony was granted a legislative assembly in 1854 only serves to emphasise the increasing influence of more practical considerations such as the mounting financial burden on

---

37. C.O. 48/348, Clerk to Newcastle, 25 Aug. 1853, ff. 11–12.
38. *Vide supra,* pp. 98–99.

Britain because of its involvement in the Colony. While various arguments for and against the granting of such political autonomy to the Cape Colony drew debate in the Commons resulting in the whole history of the Colony (including the causes and nature of the Great Trek[39]) and the past treatment of the Blackman[40] coming under discussion, that the Cape Colony *did* receive this privilege, even though the majority of the colonists were *still* Afrikaners, showed which was the more dominant consideration.

However, it is the British press that reflects most positively the swing away from philanthropy in colonial affairs. In fact, the change in attitude of the British press towards the Blackman is quite staggering when compared to its earlier pronouncements during the period 1832–1836.[41] Naturally such a turn-about in outlook had to affect English opinion of the Afrikaners and *The Spectator* (which, it will be remembered, had been a staunch philanthropist journal during the 1830's), the *Daily News* and particularly *The Times* left no doubt as to the new British sentiment.

First of all, the commencement of the 7th Frontier War (1846–48) made *The Times* realise that the natives had not yet been "beaten into civilized or trustworthy neighbours". The war had originated in "the usual manner", said *The Times,* "by depredations of marauders and the vain demand for compensation"[42] and on the whole its sympathy was with the colonists for the plight in which they found themselves.[43] As far as *The Times* was concerned the first thing to do was *end* the war, and as for the cause of the war, how could anyone *realistically* have believed it possible for treaties to be kept by savages.[44] The natives had mistakenly been treated as civilised equals with the colonists and too much was known about the injustices committed against them and not enough of the reverse.[45] It was

39. *Hansard,* 3rd Series, CXXXIII, 9 May 1854, cols. 52–88. This debate centred around the abandonment of the Orange River Sovereignty.
40. *Hansard,* 3rd Series, CXVI, 15 April 1851, cols. 226–287; 3rd Series, CXVIII, 15 July 1851, cols. 694–777.
41. *Vide supra,* 123–126.
42. *The Times,* 6 Sept. 1847. See also, *Daily News,* 4 Sept. 1847.
43. *The Times,* 6 Sept. 1847; 28 Sept. 1847; 13 Oct. 1847; 23 Dec. 1847. See also, *Daily News,* 4 Sept. 1847. Reports on the war were also carried in the columns of *The Spectator* such as, 11 April 1846; 25 April 1846; 6 June 1846.
44. *The Times,* 13 Oct. 1847.
45. *Ibid.,* 23 Dec. 1847.

necessary for the British public to realise that peace would be secured only when the natives realised the inevitable consequences of war.[46] The attitude of this newspaper and the press in general (particularly to the events of 1850–1853) showed a deep concern for the affairs of South Africa because of the financial drain it placed upon the British treasury. "We have learned," wrote *The Times* in 1847, "that a little war [in South Africa] for a year and a half is more expensive than a great war for a month."[47] Not surprisingly, it showed reservations respecting Smith's annexation of the Orange River Sovereignty,[48] while in 1851, during the troubled time of the costly 8th Frontier War on the Cape Colony's eastern frontier, *The Times* wrote: "the very mention of this property [the Sovereignty] is enough to sicken the most ambitious advocate of territorial aggrandizement".[49]

In January 1849 the first hint is noticeable that the British public was to come to view the Afrikaner differently. A correspondent to *The Times,* on referring to the Boomplaats incident when Smith succeeded in subduing the malcontent burghers of that territory, wrote: "It must to every advocate of justice and humanity be gratifying in the extreme to observe the leading journal of the day casting, with its all-powerful arm, over the helpless and injured the protecting Aegis of the press; and in no cause could it more justifiably do so than . . . the case of the South African Boers."[50] The correspondent continued:

> "You there say that 'You cannot altogether pursuade yourself that the Boers [at Boomplaats] are as much in the wrong now as the Caffres were 12 months ago'. I perfectly agree with you, and being somewhat conversant with the Colony of the Cape of Good Hope, and with the affairs of both the former and latter people, I shall endeavour, in again bringing before the public a subject which has been apparently cast aside, briefly to point out the difference between their respective positions.
>
> The Caffres for the last 50 years have been the never-ceasing foes, the irreclaimable and constant spoilators and devastators of the Colony, whose only defenders were during a long period the 'Dutch Boers', for Holland seldom maintained a military force on any portion of the frontier.

46. *The Times,* 13 Oct. 1847.
47. *Ibid.*
48. *Ibid.,* 28 Oct. 1848.
49. *Ibid.,* 10 July 1851.
50. *Ibid.,* "African", 4 Jan. 1849.

By a compact entered into with the English in 1814 the Boers were, with the land they occupied, transferred, like sheep or bullocks, from Batavian to British rule and protection.

Now, Sir, how did Britain rule and protect its new subjects? I will tell you. In the first place, she allowed them to be plundered from within by a vagrant black population, who were by us most injudiciously freed from all restraint; next she allowed them, by not taking adequate means for their defence, to be plundered by the native tribes from without; thirdly, she plundered them herself in hastily and prematurely emancipating their slaves by which the Boers were ruined, and received little or no compensation in return.

Plundered thus from all quarters, and by all hands, – a prey to petty annoyances of every description – abused, detracted, and calumniated – a deaf ear turned to their repeated and manifold complaints – left thus without hearing or redress, – they at last in despair resolved to abandon their properties and homesteads to fly the iron rule of a foreign yoke, and to seek freedom, competence, and comfort in the boundless wilderness far beyond the established limits of the colony and of civilization.

Here, at least, they hoped unmolested to be left in peace; but they were greatly mistaken. Jealous of our rights as tormentors, we vindictively followed them with fire and sword; they turned to bay – fought gallantly, and fell not wholly unavenged.

The above I believe to be a correct statement of the causes and results of our late attack on the emigrant Boers; in the justice or injustice of such a proceeding I leave the British public to decide."[51]

The 8th Frontier War of 1850–1853 evoked such strong reaction in the British press that a fresh appraisal of the 'South African problem' and the Colony's Boer population simply had to come. "Who is to pay for the triumph we are to achieve?" asked *The Times*[52] – a sentiment echoed by the *Daily News*[53] – while *The Spectator* was of the opinion that it was already too late to consider who would bear the cost of the present war on the Colony's eastern frontier – although the cost of it *should* have been "defrayed by those who had incurred it". The solution was simple: the Cape should be granted a legislative

51. *The Times,* "African", 4 Jan. 1849.
52. *Ibid.,* 7 March 1851. See also, 10 March 1851; 19 April 1851; 21 June 1851.
53. *Daily News,* 7 March 1851; 8 March 1851. See also, 9 July 1851; 8 Jan. 1852.

assembly.[54] Demonstrating a strong anti-philanthropic feeling, *The Times*, in November 1851, had the following to say on the confrontation between the colonists and the natives in South Africa: "If we are to colonize the Cape, the Caffres must gradually vanish or retire before us. It is the very essence of colonization that we should advance and they should recede; and, if their claims in this respect are to be preferred to ours, we have no business there."[55] Or, as this same newspaper wrote a month later: "We cannot, at 5,000 miles distant, charge ourselves with the formal mediation between settler and savage for the gratification of those who fear that the savage may get the worst of the bargain."[56]

In two lengthy editorials, *The Times* laid its cards on the table respecting its views on future British involvement in the affairs of Whites and Blacks in South Africa. Not much is left to the imagination:

> "Why have we passed more than 80 degrees of ocean, and hundreds of miles of inhospitable desert, in order to come in contact with people who assuredly never would have come to seek us, and the utter worthlessness of whose territory ought to have been the best protection against the invasion of a civilized enemy? Is it because our feelings were shocked by the rude and barbarous manner in which the settlers of the Cape, under the old system of 'commandoes', repelled the attacks upon their property by their savage neighbours? At any rate, the authors of these rough reprisals did not exterminate their enemies which is one of the purposes for which this civilized nation is now waging war; and, as much as the Caffres may have suffered at the hands of the Dutch farmers, they were never threatened with a doom so terrible as that which our hypocritical philanthropy now proposes to inflict."[57]

And a year later it wrote:

> "We have no alternative between quitting South Africa altogether or doing more or less violence to the interests of the

54. *The Spectator,* 29 March 1851. See also, 7 June 1851. It is interesting to note that during 1851 there were *nine* leading articles on the 8th Frontier War in *The Spectator* and no less than *19* news items. This was general throughout the press and not without reason – the British public was paying for the war!
55. *The Times,* 17 Nov. 1851. See also, 24 Nov. 1851.
56. *Ibid.,* 15 Dec. 1851. See also, 22 Jan. 1852.
57. *Ibid.,* 22 Jan. 1852.

Caffre population. The only question is how these proceedings are to be conducted, and here there are two systems open to us. The first presumes the maintenance of Imperial authority together with Imperial obligations. Under this system we are enabled to extend a certain protection to the coloured tribes, to mitigate the ferocity and control the licence of the borders to carry on wars, when wars arise, with moderation and forebearance and to give a general effect to the views entertained by a certain philanthropic section of Englishmen. But for these privileges we are compelled to pay heavily. We can only make regular war with regular soldiers, and these soldiers have to be exported, at an enormous cost over thousands of miles of ocean . . . Under the other system we should remit to the colonists, together with the duty of defending their own possessions, the liberty of conducting that defence as they thought proper. We should be released from our obligations, but at the same time divested of our authority. The borders would look to nothing but results, and would pay little attention to remonstrances of philanthropists 5,000 miles off. We should hear no more of the Caffre wars in our estimates, but we should know that the utmost licence of invasion and violence was permissible on the frontier of a British colony. The colonists, in short, can fight their own battles, if we allow them to do so in their own way; if we persist, for humanity's sake, in fighting them ourselves, we must bear the cost of our resolution. These are the two systems before us . . ."[58]

With regard to *The Times*' attitude towards the Afrikaners respecting their dealings with the natives, the comments passed in 1855 by this newspaper, after it had had the benefit of commenting upon South African affairs for more than half a century, are of the greatest possible significance. For the first time *The Times* comes close to agreeing with the Afrikaner attitude towards the treatment of the natives – and if it did not agree in so many words, it definitely found merits in the Afrikaners' methods. Referring to a situation which had arisen in the Transvaal Republic, when Makapan, chief of the Ndebele, went on the warpath in 1853 against the native clans in the Waterberg and also killed a burgher named Hermanus Potgieter, *The Times* had the following to say: "Here, like ourselves, they border upon the Caffres, and are exposed accordingly to the self-same liabilities in the shape of frontier alarms, attacks and depredations. That they do not, however, content themselves with our mild system

58. *The Times,* 18 May 1853.

of reprisals, or deal in our fashion with their savage enemies will be only too evident from the story which we are about to relate." *The Times* tells of how the Boers under Pretorius and Potgieter besieged the caves in which the numerous tribesmen lived, probably about 2 000, and for three weeks starved them out. As the natives emerged from their caves they were shot down, though some females and children escaped or were let free.[59] Now, while *The Times* was pleased that it had not been a British action, it could not help remarking on the economy of such warfare and how much more effective it was than any British expedition could have been. "Handled as those on the spot could handle them, the Caffres could be kept down with little outlay or trouble", it said, although conceding that if the British were to pursue such warfare it would be certain to cause scandals and shock certain people; however, *The Times* added, "if such an alternative be rejected, the border provinces ought to be relinquished altogether".[60] And speaking of the Black/White confrontation in general it concluded that:

> "A fierce spirit of independence seems absolutely necessary to carry this isolated [Boer] community through its dangers and its difficulties. *In this the Boers have found their safety* (italics added), and in this the English, under similar circumstances must look for it."[61]

Before arriving at some conclusion as to how the South African English regarded the Afrikaners in 1854 — both those within and without the colonies — it is necessary to remember that the decline of the philanthropic incursion into colonial politics was less noticeable in the Cape press than it had been in the British press. The reason for this is plain enough as there had always existed a strong conservative element at the Cape. The *Graham's Town Journal,* the *Cape Town Mail* and *De Zuid Afrikaan* had constantly been influenced by the practical rather than the idealistic in their opinions of Black/White relations and therefore when the scales of public opinion dipped in favour of their viewpoint it did not represent as

59. Walker, in *A History of South Africa,* p. 290, has the following to say about the incident: "It was a stern lesson, and until they [the Boers] began to fight among themselves the Transvaalers had little further trouble with the natives."
60. *The Times,* 16 March 1855.
61. *Ibid.,* 13 May 1853.

complete a turn-about in public opinion as it had in Britain. It had been the 7th and 8th Frontier Wars (1846–1847 and 1850–1852, respectively), particularly the decision of the Hottentots to side with the enemy in the latter struggle (which was received in the Colony as a direct slap in the face[62]), that had paved the way for the new conservatism among the colonists respecting the Blackman and reflecting this change was the decline of the *Commercial Advertiser* (which in fact went out of business in 1867) and the rise of typically colonial newspapers such as *The Cape of Good Hope Observer* (1849), *The Cape Monitor* (1850) and *The Cape Argus* (1857), while in 1850 *The Friend of the Sovereignty* established itself at Bloemfontein under the auspices of the *Graham's Town Journal.*

Respecting the character of the 'Emigrant Afrikaners', it will be remembered that from the start of the Great Trek the *Graham's Town Journal* and *Cape Town Mail* had not been averse to the opening up of the interior to the Whiteman. Indeed, much good, it was thought, would result from the Great Trek and the only real point of contention was the reticence on the part of the British Government to take effective control of the expansion. It will also be remembered that on the whole they had been sympathetic towards the Emigrants. In 1844 the attitude of the *Cape Town Mail* towards the Natal Afrikaners remained unchanged and it urged that the earlier contest between the Boers and Smith should be forgotten as the state of affairs in Natal, then a British colony, were most satisfactory.[63] During these years, besides harping on the old question of the need for positive British intervention in the affairs of the interior Afrikaners which required control for the sake of all, the *Graham's Town Journal* had the following to say about the Afrikaners and their dealings with the natives:

> ". . . let it always be remembered, that the Dutch emigrants are no worse than any other class of men would be in a like position, – they are impelled by circumstances, – they are unrestrained by legal and to a great extent by moral responsibility – and hence the governing principle must necessarily be selfishness, and a determination to secure by any and all means their own self-preservation."[64]

---

62. See the remarks of Sir Harry Smith, *supra,* pp. 196–197.
63. *Cape Town Mail,* 6 Jan. 1844, 11 May 1844.
64. *GHT Journal,* 13 Feb. 1845.

In January 1850 a letter signed by "A Friend to the Boer as well as the Aborigines" appeared in both the *Cape Town Mail*[65] and *The Cape of Good Hope Observer.*[66] Both newspapers judged the letter to afford "a few plain facts" concerning the condition of the Afrikaners beyond the Vaal and their relationship with the natives but they differed in their reactions. The correspondent had shown the Afrikaners there in a poor light. Maintaining that "there is no law or order among them" he depicted them as a group of desperate men who, after their defeat at Boomplaats, had crossed the Vaal and were now bent on encroaching upon and oppressing the natives. *The Cape of Good Hope Observer's* response was that "we must fear that many horrors have been perpetrated beyond the [Orange River Sovereignty] border, of which but faint rumours have ever reached the colony . . . but what have we to do with this?";[67] while the *Cape Town Mail* commented upon the charges in greater detail:

> "Some other facts of the same nature are given, — not, as the reader will observe, by way of placing the conduct of the emigrants in a favourable light, but for the contrary purpose. Yet the result is, to leave an impression that these frontier settlers form a far more orderly and respectable community than any that travellers have found among the 'squatters' and 'backwoodsmen' in the newly-peopled territories of America. What is said of the extermination and of the enslavement of the natives would probably have a very different aspect if all the facts were ascertained. It is well known that the Boers, on their first arrival in that region, found the aboriginal tribes in abject subjection to the merciless conqueror, Moselakatse, whose devastations had reduced a great portion of the country to a desert. From this subjection the feeble remnant of the earlier possessors were rescued by the Boers, who are now accused of dispossessing and enslaving them. Probably the 'slavery' to which the writer refers is merely — as he admits in the case of Militse — a regulation requiring the natives to renounce their roving life, and settle in one spot, 'as the Boers did'. This, the first step to civilization, is naturally regarded by those restless barbarians as a great grievance and oppression. It is likely enough, too, that some of the Boers have been guilty of excesses, such as are laid to the charge of 'the majority'; but it is remarkable that the acts of cruelty and extortion of which they are accused are either given as

65. *Cape Town Mail,* 12 Jan. 1850.
66. *The Cape of Good Hope Observer,* 15 Jan. 1850.
67. *Ibid.*

vague reports, or are expressly stated to have been discountenanced, and sometimes severely punished by the community at large."[68]

The opinion held of the Afrikaners in the interior by the conservative section of Cape Englishmen was expressed some years previously in 1845 when the *Graham's Town Journal* wrote:

> "It has been our fortune to hear a vast deal said about the Emigrant Boers; and it must be confessed that a considerable proportion of what has been current respecting their proceedings has not been very creditable to them. We have been told of their acts of cruelty, — of their aggression — of their violence, and of their disaffection — and we have been forced to listen to all this, without having any facts to rebut such charges, or which could warrant a belief that it was mere calumny, possessing no root in actual fact. But what then? — does it follow from this admission, that because there was an appearance of ground for such accusations we were to pass a sweeping sentence of condemnation upon the *whole* of the Emigrants . . ."[69]

As far as the *Graham's Town Journal* and the conservative section of the press was concerned they were not "apologists for the misdoings of the Boers" for they themselves condemned and deplored such abusive actions as much as anyone; yet, the real point was "we cannot shut our eyes to the fact that our own government might easily have prevented the whole". Their main argument was that while certain iregularities had occurred in the dealings which the interior Boers had had with the natives, this was insufficient to label the *whole* emigrant population as cruel or destructive.

From the remarks passed by Fairbairn in the *Commercial Advertiser* during the 1840's, however, it is clear that his attitude towards the interior Afrikaners showed no signs of mellowing. In 1844 the *Commercial Advertiser* had spoken of the necessity of those in office knowing the character of the frontier Boer — "not his personal or moral character, but the character of his mind, as it has been formed by local circumstances and the habits of his life".[70] A year later he placed the Afrikaner emigrants into what he no doubt regarded as

---

68. *Cape Town Mail,* 12 Jan. 1850.
69. *GHT Journal,* 19 June 1845.
70. *Commercial Advertiser,* 10 Feb. 1844.

the 'proper perspective' which would allow a correct impression of them to take root:

> "To those . . . who have observed with diligence the progress of the Emigration of the Boers, who know the light in which they hold uncivilized tribes, or black men generally, and their notions respecting the occupation of land, the laws of force, and the local nature of allegiance, all is clear as noon day. These Boers, with their eyes open or shut, it matters not, are merely performing another act of the tragic drama of aboriginal extermination, that has left so dark a stain on the moral character of modern Europe; and with regard to allegiance, they are simply falling off into Hordes like the Bands that used to infest the North of Asia and Europe, or some parts of Arabia, slightly civilized in form, but without either the knowledge of duty, the arts, or the religion that distinguish trust-worthy communities from the barbarian."[71]

In 1848, on touching upon the *real* character of emigrant life in the interior,[72] the *Commercial Advertiser* concluded that the situation there was sufficient to "excite astonishment and horror"[73] for there the Afrikaners were but pursuing the old pattern of encroachment upon African land and life:

> ". . . the bloody tragedy will be acted over again if the government does not take decisive steps to prevent it", the *Commercial Advertiser* wrote in 1843. "Mocke will establish a new settlement — hundreds will follow him — thousands of natives and hundreds of the emigrants will be destroyed — British troops will be obliged to pursue them — thousands of pounds will be expended — and then the patch-up system will be resorted to again, until some circumstance occasions another 'trek'."[74]

Turning from the emigrant Afrikaners, however, English/Cape Dutch relationships within the Colony itself had come a long way since Fairbairn had called all the subscribers to *De Zuid Afrikaan* "eminent growers of cabbages"[75] and during the closing years of the 1840's the Anti-Convict Agitation had underlined the need for concerted

---

71. *Commercial Advertiser,* 16 April 1845.
72. In this instance based upon an account provided by "A Traveller", in *Commercial Advertiser,* 9 Aug. 1848. See leading article of the same date.
73. *Commercial Advertiser,* 9 Aug. 1848.
74. *Ibid.,* 7 Dec. 1843.
75. *Vide supra,* p. 141.

mutual respect and co-operation. It also showed the two groups of colonists what could be achieved in this direction when necessity demanded it. Referring to this public issue which had drawn a unanimous response from all parts of the Colony,[76] the *Commercial Advertiser* proclaimed: "The people of the Cape of Good Hope have shown to the world what it is that constitutes a State – that it is not numbers, not wealth, not fleets and armies, but Public Virtue, Moral Perception, Religious Sentiment, Mutual Confidence and Fidelity."[77]

The Cape Colony was growing up and acquiring its own national attitude founded mainly upon a common understanding of the Colony's problems, coupled with the development of the economy and the prospect of a legislative assembly.

Respecting the Afrikaners on the Colony's frontiers, the *Frontier Times* wrote in 1848 as follows:

> "We are persuaded that there is no race of men in the world who are easier to manage than the Dutch African farmers. Their habits are simple. Their wants are few. Their attention is principally bestowed upon their flocks and herds, their gardens and their fields. They retire to rest heartily fatigued with the labours of the day. The Bible is their text book; they read little else. They are not politicians by trade or example. They have no fanciful grievances to complain of. They have no theoretical wrongs to redress. Their temperament is sober. Their minds are full of religious principle – and they are great respectors of authority;"[78]

while in 1851 it reported that a reciprocal feeling of good will was generally felt by the English towards "their fellow-colonists of Dutch extraction".[79] Even the once staunch philanthropic *Commercial Advertiser* took the Secretary of State to task in 1851 for having drawn a line of distinction between the English and Afrikaner colonists' attitude towards the Blackman when he had used it as an argument against granting the Colony its legislative assembly. As far as Fairbairn was concerned no such difference existed in the Colony[80] and any differences which might have existed between the English and Afri-

76. See A. F. Hattersley's *Convict Crisis and the Growth of Unity*.
77. *Commercial Advertiser*, 16 Feb. 1850.
78. *Frontier Times*, 15 Aug. 1848.
79. *Ibid.*, 8 April 1851. See also, 12 Aug. 1851.
80. See *Commercial Advertiser*, 13 Aug. 1851; 20 Aug. 1851; 3 April 1852; 15 Jan. 1853.

kaners, judged the *Cape Town Mail,* would "at once be swept away by the establishment of a popular legislature".[81]

The general trend respecting the attitude the English adopted towards the Afrikaners was also discernible in the published works dealing with South Africa. Although during the late 1840's and even the early years of the 1850's a variety of publications attached considerable importance to how the Boer emigration to Natal and other parts of South Africa had adversely affected tribal life,[82] by the early and mid 1850's the new trend in opinion became markedly dominant.

Henry Cloete's *Lectures*[83] evaluated the Afrikaners much more realistically than they had been in the previous two decades, explaining the causes of the Great Trek along much the same lines as Retief's Manifestos, while Godlonton and Irvin in their detailed *Narrative of the Kaffir War of 1850–1851*[84] advanced the strongest arguments in favour of the colonists thus helping to redeem the colonial character in British eyes. In 1855 the Rev. William Holden declared that information from Natal had too often been one-sided in the past, "tending", he judged, "to mislead the English reader, and to prevent him from drawing just inferences respecting many of the subjects brought under his consideration",[85] and in 1852, Cole, on touching upon the "notion" prevailing among the "less informed" in Britain that the colonists had encroached upon the territory of the Bantu, had said: "Nothing can be more untrue. There is not an inch of the Cape Colony that ever belonged to the Kafirs."[86] Watermeyer also added his weight to the new trend in public opinion when he said: "the accusations of cruelty and oppression of the first Dutch occu-

---

81. *Cape Town Mail,* 26 Oct. 1850.
82. See, James Backhouse, *A Narrative of a visit to the Mauritius and South Africa;* J. F. Bunbury, *Journal of a Residence at the Cape of Good Hope;* J. J. Freeman, *A Tour in South Africa.* See also, Henry Raikes, *Memoirs of the Life and Services of Vice-Admiral Sir Jahleel Brenton;* John Barrow, *An Auto-biographical Memoir.*
83. Henry Cloete, *Three Lectures on the Emigration of the Dutch Farmers from the Colony of the Cape of Good Hope, and their Settlement in the District of Natal; Five Lectures on the Emigration of the . . .*
84. See also the following works by Godlonton: *Sketches of the Eastern Districts of the Cape of Good Hope, as they are in 1842; Case of the Colonists of the Eastern Frontier of the Cape of Good Hope in reference to the Kaffir Wars of 1835–1836 and 1846.*
85. William Holden, *History of the Colony of Natal, South Africa,* p. 333.
86. Alfred W. Cole, *The Cape and the Kafirs; or, Notes of Five Years' Residence in South Africa,* p. 76.

pants, is void of foundation . . . the first settlers are not justly chargeable with the guilt of bloodthirstiness".[87]

By 1854, then, when Great Britain had effectively withdrawn her control from the interior of South Africa by way of granting the Afrikaner communities their independence, content in the knowledge that these Afrikaners were both landlocked and surrounded by native tribes, and when Natal constituted a separate British colony free from ties with the Cape, and when the Cape Colony itself had been given control of its internal affairs, what were Englishmen thinking of the Afrikaners?[88]

Holden had thought of the "Dutch *Boers*" throughout South Africa in very moderate terms, judging their "character and manners" to be "very simple, approaching sometimes to the rude",[89] while in 1844 James Backhouse, on referring to the Cape Dutch colonists had written: "an open door would be found . . . by persons acquainted with their language, who would go amongst them in the simple feeling of Christian interest in their welfare."[90] Also referring to the Afrikaners of the Cape Colony, Bunbury, while he could write that "The Cape farmers have neither the cleanliness, the industry, nor the love of money, which are said to be characteristic of the Hollanders in their own country", he was at the same time of the opinion that

> "They are not without education; on the contrary, the knowledge of reading and writing is, I believe, general among them; and in almost every house where we stopped, we saw a Bible, which seemed to be preserved with great care. The Cape farmers are

---

87. E. B. Watermeyer, *Three Lectures on the Cape of Good Hope under the Government of the Dutch East India Company,* p. 18.
88. Before investigating English opinion of first, the Cape Dutch Afrikaners and secondly, the "interior Boers" of the O.F.S. and Transvaal, it is necessary to appreciate that English/Afrikaner contact in Natal was minimal owing to the fact that by 1846 the Afrikaner population of that colony had dwindled to a mere sixty families. What this meant was that while those Afrikaners who remained in Natal were in many cases "liked and respected" (Brooks, *A History of Natal,* p. 52) by the English, they became more and more a dwindling minority as British immigration to Natal increased and as far as overall English opinion was concerned, they were of little consequence. What was to be of importance was the growth of a Natal English opinion of their Afrikaner neighbours during the second half of the century.
89. Holden, *History of the Colony of Natal, South Africa,* p. 77.
90. James Backhouse, *A Narrative of a visit to the Mauritius and South Africa,* p. 1.

said, by those who know them much better than I can pretend to do, to have a great reverence for religion, and to be very observant of all the ordinances of their Church. They are said also to have strong family affections, and a remarkable veneration for their parents; and certainly, as far as appearances and outward demeanour go (for I had no further means of judging), this appears to be quite true. The families are generally very numerous, and the sons (unless they emigrate) mostly remain in their father's house even after they are grown up and married; so that there is something very patriarchal in the aspect of society in these thinly-inhabited districts."[91]

In 1852 Cole had found the Dutch inhabitants of Cape Town "the most wealthy and respectable, and not the least intelligent part of the community",[92] but he was also of the opinion that they were not a "go-ahead" people, for while they laboured "most pertinaciously at growing bad wine they never thought of testing the capability of the Cape Colony to grow something more profitable and of better quality".[93] Of the Boers in the Cape Colony as a group, Cole had this to say:

"The Dutch Boers are in person the finest men in the colony. I have seen them constantly from six feet two to six feet six inches in height; broad and muscular in proportion. Occasionally they reach a height and size bordering on the gigantic. Their strength is immense; and though a peaceably-disposed set of men, they at all times entertain a considerable feeling of contempt for any diminituve 'Englander' . . . the characteristics of a race certainly descend to the fifth and sixth, perhaps the fiftieth generation. The Cape Dutchmen are the same frugal, industrious, sober people as those of the parent stock in Holland. Their persons are far more altered than their mental peculiarities, though the 'Dutch build' is still apparent. They are, however, terrible 'non-progressionalists' . . . Not the least pleasing characteristic of the Cape Dutch is their family affection . . . They appear to be truly 'happy families'. The Dutch formerly entertained a great dislike to British rule. I do not mean to assert that they are even yet thoroughly reconciled; but they display less repugnance to submit to it than of yore . . . I fear they had too much justice on their side in the complaints they uttered for they had not

91. C. F. J. Bunbury, *Journal of a Residence at the Cape of Good Hope,* pp. 181–183.
92. Cole, *The Cape and the Kafirs; or, Notes of Five Years' Residence in South Africa,* p. 63.
93. *Ibid.,* p. 96.

met with proper treatment at the hands of our government. Their feeling must at all events have been very strong when it induced them to leave their own farms by the hundred and 'trek', or emigrate, to the north-east, anywhere away from British misrule."[94]

As far as the old question of treatment of the natives by the Afrikaners was concerned, the remarks of Merriman in 1854 in his description of the Cape Afrikaners are most interesting:

"I learnt also to modify much my ideas of Dutch harshness towards the coloured people who serve them. It may be true that, if not restrained by law, they would often inflict severe corporal chastisement on their servants, and it is true that they seem *generally* to disregard the duty of providing them any Christian instruction; but it is also true that there is much kindness exercised towards them, in a way which English masters and mistresses seem incapable of; and I have ceased to wonder at the preference which coloured people frequently show for living in service with Dutch people rather than English. There is less of the awful distance kept up between the parties in one case than the other. The Dutchman will allow the coloured man to have all his relations and belongings come and live with him, while an Englishman rarely will. Moreover, he acts peremptorily, but speaks kindly and less haughtily to the natives than an English gentleman is used to do to his inferiors; nor has he, like the latter, any drawing room in which himself and wife are secluded. They all live (family, and to a great extent servants too) in the great 'fore-house'; there sits the vrow, usually with a coloured woman occupied in some domestic work, in the same apartment; the coloured woman has always her baby, and sometimes two, and I have even seen three, children besides, playing in the room. If the baby cries, the vrow will perhaps send one of her own children to nurse it; whatever dainties the Dutch children have to amuse or keep them quiet between meals, the little blackies, if present, participate in on equal terms. Yet I could easily tell tales, which might carry weight if repeated at Exeter Hall, about divers slaps and approbrious words which I have witnessed an angry noie (mistress) bestow occasionally on these little creatures. What farmer's wife does not get in a pet sometimes?"[95]

---

94. Cole, *The Cape and the Kafirs; or, Notes of Five Years' Residence in South Africa,* pp. 122–125.
95. Archdeacon Merriman, *The Kafir, the Hottentot, and the Frontier Farmer,* pp. 147–151.

With the attitude of the British press to South Africa in general already having been outlined above, it is not necessary to elaborate further upon their views on the Afrikaners outside the colonial boundaries. The Cape press, too, manifested much the same outlook. During the late 1840's the English Cape press in general disassociated itself from the hysteria which had attended earlier reports of abuses or hardships which fell to the lot of the natives and it may be said that in the main the colonists, both English and Afrikaner, accepted as the normal course of events that in his contact with the Whiteman, the Blackman would come off second best. Such an attitude did much to draw the two European groups within the Colony closer together and even the reported molestations of English travellers by the Boers in the trans-Vaal territory was received by the press with tolerance. In 1850, before talk of abandoning the Sovereignty reached the Colony, *The Friend,* which on more than one occasion referred to the Transvaal Boers as their "brethren",[96] did not credit such actions to the general body of the Afrikaners there – though it admitted that such actions might have sprung from those "whose recollection of former grievances may [have influenced] their calmer judgement" – and it therefore advised all travellers who might be passing through the trans-Vaal country "to manifest towards the Boers most friendly feelings and deportment – for we should never forget that, from a sense of wrongs endured in the Colony (we know not however whether this applies to all) they have been led to cherish towards us feelings which we are confident will be modified by the power of religion, and soothed by the happy influence of time".[97] The *Cape Town Mail,* on the occasion of a similar incident in 1850, wrote with philosophical calm: "In a few years hence, we shall see the 'Trans-Vaal Boers' as desirous of a closer connection with their brother colonists as they are now averse to it. Why, then, should we spend our strength in shaking the green fruit, when we have only to wait till the pear is ripe, and it will fall into our hands?"[98]

96. Such as *The Friend,* 10 June 1850, 16 Sept. 1850.
97. *The Friend,* 10 June 1850.
It is perhaps necessary to point out that further molestation of English travellers during 1851 caused *The Friend* (28 April 1851) to react in a less understanding manner against this type of action by certain of the Afrikaners in the Transvaal. However, on 26 May 1851 it spoke of the "comparative harmony" and "good understanding" which existed between the Sovereignty and the trans-Vaal Boers.
98. *Cape Town Mail,* 10 Aug. 1850.

Such might well have been the tenor of the relationship between the Cape English and the republican Afrikaners had not Britain's policy been aimed at withdrawal from the interior of South Africa. As has been shown in the preceding chapters, the Cape press as a block had advocated that Great Britain be at the helm of any expansion towards the hinterland, and while the granting of independence to the Afrikaners beyond the Vaal in 1852 caused but little real reaction in the Cape press, the prospect of Great Britain abandoning the Sovereignty drew strong reaction from all[99] – especially the *Graham's Town Journal* and *The Friend* who had always been so keenly interested in the development of the interior. Obviously, the object to aim for was to persuade the authorities to revoke their decision to abandon and here, as a result of a propaganda programme introduced against the Transvaal Republic, a grim picture was painted or rather predicted if Great Britain did, in fact, withdraw – a picture equal to Barrow's earlier descriptions of the Cape Colony[1] only now the champions were the missionaries Edwards and Inglis.[2]

A. N. Pelzer, on referring to one of the major reasons for the Transvaal not attracting as many emigrants as hoped during its early years, has the following to say about the propaganda campaign conducted against the interior or, at least, the Transvaal Afrikaners:

> "Die voortou is hierin geneem deur 'n onaansienlike maar uitgesproke vyandig-gesinde Engelse ou koerantjie, die sgn. Friend of the Sovereignty, wat gedurende die soewereiniteitsdae vanuit Bloemfontein met lasterpropaganda die hele wêreld teenoor die Suid-Afrikaanse Republiek in die harnas wou jaag. Getrou soos slawe het die vyandige pers in die Kaapkolonie die een onware berig na die ander oor die nuus-arme Republiek oorgeneem en hulle deeltjie bygedra om dit wêreldkundig te maak."[3]

Referring to the charge of libel brought by the Transvaal Volksraad against these two men resulting from their allegations that slavery,

99. See *GHT Journal*, 3 Sept. 1853.
1. *GHT Journal*, 2 July 1853; 3 Sept. 1853; 1 Oct. 1853. A similar picture had been presented prior to the signing of the Sand River Convention. See, *The Friend*, 16 Sept. 1850; 28 April 1851. From the *Natal Mercury* (4 Oct. 1854) came the opinion that ". . . abandonment means not only *Black* slavery, or an exterminating policy towards the coloured race. It means also the *British*, annihilation of religious and civil liberty".
2. See, *The Friend*, 20 Jan. 1853.
3. A. N. Pelzer, *Geskiedenis van die Suid-Afrikaanse Republiek, Deel I, Wordingsjare*, pp. 39–40.

child-stealing, etc. were taking place in the Transvaal, Pelzer concludes:

> "Albei, maar veral Inglis, het daarna dankbaar van die kolomme van die reeds genoemde Friend of the Sovereignty gebruik gemaak om al hulle haat en venyn wêreldkundig te maak. Alleen sou hy in sy agitasie nie staan nie: in die Kaapkolonie was die hele georganiseerde Londense Sendinggenootskap trou ondersteun deur die sgn. Evangeliese Verbond, oorgehaal om hulle kontakte in Londen in te lig oor beweerde gruweldade van die Transvalers teenoor onskuldige inboorlingstammetjies . . . Die reeds genoemde organisasies en talle ander wat met hulle in verband gestaan het, het hulle tyd nie onledig deurgebring nie maar ywerig probeer om die Britse regering tot inmenging in Transvaal aan te spoor . . . Die Sandrivierkonvensie moes ontken word, Transvaal moes by Groot Brittanje ingelyf word – die sendelinge het dit geëis en saam met hulle die Britse handelaarsmous. Die Sandrivierkonvensie was vir hulle 'n hinderlike las wat hulle bedrywighede oor 'n groot en uitgestrekte gebied oorkant die Vaalrivier ernstig aan bande gelê het – 'n las temeer omdat dit soos 'n geweldige groot struikelblok die pad na die Noorde en die pas-ontdekte Ngamigebied, versper het."[4]

This smeer campaign against the integrity of the Afrikaners of the Transvaal, centred around alleged slavery and child-stealing and undertaken for the sole purpose of trying to persuade Great Britain not to relinquish control of the interior of the country, was nothing more than the resurrection of the prejudices of the past and was once again to influence British policy when the Transvaal Afrikaners posed what was thought to be a political threat to Imperial interests in South Africa during the second half of the century.

Conclusion

When reflecting upon English opinion of the Afrikaner a number of factors come to mind. First, it must be appreciated that the Boers constituted a pastoralist society, while the English comprised an agriculturalist or urban society. The Boers, the pioneers of South Africa, held the outlook, interests, mentality, etc. of an essentially conservative society, whereas the English came from a background of empire builders. Where the Afrikaners were town dwellers, such as

4. Pelzer, *Geskiedenis van die Suid-Afrikaanse Republiek, Deel I, Wordingsjare,* pp. 41–42.

those in Cape Town, or where the English were country folk, such as the majority of the Settlers (who, in addition, shared a common frontier environment with the Boers), the differences between the Afrikaners and the English were less marked; but when the Englishman from Cape Town (or London!) met the Afrikaner from the distant frontier, then no comparison could be made. Also of importance were the differences emanating from the religious outlooks of the two races. On the one hand was the liberalism of the English, stemming as it did from the humanitarianism and philanthropy of the evangelical revival which swept Europe during the second half of the eighteenth century; on the other was the conservatism of the essentially rural Afrikaner people whose religious traditions were based on dogmatic Calvinism which had refrained from any participation in the above-mentioned religious movement. Finally, there was the effect of environment upon the opinion-making process of the English. Whilst in Cape Town or London the threat of native incursions on the frontier was a matter which invited speculation and argument, on the frontier itself it was a matter which called for action. Likewise the question of the eastern districts' dependence upon Hottentot labour was a major problem to those concerned and not one to be theorised on. That the *Graham's Town Journal* had to come into existence in opposition to the *Commercial Advertiser* attests to the fact that different environmental circumstances create different viewpoints.

The remarks passed by *The Observer* in 1802 respecting the "deplorable situation" in the Cape Colony, following upon the publication of John Barrow's *Travels,* and the remarks of *The Times* during the 1850's advocating a new approach towards the affairs of South Africa, indicate the extent to which English opinion of the Blackman changed over a period of fifty years and owing to the fact that English opinion of the *Afrikaners* corresponded directly with their attitude towards the *Blackman,* it is not surprising to find that during the same period British opinion of the Afrikaners also swung from the one extreme to the other.

When the British first landed in 1795, their interest in the internal affairs of the Cape Colony had been confined to their own security and yet even during those early years philanthropic considerations were beginning to gather momentum so that by the late 1820's and throughout the 1830's and 1840's English opinion of the Afrikaners was based primarily upon their estimation of what the relationship between White and Black should be. Herein lies the reason, or at least a large part of it, for the Afrikaners' poor image amongst the English – an image which was to pursue the Afrikaner frontiersmen throughout the years of the Great Trek. However, during the late 1840's and 1850's, because of the costly frontier wars and the burden they placed upon the British taxpayer, public reaction in Great Britain to the philanthropic incursion into colonial affairs grew to such an extent that the Government was called upon to withdraw itself from all involvement in those territories outside the colonial boundaries of the Cape and Natal, which in fact it did, at the same time adopting a no-nonsense policy towards the bordering native tribes. With this general turn-about in British policy it therefore followed that the critical and defamatory opinions passed by the earlier philanthropists on the Afrikaners and impressed upon the British public required reappraisal and as a result public opinion of the Afrikaner in Great Britain assumed a moderation unknown in the past, while in South Africa itself the more sympathetic views held by the conservative section of the population were further consolidated.

Bibliography

I–ARCHIVAL SOURCES

(A) Unpublished Source-material

(i) *Public Records Office, London*

COLONIAL OFFICE RECORDS

Cape of Good Hope

ORIGINAL CORRESPONDENCE, official officers and miscellaneous Despatches to the Secretary of State.
Colonial Office 48/1–48/360. (1807–1854)

ENTRY BOOKS, letter books of official, officers and miscellaneous Despatches to Cape Governors.
Colonial Office 49/1–49/2. (1795–1806)

(ii) *British Museum, London*

JOURNAL and memoranda of Sir Robert Wilson on service at the Cape, 1805–1806.
ADD. MSS. 30096-7.

WELLESLEY PAPERS, Series II, containing scattered South African papers, including letters from Governors and officials at the Cape (1797–1802) and correspondence with the Barnards (1797–1802).
ADD. MSS. 37274-318.

(iii) *Cape Archives Depot, Cape Town*

ORIGINAL CORRESPONDENCE, general, miscellaneous and foreign Despatches received from the Secretary of State.
Government House 1/1–1/50. (1807–1854)

(iv) *Natal Archives Depot, Pietermaritzburg*

HER MAJESTY'S COMMISSIONER, Mr. Henry Cloete, correspondence.
Surveyor General's Office II/I. (1842–1845)

(B) Published Source-material

(i) *Literary works*

ANDERSON, H. J. (ed.), *South Africa a Century Ago (1797–1810)*, Cape Town 1925.

MOODIE, D., *The Record; or, a Series of Official Papers relative to the Conditions and Treatment of the Natives Tribes of South Africa*, reprint, Amsterdam 1960.

THEAL, G. M. (ed.), *Records of the Cape Colony . . . 1793–1806*, vols. i-vi, London 1897–1900.

(ii) *Reports*

Report from the Select Committee on Aborigines, August 1836, Blue Book VII (538), 1836.
Report of the Parliamentary Select Committee on Aboriginal Tribes (British Settlements), reprinted, with comments, by the Aboriginal Protection Society, London 1837.
Reports of the Directors to the Members of the Missionary Society (London Missionary Society), (at the 10th to the 60th General Meeting), 51 vols., London 1804–1854.
The Annual Reports of the Aborigines Protection Society (at the 1st to the 4th Annual Meetings), 3 vols., London 1838–1841.

(iii) *British Parliamentary Debates*

HANSARD, 1795–1854.

II – LITERARY SOURCES

(A) Contemporary Periodicals and Newspapers

IN GREAT BRITAIN

Blackwood's Edinburgh Magazine, 1817–1854.
The Atlas, 1826–1854.
The Colonial Gazette, 1838–1839.
The Colonial Intelligencer; or, Aborigines' Friend, 1847–1854.
The Daily News, 1846–1854.
The Manchester Guardian (until March 1828, *The Manchester Guardian and British Volunteer*), 1824–1854.
The Observer, 1795–1854.
The Quarterly Review, 1809–1854.
The Spectator, 1828–1854.
The Times, 1795–1854.

IN SOUTH AFRICA

The Cape Frontier Times, 1840–1854.
The Cape Monitor, 1850–1854.
The Cape of Good Hope Observer, 1849–1851.
The Cape Town Gazette and African Advertiser, 8 Jan. 1814.
The Cape Town Mail, 1841–1854.
The Friend of the Sovereignty, 1850–1854.
The Graham's Town Journal, 1832–1854.
The Natal Mercury, 1852–1854.
The South African Commercial Advertiser, 1824–1854.

(B) Contemporary and Near Contemporary Works, Travellers' Accounts and other Personal Recollections

ANON., *An Account of the Colony of the Cape of Good Hope with a view to the Information of Emigrants*, London 1819.

ANON., *A Guide to the Cape of Good Hope, describing its geographic situation, climate, etc.*, 1819.

ANON., *Considerations on the means of affording Profitable Employment to the redundant population of Great Britain and Ireland, through the medium of an improved and correct system of colonisation in the British Territories of Southern Africa*, 1819.

ANON., *Notes on the Cape of Good Hope, made during an Excursion in that Colony in the Year 1820*, London 1821.

BACKHOUSE, J., *A Narrative of a visit to the Mauritius and South Africa*, London 1844.

BANNISTER, S., *Humane Policy, or Justice to the Aborigines of New Settlements essential to a due expenditure of British Money, and to the best interests of the Settlers*, London 1830.

BARROW, J., *An Account of Travels into the Interior of Southern Africa in the Years 1797 and 1798*, 2 vols., London 1801 and 1804.

BARROW, J., *An Autobiographical Memoir*, London 1847.

BIRD., W. W. ("A Civil Servant"), *State of the Cape of Good Hope, in 1822*, London 1823.

BOYCE, W. B., *Notes on South African Affairs from 1834 to 1838 with reference to the civil, political, and religious condition of the colonists and aborigines*, Grahamstown 1838.

BUNBURY, C. F. J., *Journal of a Residence at the Cape of Good Hope with excursions into the Interior, and notes on the Natural History, and the Natives Tribes*, London 1848.

BURCHELL, W. J., *Hints on Emigration to the Cape of Good Hope*, London 1819.

BURCHELL, W. J., *Travels into the Interior of Southern Africa*, 2 vols., London 1822 and 1824 (ed. by I. Schapera, 2 vols., London 1953).

CAMPBELL, J., *Travels in South Africa*, London 1815.

CLOETE, H., *Three Lectures on the Emigration of the Dutch Farmers from the Colony of the Cape of Good Hope, and their settlement in the District of Natal*, Pietermaritzburg 1852.

CLOETE, H., *Five Lectures on the Emigration of the Dutch Farmers from the Colony of the Cape of Good Hope and their settlement in the District of Natal — until their formal submission to Her Majesty's authority, in the Year 1843*, Cape Town 1856.

COLE, A. W., *The Cape and the Kafirs; or, Notes of Five Years' Residence in South Africa*, London 1852.

DE MIST, J. A., *The Memorandum containing recommendations for the form and administration of Government at the Cape of Good Hope, 1802* (English trans. of the *Memorie* by K. M. Jeffreys), Van Riebeeck Society publication, No. 3, Cape Town 1920.

FAWCETT, J., *An Account of Eighteen Months' Residence at the Cape of Good Hope in 1835–1836*, Cape Town 1836.

FISHER, R. B., *The Importance of the Cape of Good Hope as a Colony to Great Britain, independently of the Advantages it possesses as a military and naval station and the key to our territorial possessions in India*, London 1816.

FREEMAN, J. J., *A Tour in South Africa with notes of Natal, Mauritius, Ceylon, Egypt and Palestine*, London 1851.

GARDINER, A. F., *Narrative of a Journey to the Zoolu Country, in South Africa*, London 1836.

GODLONTON, R. (as editor, *Graham's Town Journal*), *Sketches of the Eastern Districts of the Cape of Good Hope, as they are in 1842*, Grahamstown 1842.

GODLONTON, R., IRVINE, E., *A Narrative of the Kaffir War of 1850–1851*, London 1851.

GODLONTON, R., *Case of the Colonists of the Eastern Frontier of the Cape of Good Hope in reference to the Kaffir Wars of 1835–1836 and 1846*, Grahamstown 1879.

HOLDEN, W. C., *History of the Colony of Natal, South Africa*, London 1855.

ISAACS, N., *Travels and Adventures in Eastern Africa, descriptive of the Zoolus, their Manners, Customs, etc. etc., with a Sketch of Natal*, 2 vols., London 1836.

KAY, S., *Travels and Researches in Kaffraria*, London 1833.

LATROBE, C. J., *Journal of a Visit to South Africa in 1815 and 1816, with some account of the Missionary Settlements of the United Brethren near the Cape of Good Hope*, London 1818.

LE VAILLANT, *Travels into the Interior Parts of Africa*, i, London 1796.

LICHTENSTEIN, H., *Travels in Southern Africa in the Years 1803–1806* (trans. by A. Plumtre), London 1812.

MENTZEL, O. F., *A Geographical and Topographical Description of the Cape of Good Hope*, 2 vols., (ed. by H. J. Mandelbrote), Van Riebeeck Society publication, No. 6, Cape Town 1925.

MERRIMAN, ARCHDEACON, *The Kafir, the Hottentot, and the Frontier Farmer*, London 1854.

MOODIE, J. W. D., *Ten Years in South Africa, including a particular description of the wild sports of that Country*, 2 vols., London 1835.

PALLANDT, A. VAN, *General Remarks on the Cape of Good Hope*, Cape Town 1803.

PERCIVAL, R., *An Account of the Cape of Good Hope*, London 1804.

PHILIP, J., *Researches in South Africa*, 2 vols., London 1828.

PHILLIPS, T., *Scenes and Occurrences in Albany and Caffer-Land, South Africa*, London 1827.

PRINGLE, T., *African Sketches and a Narrative of a Residence in South Africa*, London 1834.

RAIKES, H., *Memoir of the Life and Services of Vice-Admiral Sir Jahleel Brenton*, London 1846.

ROSE, C., *Four Years in Southern Africa*, London 1829.

ROSS, G., *The Cape of Good Hope Calendar and Agricultural Guide; containing a correct account of all the public offices, military forces, and other establishments in that Colony. Together with a brief description of its soil, agriculture, and commerce. Intended for the use of those persons who may become settlers*, 1819.

SPARRMAN, A., *A Voyage to the Cape of Good Hope, towards the Antarctic Polar Circle and round the World but chiefly into the Country of the Hottentots and Caffres, from the Year 1772 to 1776*, 2 vols. (trans.), London 1785.

STEADMAN, A., *Wanderings and Adventures in the Interior of Southern Africa*, London 1835.

THOMPSON, G., *Travels and Adventures in Southern Africa*, 2 vols., London 1827.

WATERMEYER, E. B., *Three Lectures on the Cape of Good Hope under the Government of the Dutch East India Company*, Cape Town 1857.

WILSON, J., *An Emigrant's Guide to the Cape of Good Hope*, 1819.
WRIGHT, W., *Slavery at the Cape of Good Hope*, London 1831.

(C) General Works

BROOKS, E. H., WEBB, C. DE B., *A History of Natal*, Pietermaritzburg 1967.

CAMBRIDGE, *History of the British Empire, Vol. ii, The Growth of the New Empire, 1783–1870* (ed. by A. P. Rose, A. P. Newton, E. A. Benians), Cambridge 1940.

CAMBRIDGE, *History of the British Empire, Vol. viii, South Africa, Rhodesia and the High Commission Territories* (ed. E. A. Walker), Cambridge 1963.

FAIRBRIDGE, D., *Lady Anne Barnard at the Cape of Good Hope, 1797–1802*, Cape Town 1924.

FORBES, V. S., *Pioneer Travellers in South Africa, 1750–1800*, Cape Town 1965.

FURNAS, J. C., *The Americans – A Social History of the United States, 1587–1914*, London 1970.

HARINGTON, A. L., *The Graham's Town Journal and the Great Trek, 1834–1843*, unpubl. thesis, Uni. of South Africa, 1968.

HARTZ, L., *The Founding of New Societies*, New York 1964.

HATTERSLEY, A. F., *Convict Crisis and the Growth of Unity*, Pietermaritzburg 1965.

HOCKLY, H. E., *The Story of the British Settlers of 1820 in South Africa*, Cape Town 1949.

HOWISON, J., *European Colonies, in various parts of the World, viewed in their Social, Moral, and Physical Condition*, i, London 1834.

KOTZÉ, C. R., *Owerheidsbeleid Teenoor die Afrikaners, 1806–1820*, unpubl. thesis, Uni. of Stellenbosch, 1958.

LLOYD, C., *Mr. Barrow of the Admiralty*, London 1970.

MACCRONE, I. D., *Race Attitudes in South Africa*, Johannesburg 1957.

MACMILLAN, W. M., *Bantu, Boer and Briton*, Oxford 1963.

MALHERBE, E. G., *Education in South Africa (1652–1922)*, Cape Town 1925.

MANNING, H. T., *British Colonial Government after the American Revolution, 1782–1820*, New Haven 1933.

MOORE SMITH, G. C. (ed.), *The Autobiography of Lieut.-General Sir Harry Smith*, 2 vols., London 1902.

MULLER, C. F. J., *Die Britse Owerheid en die Groot Trek*, Cape Town 1947.

NEUMARK, S. D., *The South African Frontier*, Stanford 1956.

PRELLER, G., *Andries Pretorius: Lewensbeskrywing van die Voortrekker Kommandant-Generaal*, Johannesburg 1940.

PELZER, A. N., *Geskiedenis van die Suid-Afrikaanse Republiek, Deel I, Wordingsjare*, Cape Town 1950.

SCHOLTZ, G. D., *Die Ontwikkeling van die Politieke Denke van die Afrikaner, Deel I, 1652–1806*, Johannesburg 1967.

SCHOLTZ, G. D., *Die Ontwikkeling van die Politieke Denke van die Afrikaner, Deel II, 1806–1854*, Johannesburg 1968.

SCHOLTZ, G. D., *The Origin and Essence of the Race Pattern in South Africa, Digest of South African Affairs*, Fact Paper 61, Pretoria 1958.

SPILHAUS, M. WHITING, *South Africa in the Making, 1652–1806*, Cape Town 1966.

THEAL, G. M., *History and Ethnography of South Africa before 1795*, Vol. III, London 1910.
THEAL, G. M., *History of South Africa since 1795*, Vol. I, London 1908.
VAN JAARSVELD, F. A., *Die Eenheidstrewe van die Republiekeinse Afrikaners, Deel I, Pioniershartstogte (1836–1864)*, Johannesburg 1951.
VAN JAARSVELD, F. A., *Die Tydgenootlike Beoordeling van die Groot Trek, 1836–1842*, C. 36, Communications of the Uni. of South Africa, Pretoria 1962.
VAN JAARSVELD, F. A., *The Afrikaner's Interpretation of South African History*, Cape Town 1964.
VAN JAARSVELD, F. A., *The Awakening of Afrikaner Nationalism*, Cape Town 1961.
WALKER, E. A., *A History of South Africa*, London 1941.
WALKER, E. A., *The Great Trek*, London 1938.
WILLIAMSON, J. A., *A Short History of British Expansion*, London 1964.
UYS, C. J., *In the Era of Shepstone*, Lovedale 1933.

Index